The Evolution of American Taste

Other books by the author
Edward Eggleston: Author of The Hoosier School-Master
The Ku Klux Klan: A Century of Infamy
Centennial: American Life in 1876
The American Revolution: Mirror of a People

Page 1: *Tavern sign for town crier
James Wilson's Bell in Hand tavern;
Boston, Mass.; 1795. Bell in Hand
was a temperance tavern.*
Pages 2–3: *Shingle-style vacation
home; Kennebunkport, Maine; ca. 1900.*
Pages 4–5: *Central University
Library, University of California,
designed by William Pereira; San
Diego, Calif.; 1970.*

The Evolution of American Taste

WILLIAM PEIRCE RANDEL

A
Rutledge
Book
Crown
Publishers, Inc.
New York

EDITORIAL
Fred R. Sammis
John Sammis
Jeremy Friedlander
Beverlee Galli
Jay Hyams
Susan Lurie
Candida Pilla
ART DIRECTION
Allan Mogel
PRODUCTION
Lori Stein

Copyright 1978 in all countries of the
International Copyright Union by Rutledge
Books, Inc., and Crown Publishers, Inc.
All rights reserved.

Prepared and produced by Rutledge Books, Inc.,
25 West 43 Street, New York, N.Y. 10036.

Published in 1978 by Crown Publishers, Inc.,
One Park Avenue, New York, N.Y. 10016.

Library of Congress Cataloging in Publication Data

Randel, William Peirce, 1909-
    The evolution of American taste.

"A Rutledge book.",
Includes index.
    1. United States—Popular culture.   2. United
States—Social life and customs.   I. Title.
E169.1.R27   973   77-18525
ISBN 0-517-52180-6

Printed in Italy by Mondadori, Verona.

Introduction 6
I **The Old World Transplanted (1607–1714)** 9
II **The Georgian Age (1715–1775)** 39
III **The Federal Decades (1776–1825)** 67
IV **The People's Choice (1826–1875)** 93
V **From Centennial to World War (1876–1914)** 125
VI **Twentieth Century Limited (1915–1945)** 159
VII **Anything Goes (since 1945)** 187
   Index 210
   Acknowledgments 212

Introduction

The Europeans who immigrated to America found many new things in the new land—new food, new terrain, new weather, a new race of people. But there was one very important old thing that they didn't find here, something that they left behind in Europe and try as they might couldn't transplant to America: a class structure, a well-ordered society of haves and have-nots. The immigrants tried to re-create the Old World in the New, but the Old World structure was based upon the Old World realities of land that for centuries had been divided up and owned, leaving most Europeans little room for change. But in America there were too many trees, too many rivers, too much land to make such an ordered society necessary—or even possible. The ideas of political freedom spawned in England were multiplied a thousandfold by a new sense of freedom: the freedom of each man to be whatever he might aspire to be.

The American Revolution declared that all men are created equal, and that idea made it very clear that the differences between the rich and the poor had nothing to do with blood—they were a matter of outward trappings. The evolution of American taste is a history of how Americans have made those trappings available to every man, thereby making every man his own tastemaker.

For more than a hundred years, the attempt to re-create the Old World kept the colonials turned to Europe for all direction in matters of taste. But the evolution of American taste had begun with the first settlements. In the narrow ribbon of colonies along the coastline—fed supplies and information from Europe through its seaports—people could try to maintain European standards. But not everything could be imported from Europe, and not everyone had the economic means to defer to European standards. Clothing, tools, and household implements were more available and less expensive if homemade or made by local artisans. Although modeled after European examples, each item handmade in America differed, however slightly, from its European counterpart.

As the nation expanded westward, this self-sufficiency, of necessity, became more pronounced. Too far from seaports to be reached by European supplies—even if they could have afforded them—and too far to learn of changing styles in Europe—even if they had wanted to defer to them—the Americans in these remote western areas created their own forms. The unique differences found between regions in so large a country as America also encouraged new forms, some forced by climate, others the result of population concentrations arriving from countries other than England, still others reflecting local commitments to certain creeds. As a result, instead of one standard of taste prevailing everywhere in America, there was a dominant cultivated taste accompanied by various deviant tastes, or subtastes.

Once they stopped looking to Europe for direction, Americans looked to themselves. The people became their own tastemakers, and no one group has ever successfully gained control of American taste.

Taste has not evolved at a steady or uniform pace. It has changed faster in some areas of the culture than in others. In serious music, even today, deference to Europe holds strong, but all the world defers to our popular music. Architecture shows a curious split—ultramodern for public buildings, quaint and nostalgic for most dwellings.

This book is meant to be an overview of changing national styles and tastes, written not for specialists but for intelligent readers who share the author's interest in America past and present. Ours has been a fantastic development, at breathtaking speed. It is conceivable that no other people has ever come so far in so short a time. This survey of the changes in American taste falls into the general area of social history. If it contributes something to our self-awareness as Americans, and if it creates fresh sympathy for our forebears, the author will feel that his labors have not been in vain.

The Old World Transplanted

(1607–1714)

When people move from one place to another, whether as travelers or migrants, they invariably take their culture with them. Among the Europeans who ventured across the Atlantic in the early 1600s to settle in America, those who were sufficiently well-to-do could take with them almost all of their tangible possessions—furniture and clothing, books and cherished heirlooms, tools and household utensils, even livestock —except for their houses, which would have overtaxed any of the ships then afloat. Most of those first immigrants, however, could take much less, and the least fortunate—military prisoners, transported criminals, indentured servants—seldom arrived with more than the clothes on their backs. But none of these people, whatever their status, could have left behind another kind of baggage: the intangibles of language, skills and interests, familiar methods, social and ethical values, standards of behavior, and that faculty of judgment known as taste.

Once the voyage ended, some of the preconceptions these immigrants had about North America had to be modified at once if they were to stay alive, let alone create permanent settlements. By the simple arithmetic of adaptation, each habit or method modified, however slightly, reduced the old culture and added to one that was new and would, in time, be recognized as distinctively American.

This process of discarding familiar cultural baggage was very slow during the seventeenth century and was limited to making the adjustments—most of them forced by the environment—that could not be avoided. Motives for immigrating differed, colony by colony, class by class, but there was a general desire among the new arrivals to transplant the Old World just as it had been when they left it. An era characterized by cultural lag had begun, a phenomenon that would continue, especially at the level of cultivated taste, well into the nineteenth century. It commonly took a decade or more for a new European style to cross the Atlantic and be accepted by American taste.

"Famine is never known"

But change was inevitable. The first divergence from European culture was in diet, the changes evolving in much the same way during the first year or two of every new settlement. At Jamestown, what food remained after the long ocean voyage dwindled so fast that it had to be rationed. The dole, as Captain John Smith recalled later, was "half a pint of wheat and as much barley boiled with water for a man a day, and this having fried some 26 weeks in the ship's hold, contained as many worms as grain." He added that "our drink was water, our lodgings, castles in the air." But just when the situation became desperate, "God so changed the hearts of the savages that they brought such supply of their fruits and provisions" that starvation was averted.

"And now with winter approaching, the rivers became so covered with swans, geese, ducks, and cranes that we daily feasted with good bread, Virginia peas, pumpions and putchamins, fish, fowl, and diverse sorts of wild beasts as fast as we could eat them, so that none of our tuftaffety [fastidious] humorists desired to go for England." Perhaps it took a spell of having to survive on wormy gruel for those first of all the immigrants to develop an appetite for lima beans, pumpkins, and persimmons, and strange new game and seafood; in any event, they took to the food provided by the Indians and nature, discovered how palatable it was, and quickly acquired a taste for it.

A dozen years later, another group bound for Virginia but forced by foul weather and treacherous currents near Cape Cod to land in Massachusetts had the same experience of Indian hostility being replaced by friendship. Their harvest feast of native foods set the standard for today's Thanksgiving menu.

The rich variety of food found on the East Coast in the 1600s is confirmed by a secular reporter, William Wood, in his *New England's Prospects*, published in England in 1634. Hear him on the region's seafood: "Codfish in these seas are larger than in Newfoundland, six or seven making a quintal . . . some be three and some four foot long, some bigger." Other fish in abundant supply were mackerel, bass, and alewives. "The oysters be great ones in form of a shoe-horn [and] without the shell is so big that it must admit of a division before you can well get it into your mouth." Clams were also plentiful but with so much other food available were "a great commodity for

Pages 8-9: *Embroidered picture; ca. 1740. Courtesy, Museum of Fine Arts, Boston. Opposite:* Philipsburg Manor; *North Tarrytown, N.Y.; ca. 1683.*

11

the feeding of Swine."

Nor did the supply show any sign of diminishing sixty years after Jamestown was founded. George Alsop, writing about Maryland in 1666, tells of the rapid increase in imported domestic animals—cows, sheep, and hogs—and also of the abundance of native wildfowl: "The Turkey, the Woodcock, the Pheasant, the Partridge, the Pigeon, and others, especially the Turkey, whom I have seen in whole hundreds in flights in the woods of Mary-Land, being an extraordinary fat Fowl, whose flesh is very pleasant and sweet." Swans, geese, and ducks "arrive in millionous multitudes" in September and stay until mid-March. The soil in Maryland, he adds, is so rich that it needs no fertilizing to produce bumper crops of wheat, rye, barley, oats, and peas year after year, "so that Famine (the dreadful Ghost of penury and want) is never known with his pale visage to haunt the Dominions of Mary-Land."

Like taste in general, which implies discriminating among alternatives, taste in its narrower meaning as one of the five senses depends on having a range of possibilities from which to choose. The immigrants did not abandon their familiar European foods, those they could bring in the form of seeds and livestock, but with the help of friendly Indians and by means of their own trial-and-error methods, they greatly increased the variety of edibles to be ranked on the scale of preference. With certain regional differences, north and south, the native foods they adopted with the most enthusiasm —the Atlantic salmon, for example, and soft-shell crabs, cranberries and blueberries, cowpeas, and Indian corn in all its varied uses— represent a marked divergence in taste from Old World tradition.

Apart from the fishfry and the clambake, the newcomers adopted very few of the Indian methods of food preparation and cookery. For the most part they continued their familiar practice of cooking over flames or hot coals in large fireplaces, using traditional utensils. They ate seated at tables, with metal or wooden knives and spoons and with their fingers, from dishes of pewter or crockery or wood, just as they always had, and their meals were at fixed hours. Transplanted taste determined *how* they ate. What was new and very welcome were the delicacies nature provided, and their abundance. American taste, to state the simple truth, first diverged from European taste in the area of diet.

Architecture for weather both hot and cold

Nature was less beneficent, though no less bountiful, in the weather it provided. A much wider range in seasonal temperature than in western Europe and a greater frequency of severe storms forced the settlers to build with attention to sturdiness and to provide clothing for both very hot and very cold weather. Some of the immigrant groups had a pretty good idea of what the climate would be where they intended to land, but for the Pilgrims, for instance, who fully expected to settle in Virginia, accommodating to the harsher Massachusetts winters posed unexpected problems.

No Englishman, however, could have been adequately prepared for the extremely warm weather to be found in the lowlands of South Carolina. Houses in New England, which had to be at least somewhat resistant to winter's cold, could be built with very little change from the clapboard houses in the medieval style of Jacobean England that the immigrants had known. But in the Deep South, where interiors

needed to be reasonably cool, the construction of a house had to depart considerably from the English method. In both regions, the basic answer was thicker walls, but in the South larger windows were desirable, to admit air currents on sultry days, and it was wise to build in the shade of large trees.

But both North and South, the design of most houses closely followed English practice of the time of King James. The same basic forms held firm in colonial taste, moreover, for the rest of the seventeenth century, despite the great changes in England. Before 1700, there was no great city anywhere in the colonies to burn as London did in 1666, and no need or opportunity, as a consequence, to rebuild in a distinctive new style of architecture. There were no American theaters where licentious Restoration plays could be performed, nor was there a leisure class to adopt the lavish dress and manners that marked the reign of Charles II. Worsening relations with the Indians, especially in New England, demanded more attention but had no effect on taste. Villages burned during King Philip's War (1675–76), fought between the Wampanoag Indians led by King Philip and the English immigrants, and outlying houses set to the torch by local Indians at other times were rebuilt somewhat more sturdily but with no change in form. The colonials were British subjects, and most of them were proud to be, but their own serious problems, and their remoteness from their cultural source, retarded their awareness and acceptance of change in styles abroad, prolonging the cultural lag.

The blacksmith as tastemaker

Tools for building, and for every other purpose, were in short supply. New arrivals, year by year, compounded the shortage, and

Top: *John Whipple House; Ipswich, Mass.; 1639–40. Left: Kitchen, Jane Dillon House; Easton, Conn.; ca. 1710. Above: Etching of houses in Albany, N.Y.; 1789. Below, far left: Peel handle, example of early ironwork. Below, left: Church weathervane, wrought iron with gilded banner and finial; Concord, Mass.; 1673.*

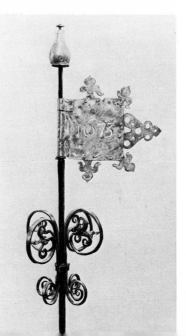

prospective immigrants were advised not to leave home without whatever tools they owned or could acquire. Imports through the few established trade channels sold out quickly, and ordering directly from European suppliers meant long delays. In villages remote from the seaports, replacement from abroad was virtually impossible, forcing people to improvise as best they could.

In New England, if less so in other colonies, every villager was expected to know at least the rudiments of some trade. With money even scarcer than tools, neighbors exchanged services in the now-lost system of local self-sufficiency. The one skill no village could do without was blacksmithing, and the man with that skill was ordinarily the first to have a shop of his own, thus becoming a full-fledged tradesman. When neighbors brought him enough plows broken beyond their own ability to repair, with even minimal imagination he would work out some way to make plows stronger, more suitable to glaciated fields. If in addition he had a spark of artistic talent, he would be likely, sooner or later, to change the basic design. By the early 1700s, the American plow was stronger and easier to handle than any made in Europe. It was also different in appearance. The same creative impulse gave a new look to small iron implements and hardware—trivets, warming pans, griddles, handles of tongs and peels, latches and hinges. Divergence in an established style is usually slight at the outset, and departures from European design were often so minute that only expert collectors can readily detect them.

The first ironworks, built in 1621 at Falling Creek, Virginia, was soon destroyed by Indians. For the next quarter-century, smiths had to depend on the lim-

ited scrap available or on iron imported from Europe, which was expensive. Home-builders, unless they were wealthy, resorted to using wood for much of their hardware, and wooden utensils can still be found in surviving "oldest houses" open to the public. It was crude but serviceable, and it had a style of its own, quite different from the forms that blacksmiths could produce.

In 1646, when the Saugus Iron Works opened for business near Boston, iron came into its own.

John Winthrop, Jr., son of the Massachusetts governor, set off for England to find skilled ironworkers and persuade them to emigrate. Once settled at Saugus, they soon were turning out bars that blacksmiths could forge into tools and thin rods that could be made into nails. Saugus also produced large pieces made of iron—pots, kettles, and firebacks, for which potters made molds.

This was the beginning of America's iron industry, which by the middle of the eighteenth cen-

Opposite top: *Van Cortlandt Manor House; Croton-on-Hudson, N.Y.; 1690–95.* Opposite center: *Medway Plantation; near Pine Grove, S.C.; 1686.* Opposite bottom: *Swedish log cabin; Darby Creek, Pa.; 1643–53.* Below: *Delft bowl; Holland; 1689–1714. Brass candlesticks; England; 1760. Wineglasses; England or America; 18th century.*

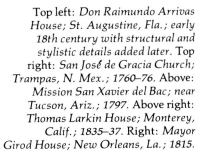

Top left: *Don Raimundo Arrivas House; St. Augustine, Fla.; early 18th century with structural and stylistic details added later.* Top right: *San José de Gracia Church; Trampas, N. Mex.; 1760–76.* Above: *Mission San Xavier del Bac; near Tucson, Ariz.; 1797.* Above right: *Thomas Larkin House; Monterey, Calif.; 1835–37.* Right: *Mayor Girod House; New Orleans, La.; 1815.*

tury was highly productive and efficient. Everything depended on handwork, which, being individual, led to deviations in design and eventual distinctiveness in style. Museums of early Americana furnish ample evidence of this impulse on the part of workers to create their own designs, whether integral or decorative. Of the great variety that might be cited, one may be singled out—a door latch with upper and lower plates shaped like the head and sword of the native swordfish.

Until about 1850, when machinery took over most production, American blacksmiths and ironworkers continued to create what must be called the first important indigenous style, in the design of bolts and locks, door pulls and knockers, balcony rails and gates, shutter fasteners, weathervanes, cranes and andirons, trammels and toasters, foot-scrapers, and wagon hardware.

Villagers in the 1600s had to build their own houses and keep them in repair, manage homestead farms, and clothe and feed their families in addition to making a living. Only when the population grew and with it the demand for specialized services did some of them set up shops and become tradesmen. But that took time. In his book *Sticks and Stones,* Lewis Mumford, an historian and critic of architecture, said about colonial carpenters that "their profound ignorance of 'style' made for freedom and diversity." The same may be said of blacksmiths and other villagers with particular skills both before and after they became full-time tradesmen.

Imported artifacts and those made by the few urban craftsmen on traditional models helped maintain Old World taste in America. What was country-made, by part-time tradesmen with little or no knowledge of changing taste abroad, was an unself-conscious but significant contribution to a distinctive national culture.

The Dutch in America

If Mumford singled out carpenters, it was because of their eventual contribution to architecture, the most substantial element in any culture. At the outset, colonial builders had no more interest in new forms of building than did the people they worked for, and they were hardly the conscious tastemakers that designers often were later. Virtually every structure surviving from the seventeenth century is a faithful reproduction of one or another style favored in Europe. In construction, at least, the hope of transplanting the Old World to the New was amply fulfilled.

New Amsterdam, for example, even after the English took it over in 1664 and renamed it New York, could have been any small, crowded harbor town in the Netherlands, devoted to trade and the comfortable living the profits assured. It may well be, as we are told in *The Great Gatsby,* that "for a transitory moment" the first Dutchman to see America "held his breath in the presence of this continent," but the Dutch settlers had visions only of commercial success. In 1653, fear of land attack by Indians and/or the English led the prudent burghers to erect a wall across the island, along what is now Wall Street. The original crowding, south of that line, was not for protection. Tradition alone explains the compactness of New Amsterdam.

Transplanted taste also accounts for the use of brick, which the Dutch considered superior to stone, for the dwellings, the warehouses, and the modest Stadt Huys, all hemmed in by the North (or Hudson) River on one side and the East River on the other. Traditional taste also explains the stepped gables at either end of the pitched roofs, a style long popular in the Low Countries.

Apart from the crowding, which would have been distasteful to settlers of other nationalities, New Amsterdam was an attractive village. Bricks of different colors— red, salmon, yellow, purple—were laid in traditional patterns that gave exterior walls a pleasing design. The houses were set so that their gable ends faced the street. They had no front yards, and a low stoop led to the main door, which was likely to be outlined with glazed tile. Sometimes the stoop of stairs going up to the house was raised over a set of stairs going down into a semibasement level.

Inside the house, one front room was often an office from which the owner transacted his affairs or a retail shop managed by his wife and daughters. The rest of the house was cut up into small rooms, all furnished in styles set in the Netherlands. In back was a garden, varying in size from house to house, for kitchen vegetables and fruits and for welcome shade in summer.

Across the tidal waters in upper New Jersey and on Long Island, and all up the valley of the North River, were the farms that supplied the minuscule city with its food and the raw materials of trade. A few of the farmhouses survive, but alterations made over the centuries have destroyed the original character of many of them. Typically, their walls were of fieldstone that may have been whitewashed. They were long across the front and often a single room deep. A generous gambrel roof swept out over a deep front porch, making the rooms behind it rather dark. One such dwelling that was built quite late, in the eighteenth century, somehow resisted change and still retains the

old Dutch character—the Dyckman House, near the northern tip of Manhattan.

Rooms in early Dutch houses, both rural and urban, were neat and comfortable. Dutch taste in colonial America was more sophisticated than that of the Anglo-Americans for a simple reason—culture was more advanced in the Netherlands. The English at that time looked to the Dutch for inspiration in matters of style, and much of what English immigrants took with them across the Atlantic had crossed the English Channel somewhat earlier. The migrating Dutch, in contrast, took along styles that had not yet become popular in England. Furthermore,

these first Dutch settlers included skilled artisans who could maintain the high level of cultivated taste, whereas the English stress was on basic, practical skills such as carpentry and blacksmith work.

Even after the English took over the colony and renamed it for the Duke of York, the Dutch maintained their priority in excellence of goods, whether the objects were imported or locally made. Typically Dutch were the *kas,* a large, carved wardrobe for the storage of clothing; handsome high chests; painted cupboards; splat-back chairs; fine linen and silverware; decorated tools; and crockery with colorful designs. Rooms in the rural homes of prosperous Dutch

Opposite: *View of gallery, St. James Church; Goose Creek, S.C.; 1711–19.* Left: *Front stairway, Francis Wyman House; Burlington, Mass.; late 17th century.* Above: *Wainscot chair; Ipswich-Rowley, Mass.; 1680–1700. Courtesy, Museum of Fine Arts, Boston.*

Top left: *Country chair;
American; 18th century.* Top right:
*Press cupboard; Ipswich, Mass.;
1680–90. Courtesy, Museum of Fine
Arts, Boston.* Left: *Hadley chest,
made for Abby Wyman; Conn.;
1690–1710.* Above: *Country tape
loom; American; 18th century.
Baroque pewter candlestick; English
or Dutch; 17th century.*

farmers approached in elegance the more formal rooms in New Amsterdam town houses, for some of the pieces were made by the same skilled artisans.

Burghers and farmers differed more in their dress and their food and drink than they did in selecting furnishings for their homes. New Amsterdam's socialites imitated the fashions of the merchant class in the Netherlands. The men wore the breeches, low shoes with silver buckles, fancy waistcoats, and bright-colored surcoats that were to dominate Anglo-American taste only after 1700, and their wives adopted the fashions of the Continent long before they reached Boston or Philadelphia via London. Dutch farmers had little occasion for such finery and preferred the plain clothes of durable homespun worn by farmers everywhere. As for food, the Dutch of both classes shared with other colonials the variety and abundance of native foods, but the urban Dutch imported more Old World delicacies and had a special appetite for Holland gin, less highly distilled than the London variety. Only after intermarriage and commercial contacts reduced isolation and gave New York a cosmopolitan flavor did the Dutch and English cultures begin to merge.

Patroons and merchants

As a device for encouraging Dutch farmers to immigrate, the West India Company offered huge tracts bordering the Hudson River to any of its stockholders who could entice at least fifty adults to settle and work the land. Few of these patrons of migration, called patroons, profited much from the scheme. The most successful was Kiliaen Van Rensselaer, a wealthy Amsterdam diamond merchant who claimed for himself a large tract of land well north of New Amsterdam, continued to enlarge

it until he owned seven hundred thousand acres, found people to settle there, and gave the name Rensselaerswyck to its principal village, across the Hudson from Albany.

After the Dutch ceded New Netherland in 1664, patroons could no longer expect such favors; but the English continued the practice for eminently successful merchants. In 1697, Stephanus Van Cortlandt, New Amsterdam-born, received a royal grant from London for eighty-seven thousand acres just north of Manhattan. The commodious rural retreat he built at Croton-on-Hudson was in the Dutch farmhouse style, and was richly furnished. Restored and now a museum, it is an admirable illustration of just how well the Dutch, when they had enough money, could transplant the Old World to the New. John, nephew of Stephanus, built in 1748 an even grander mansion, of gray stone, in what is now Van Cortlandt Park, the largest of New York City's parks with 1,132 acres but representing only a small fraction of the former family domain.

Another eventual "lord of the manor," the title favored by the English, was Frederick Philipse, a Dutch immigrant who was able to amass a fortune in trade and to buy extensive property between the Hudson and Bronx rivers. About 1682, he built a mill and house in Yonkers, and soon afterward began construction of his "northern seat" at North Tarrytown on the Pocantico. Both were part of Philipsburg Manor after the government in London finally recognized his patent in 1693, and both were confiscated during the Revolution.

New Sweden

Fourteen years after the founding of New Netherland, Sweden claimed a tract straddling the

lower Delaware River, named it New Sweden, and sent out groups of settlers, many of them from its Finnish province across the Gulf of Bothnia. The colony lasted only seventeen years, being absorbed in 1655 by the land-hungry Dutch. In so short a period, the hardy Swedes could introduce little that endured in American culture, and they were soon assimilated, by intermarriage, into the general stock of the population. Like every other immigrant group, they built in the style of their homeland—which for them meant with logs. Left round or hewn square with special tools and tightly joined where their ends overlapped, the logs were much thicker than most exterior siding and would have served well in northern New England, where winter weather is often severe. The English sometimes used logs for crude sheds, and commonly for forts, but for dwellings the log house was alien to English tradition. Even if an Anglo-American, seeing log houses in New Sweden and realizing their advantages, had thought of building one for his family, he would not have known how to and would have lacked the needed tools. Practicality and suitability, in this instance as in many others, carried less weight than transplanted tradition.

Log construction was abandoned when New Sweden collapsed, and very few of its log buildings survive. A century later, however, the use of logs was revived by German and Scotch-Irish immigrants pushing farther westward, to regions so remote from sawmills that boards for walls and floors and roofing were not available at any price. As raw frontier yielded to permanent civilization, what began as necessity gradually became a matter of choice. Today there is some limited interest in log structures—vacation homes, occasional year-round residences, hostelries in the tradition of Old Faithful Inn at Yellowstone National Park. Thick log walls are no longer more efficient as insulation than other materials, and use of them reflects not pioneer practicality but individual taste—and a tinge of nostalgia. There is only the most tenuous relation between these modern log buildings and those of the first Swedes and Finns in America.

The Spanish advantage

In other parts of North America, France and Spain could transplant their culture with little fear of its obliteration by Anglo-Americans. St. Augustine, in Florida, founded by the Spanish in 1565, was sacked by Sir Francis Drake in 1586, only to be rebuilt in the same style and with the same local timber. But when a fire leveled the town again in 1702, it seemed prudent to try building with the abundant shellstone known as coquina, which does not burn. The new material proved just as well suited as wood to the Spanish love of whitewashed outer walls, projecting balconies, low roofs, and interior garden patios.

In the arid Southwest, where timber was scarcer than in Florida, adobe proved equally adaptable to traditional Spanish styles. A mixture of local soil and water, adobe was the common building material of the Indians of the region. They spread one layer, let it bake under the hot sun until it was hard, and then added other layers until the wall was thick and strong enough to support a roof or, less commonly, one or more upper stories. The beam ends of that roof (or added floors) projected beyond the outer wall, giving the final touch to what we know as the pueblo.

Unlike the English in the East, who adopted the crude bark shelters of the local Indians only until they could build with English methods, when the Spanish began to expand their settlements north of Mexico, about 1600, they wholeheartedly adopted the adobe style and method for dwellings and other secular buildings. The Palace of Governors in Santa Fe, the oldest surviving public building in the United States, in its present restored condition, is a good example of a one-story pueblo except for its numerous doorways.

For religious structures, the Spanish formed adobe mud into bricks of various sizes, let them bake in the sun, and then pieced them together, constructing some of the most beautiful churches in the country. They varied in ornateness. The Mission Church at Ranchos de Taos, northeast of Santa Fe, New Mexico, is a veritable miracle of simplicity, while San Xavier del Bac, near Tucson, Arizona, is heavily baroque in the Counter-Reformation style, the Catholic answer to Renaissance secularism. Completed in the 1790s, with the adobe bricks kilnburnt instead of sun-dried and covered with white lime stucco, it is richly ornamented, especially at the main entrance between its two towers and around the high altar.

Spain had a substantial time advantage over the other colonizing nations: it had extended its culture to America early in the 1500s—it had a printing press in Mexico City almost a century before New England had its first. The culture that Spain spread northward to the present United States was a direct transplantation not from Europe but from Spanish America, where it had already acquired some indigenous characteristics. In penetrating California, somewhat later than the present states of Arizona and New Mexico, the Spanish built a chain of missions along the coast—the first at San Diego in 1769, then Santa Barbara, Monterey, and San Francisco, with smaller missions along the way. Each served as focal point for a small community of simple adobe houses with dirt floors and casement windows, seldom with glass. The interiors of the mission buildings themselves were almost as primitive. The floors were of uneven stone or brick, the rooms were small, some of them hardly more than cells, and only in the chapels was there decoration. Furniture was sparse and crude in design.

When easterners moved to California in the late 1830s, they too used adobe for the first buildings they needed. But being easterners, and mostly from New England, they were not long content with one-story adobe houses a single room deep and with interior patios. Some of them put up boxlike, two-story adobe houses, added a double porch for protection from the sun, and replaced the old casement windows with double sash. The result, a cross between Spanish and New England styles, was subsequently labeled "Monterey Colonial." It gave way during the Gold Rush to Victorian styles popular elsewhere in the nation but returned as a revival form, one of many, in the twentieth century.

France in America

About the time Spain was expanding its culture into California in the eighteenth century, it lost Florida to the British, as a kind of ransom for retaining control of Cuba. France, meanwhile, as England's chief rival for control in the East after the Dutch lost New Netherland, had transplanted its culture most successfully in Quebec. It also controlled the Mississippi River long enough to give New Orleans, its major port, an enduring French character, very evident today in the solid stone buildings and extensive iron grillwork of the old quarter, dating from 1712.

Smaller outposts along the great river lost much of their early flavor in the rapid material expansion after 1800, but the old section of Ste. Genevieve—the oldest town in Missouri—settled by French immigrants from Quebec still somewhat resembles a provincial town in France.

In general, however, French culture never had as direct or as wide an influence in the United States as did the Spanish, perhaps because French culture did not enjoy as long a period as the Spanish to develop in isolation and to plant its roots firmly on the continent. French forms did influence national taste in the nineteenth and twentieth centuries, but by sudden, fresh impact rather than long continuity.

Prototypes in pockets

In addition to remote areas where non-English cultures could flourish until absorbed by the Anglo-Americans, small cultural pockets existed and had varying local influence. The Huguenot colony at New Rochelle, on Long Island Sound less than twenty miles from Manhattan, from the time of its founding in 1688 added a French element to the development of Westchester County and helped to make New York the most cosmopolitan of all the colonies before the Revolution.

A single individual could also exert a regional influence. One of the earliest to do so was Jan Van Arrsens, who reached America about the same time as the Huguenots. This Dutch immigrant, also known as Seigneur de Weirnhoudt, led a small group of his countrymen to South Carolina, where in 1686 he built a substantial house named Medway. Under his close supervision, his workmen made bricks from local clay for the foundations and walls. The bricks, called "Carolina Gray," were of

poor quality, and were covered by stucco to hide their deficiencies. What gave Medway its special character was the unmistakable Dutch exterior, especially the stepped-gable roof ends. Medway faces two directions, with a broad central hall that leads from one main door to the other. Until the time of the Revolution, this basic floor plan was adopted for numerous other houses in that part of South Carolina. Many of them, like Medway itself, survive as examples of the successful transplantation of seventeenth-century Dutch taste.

Another house in South Carolina, Middleburg, illustrates influence from the West Indies. Erected in 1699 by Benjamin Simons, one of a group of Huguenots who organized a settlement near Pompion Hill, it may be the oldest wooden house in the state. Its main beams follow English tradition, but more conspicuous are its Caribbean details, especially the careful placement of windows to catch every breeze and the use of broad porches for shade. (Either Simons or one of his carpenters must have spent time on one of the Caribbean islands.) Middleburg is a prototype of the so-called single house of coastal South Carolina, popular for many years in Charleston but not found elsewhere north of the West Indies.

Both Medway and Middleburg were built before South Carolina had any large, ethnic population. If they had a stronger impact on subsequent taste than most deviant designs, it was largely because of their priority.

Re-creating England

People of English descent, eventually dominant everywhere on the Atlantic seaboard, had no more desire to abandon their familiar culture than did the people of other national origins. So firmly were

they attached to that culture, moreover, that not until the very end of the seventeenth century did they begin, with considerable reluctance, to accept some of the newer forms already popular in England. Colonial taste in the 1690s differed little, from ample evidence, from that of sixty years before.

Enough houses from that century survive in the former English colonies to give a clear notion of what most people considered to be in the best of taste, whether or not they could afford to shape it. The greater part of the English immigrants had been from counties in southeastern England, and, reasonably enough, they chose to build in the style that was favored there when they left: steep, pitched roofs; tall, massive chimneys; casement windows with leaded panes, often shaped like diamonds; and irregular facades—all in the tradition dating from the late Middle Ages.

Most of the differences that existed in these structures from region to region were external. For instance, in New England, wood was used almost exclusively as a building material; stone was fairly common in the middle colonies; and brick was favored in the South. There were also differences according to social class, carried over from England, and, of course, a range in cost from mansions only the most prosperous could build to the very humble homes of the poor. But the differences were too limited to permit any doubt of their common English origin; all were rectangular, with the entrance on the long side.

In New England, blessed by nature with fine stands of timber and numerous rivers and streams but without the lime necessary for the mortar needed in masonry construction, the logical course was to carry on the Elizabethan tradition

of building framed wooden houses. South Berwick, Maine, claims the first water-powered sawmill in the colonies, erected in 1623 to supply the carpenters of Portsmouth, New Hampshire's major settlement, a few miles downstream. Until every community had a sawmill nearby, as most soon did in New England, hewing beams and boards was arduous work; but transplanted taste for framed buildings ruled out any other method.

Most of the first framed houses in New England were one story high, with a single ground-floor room and a copious garret under the steep roof. In Ipswich, a town northeast of Boston that can boast numerous houses built before 1700, the finest example is the John Whipple House, which had two full stories in its original form, with one room on each floor. The chimney was against the east wall, not obtruding until it cleared the pinnacle of the roof. Additions made about 1670 beyond the chimney wall and toward the rear are evidence of a growing family, affluence above the average, and a

continuing indifference to a facade that was regular. The massive front door, at the right front corner of the original house, was well left of center after the enlargement. The windows vary in size and are spaced unevenly. Some are fixed so that they can never swing out like the casement windows in several of the other rooms.

The present east wall of the Whipple House has a second-story overhang, a purely decorative feature brought from England where it had long since lost its purpose, if it ever had one. Since these projections were fairly common in New England before there was any widespread fear of Indian attack, they were not added for protection and their existence, contrary to contemporary thinking, does not mean that the house was at any time a garrison. During and after King Philip's War, the first serious Indian trouble in New England, certain buildings in outlying villages were designated as garrisons because of their roominess, stout walls, and strategic location. Some had overhangs; others did not. In

any event, "garrison house" and "overhung colonial" are synonyms only in the minds of modern realtors and their customers.

Overhung or not, most New England houses that were built before 1700 and are still standing represent wealth that was well above the median. Lower-income families could less afford to add rooms and gables or to keep their houses in prime condition generation after generation. The hovels of the very poor, as shoddily built as cheap homes in any period since, have long since disappeared.

Many of the costly houses have also disappeared, some of them victims of fire. Simon Bradstreet lost his fine house in Salem to fire, as his wife, Anne, recorded in one of her last and best poems, "Verses upon the burning of our house, July 10, 1666." Of its nine stanzas, the fifth is especially poignant:

> Here stood that trunk, and
> there that chest;
> There lay that store I counted
> best;
> My pleasant things in ashes lie,

And them behold no more shall I.
Under thy roof no guest shall sit,
Nor at thy table feast a bit.

Good Puritan that she was, Anne Bradstreet ended the poem with the dream of a more glorious abode in heaven, but Simon could not wait. Within a year he moved Anne and their eight children to the commodious new house he had ordered built in North Andover, with as many trunks and chests and pleasant things as Anne could ask for, and all with due regard for the same Elizabethan taste as the former house had displayed. Highly placed Puritans, it must be understood, were not held strictly to the rules prohibiting finery. In fact, wealth was regarded as a mark of being chosen by God.

Bradstreet was a man of distinction, with a long career of public service capped by twelve years as governor of Massachusetts. Owners of other fine houses in the seventeenth century were usually men of comparable stature—judges, merchants, landlords of rental property, shipowners, foreign-trained physicians, pastors of fashionable churches, military officers. Such men were held in high regard and could set standards of taste for their admirers to emulate if they could afford it. Their firm preference for the domestic style of the Elizabethan and King James periods, more than half a century earlier, assured its long popular favor. Whether any of these gentlemen were conscious of forming or maintaining taste, they were pioneers in a long line of American tastemakers.

What others of English origin were doing elsewhere along the Atlantic seaboard was of minimal interest to New Englanders. Strangers were not welcome in the region, and neither were their ideas or standards, which were viewed as potentially dangerous to Puritan theology and to the persistent vi-

sion of a new Zion in the wilderness.

The Philadelphia checkerboard
Even so, people in distant English colonies shared with the Puritans many of their tastes and patterns of living. Philadelphians might have been hated for their Quaker faith and behavior, but they lived under the same pitched roofs as Bostonians, cooked and kept warm at the same huge fireplaces, favored the same traditional utensils and massive furniture, and looked out through the same leaded windows.

The view from those windows, however, was not the same as it was in a New England city. Instead of streets converging in hit-or-miss fashion on a central open space called the Common or the Green, and instead of houses being set on lots of varying shapes and sizes, Philadelphia's street plan (like that of New Haven, Connecticut, laid out as early as 1638) was like a checkerboard, with corners at right angles, every block a square, and the houses on rectangular lots, each sixty feet wide. William Penn, in drawing the plan for his city in 1682, had simply imposed on it a logic of symmetry borrowed from Renaissance plans. This logic was unknown to the English tradition of haphazard streets, which grew out of England's medieval agrarian and manorial past.

The only way average Philadelphians could enlarge their homes was to add rooms at the rear, thereby reducing what little space they had for lawns or gardens. If such crowding became unbearable, there were two alternatives: to move beyond the city limits or—by the mid-eighteenth century—if there was money enough, to build second homes along the wooded banks of the Schuylkill River.

Across the Delaware, as popula-

tion increased, Dutch and English mingled to a degree that might have been hard to imagine in New England, and their homes were symbolic of the harmony. Dutch and English farmhouse styles were more or less combined, and the furnishings showed no sharp distinction. The familiar canard used to describe New Jersey—that it is a populated area between New York and Philadelphia—has a valid historical base. The early blending of styles there anticipated the eventual homogenization of American culture.

In northern Maryland, taste ran to stone dwellings crowded close together along narrow streets in villages or dwarfed on outlying farms by some of the largest barns in America. Maryland's principal town was not yet Baltimore, which was founded in 1729, but a community settled in 1648 by Puritans from Virginia, who first called it Providence, then Anne Arundel, and finally, in 1694, Annapolis. Like their coreligionists in New England, they liked spacious grounds, laying out ample lots on streets that radiated from two central squares. In the next century, men with money built on those symmetrical lots the handsome mansions that give the city much of its present charm.

The old dominion
Among other reasons for the founders of Annapolis having left Virginia may have been their aversion, as Puritans, to the love of external beauty displayed in Virginia, and throughout the entire South, by the Anglican majority. They would not have forgotten how much this difference of opinion had divided the Church of England or with what zeal an Anglican bishop had harried many Puritans out of the land. Southern taste, in any event, leaned as far toward ornament as New England

taste did toward plainness. One prime example is Bacon's Castle, in Virginia's Surry County, almost an anomaly for its period but certainly a joy to the senses.

This house, the only High Jacobean structure remaining in the United States, got its name from its seizure in 1676 by Nathaniel Bacon, leader of a rebellion over Virginia's high taxes. It was actually the home of Arthur Allen, who built it in 1655. How he could afford it and why he desired such elegance are less important than his personal taste, which was obviously sophisticated. He achieved perfect symmetry. With a projecting stairwell in the rear matching the front entrance porch, the ground plan resembles a cross. At either gable end, the light-colored brick wall rises to alternating steps and curves topped by clustered chimneys of three separate flues (to keep rain out of the fireplace). Inside, the main hall has vaulting suggestive of a medieval chapel. Even though the house is no wider than some of the dark, added-on-to wooden houses in New England, its overall splendor and richly decorative details suggest the late sixteenth-century rural retreat of a lesser English nobleman.

The Adam Thoroughgood House, near Virginia Beach, and the Rolfe-Warren House (alias Smith's Fort Plantation), near Surry Court House, are among the few surviving houses comparable to Bacon's Castle. Most High Jacobean houses built before 1700 were abandoned when the surrounding farmland lost its fertility through improper crop rotation. Some stand in roofless ruin, reminders of the southern eagerness to emulate the landed gentry of England and the extinction of that hope two centuries later. These settlers of Virginia had not been gentry in England, but the few who could secure land enough, and slaves to work it, did achieve a reasonable equivalence of the lifestyle of English country gentlemen. Successful enough to build fine houses and to develop a highly cultivated taste, these were later called the First Families of Virginia.

Churches in English America

The earliest churches in all the English colonies were built, like the houses, in familiar English styles. But they differed from region to region, reflecting the wide variety of religious attitudes. In Virginia, where the Anglicans kept up their ties with the Church of England, the churches were deliberately modeled after old stone churches in English villages but were built of brick rather than of stone. The larger ones usually had square towers above the main entrance at the west front. The oldest still standing, St. Luke's, not far from Smithfield, was built in 1632 in the late Gothic style then prevalent in England. The windows have double-pointed arches and between them, on either side, are buttresses. The rear (east) wall is distinctive for its stepped gable, a feature that Flemish immigrants had introduced to England. Most other early churches in the South, whether in ruins or still in good condition, reflect the strong desire of their parishioners to worship as the gentry did in England. The structure had to be the same, and so did the time-honored sacraments, the order of worship as prescribed by the *Book of Common Prayer*, the seating by rank, and the taste for beauty of worship shared by all good Anglicans.

In New England and wherever Quakers and other lovers of simplicity were numerous, worship was in plain meetinghouses, usually made of wood and not much different in design from dwellings or barns. Old Ship Meeting House, built in 1681 in Hingham, Massachusetts, is unusual for its massive interior beams that arch like the ribs of a ship's frame and were no doubt installed by shipwrights. The stone Holy Trinity Church in Wilmington, Delaware, built in 1698 and better known as Old Swedes, is plain both inside and out, expressing a wish for clear and uninterrupted communion with God.

Furniture

Differing religious views had less effect on furniture. For much of America's history, styles of furniture have changed rather rapidly, in every region, in response to shifting taste abroad. But not before 1700. Even the best pieces, whether imported or made in the colonies and whether put together by turning or joining, showed little change during the seventeenth century. The popularity of their classical ornamentation—carving in the form of flowers and urns, chair and table legs turned to resemble Greek columns—might suggest a break with the recent past, but it was actually the continuation of a taste prominent during the reign of Elizabeth. In its basic elements—legs, backs, surfaces—seventeenth-century furniture in America was essentially medieval.

Generally dark and heavy, the furniture brought by the first immigrants and subsequently imported or locally reproduced was stylistically appropriate to the houses most colonials lived in. Until taste in architecture changed, there was no practical reason for discarding that furniture for unfamiliar new styles. Fresh immigration brought increasing numbers of men trained in woodworking to America's shores, but not until after 1670 did any of them successfully introduce new kinds of furniture. The first was the chest of

Detail, slate tombstone of John Foster, mathematician and printer; Dorchester, Mass.; 1681. Foster died at the age of 33. The tombstone is attributed to "the Stone Carver of Boston."

drawers, which in time replaced the chest with hinged top for storage of clothes and linens.

For families with the means to choose, a plentiful supply of chairs was considered essential. Backless stools and benches were common in most households. The peak of good taste was the wainscot chair, rather cumbersome and uncomfortable without the usual cushion. It sometimes had turned legs in front, but usually all the essential parts were square except for the curving armrests. The seat was a solid piece of wood, and the back, also solid, was carved with considerable elaborateness. Not many people owned wainscot chairs; they were evidence of their owners' prominence in the community.

More numerous, and hardly lower in cultivated taste, were the lighter, less expensive turned spindle chairs with rush or splint seats. Two of these, later named the Brewster and Carver chairs after two famous New England families, were made almost entirely of spindles. Also in good taste were the slat-back chair, with one or more horizontal back slats for support, and the utilitarian table chair, convertible into a table by lowering the broad back on its hinges.

Tables as such also varied. The simple trestle type, with legs like inverted T's, and the sawbuck type with crossed legs could accommodate large families. Their tops were thick and made of a single, broad plank—or two, after trees of immense girth became rare. Toward the end of the century a new type, introduced from England, gained favor—the gateleg table. With the hinged legs at either side closed and the leaves down, this table occupied little space, a consideration at a time when most rooms were small.

It may seem odd that closets did not exist until much later. The boxlike chests with hinged tops that were first used for storage were sometimes undecorated and at other times elaborately carved with Elizabethan motifs or ornamented with surface paint, or both. The designs varied from region to region and from one individual maker to another. A tulip with two petals and a single large leaf, for example, is the sign of what is now called a Hadley chest, one of several types made in the Connecticut valley. Today, whatever paint there may once have been is gone, and the beauty of the wood itself attests to the taste of the period.

Press cupboards were expensive to make and, being limited to affluent households, were symbols of superior status. Late in the seventeenth century, the elaborate carving that had characterized them up to that point yielded somewhat to the use of turned spindles, which were easier to make. This change in construction reflected a definite shift in taste, first in England and, twenty years later, in America. The replacement of carving with spindles also occurred in other pieces, notably cradles.

Needlework

Needlework design followed Elizabethan practice, which stressed such motifs as scrolls and plant forms and East Indian trees and birds introduced to England by globe-circling traders. Such designs were commonly taken from pattern books printed in Europe and on sale in colonial bookshops. In some cities, instruction in needlework was offered to young ladies, who, if ambitious enough, would depart from the book patterns to include native trees and flowers, although originality and creativity were not considered necessary or even desirable traits. The colors used depended on what was available rather than what taste might have favored. Indigo for blue dyeing was inexpensive, but Venetian red, made by a secret formula, had to be imported and was quite expensive.

The bed in the main room of a typical seventeenth-century house was often covered with a bed rug. The word *rug* then meant any cover, a sense restricted today to steamer rugs. Worked with wool, these bed rugs were not greatly different from the hooked rugs of the nineteenth century, with bright colors that enlivened any room. As a covering, moreover, they were practical because the wool provided good warmth on cold nights. The proud makers of these bed rugs often signed them with their initials and the year of their completion. Coverings for tables were called "table carpets"; rugs were almost nowhere used on the floor.

Needleworking was at first a practical necessity, but with a growing amount of leisure time, late in the century, it was no longer limited to mending and making necessary coverings. Ladies had time to develop skill in embroidery work, especially crewel, as well as to create elaborate designs and sometimes an individual pictorial scene to stitch. Since the wool yarn used for crewel work was thin and, like the best colors, had to be imported, needleworkers were encouraged to economize by using spare designs and few stitches. Taste for crewel was strong

Opposite: Eleanor Darnall, *at about 6 years of age, by Justus Englehardt Kühn; Maryland; ca. 1710.* Above: Cotton Mather, *by Peter Pelham; Boston, Mass.; 1727. The first mezzotint made in America.* Left: Robert Gibbs, *at 4½ years of age, by an unknown limner; 1670. Courtesy, Museum of Fine Arts, Boston.*

enough, however, to override economic prudence. Otherwise there would not have been so many crewel hangings made to enclose bedsteads or so many crewel chair cushions, tablecloths, and coverlets. Like paint on furniture, they gave color and light to dark interiors. Somewhat easier than crewel was Turkey work, which produced a knotted fabric that imitated Oriental rugs; it was often used as a fringe at the top of a cupboard, partly to keep dust off its contents but chiefly as decoration. Turkey work was also thought tasteful for chair cushions and table carpets when finished with large corner tassels.

Silverware

The objects displayed on cupboard shelves were valuable utensils, pieces of porcelain, pewter, or silver. Many of the silver pieces were made in England or elsewhere in Europe, as was virtually all ecclesiastical silver. Early goldsmiths (this term was used for workers in both gold and silver) were few in number and not skilled enough, until the next century, to turn out many pieces acceptable to cultivated taste.

The best colonial work, simpler than the imports, has strong appeal to modern taste, but for costly objects, ornateness was high in favor in the 1600s. Those pieces made by colonial silversmiths that copied or were greatly influenced by ornate English designs were the most sought after, even in Puritan New England with its proverbial love of plainness. Southern plantation owners commonly imported their silver from England or bought it on visits there. In all the colonies, the less affluent—meaning most of the population—had to make do with pewter or crockery.

Short shrift for the fine arts

In a country made up of separate political jurisdictions, unified only by their common allegiance to the English Crown, and with most available energy preempted by practical needs, the fine arts got short shrift compared with the useful arts. There was little encouragement for independent artists.

Sculpture was hardly more than low-relief carving of gravestones, and little of it remains, for most of the stone used crumbled in a few decades. The best stone was slate imported from Wales, where the marginal decoration was often added before shipment. If taste ran to symbols of mortality—Father Time with his scythe, skulls and crossbones, gaunt skeletons—it was a lugubrious tradition not limited to America. For slate not thus decorated abroad, local carvers often added floral or other motifs to the margins, as well as incising the name and date of the deceased and whatever biblical passage or poetic lines the survivors asked for.

Only rarely was there an attempt at a gravestone portrait. Some of the funereal workmanship was artistic, but most of it was crude. So were the few other pieces of sculpture: weathervanes of wood, more whittled than carved, and three-dimensional tavern signs. One glorious exception to this general amateurism is a vane made in 1673 by a local smith for a church in Concord, Massachusetts. Its wrought-iron upright supports a gilded metal banner with the numerals of the year cut out, pierced decorations along the edges, and a finial above it.

Music was also limited. Puritans sternly opposed it except for the Psalm tunes—of which, by one count, there were thirty-nine—for congregational singing. Quakers had no music at all in their unstructured services. Anglicans were more liberal, but most of their music was secular—familiar sixteenth-century compositions played for private family entertainment or for stately court dances on special occasions. Musical instruments were scarce. There were lutes of assorted shapes, a few harpsichords and virginals, and somewhat more violins and flutes—all, of course, imported. Redcoat parades and annual militia musters were enlivened by old martial airs, played by fifers against a drum background. Dancing at weddings, where it was not forbidden, was to tunes of itinerant fiddlers. Taste in music was narrow in range and a transplant of archaic tradition; and this is ironic, even sad, for Europe in the late seventeenth and early eighteenth centuries was enjoying a virtual explosion of excellent music.

The portraits of members of the wealthier class were brought as baggage or were painted in England or Holland during return visits. In America, limners, now usually unknown by name, painted portraits in the stiff medieval style. For the most part the faces, looked at from a frontal perspective, are severe in expression. A large white collar (or fichu), perhaps edged with lace and a cap to match, for a woman and for a man a stock (or neckcloth) of white material provided contrast with the usual black garment. Children were dressed the same as adults. As the century progressed, the women's clothing shown in portraits is less severe and the artists' conceptions less rigid.

Etchers copied the portraits. In 1727, Peter Pelham, who had settled in Boston the year before, introduced the mezzotint process to America with his *Cotton Mather*, based on a portrait of the illustrious divine that he had painted earlier. Mather, in a large wig, is revealed as something of a dandy in dress. Another migrant painter, Justus Kühn, was active in Maryland from 1708 until his death in 1717. His portrait of Eleanor Darnall has an imaginary background, a device used by many of the limners. Colonial portraiture even by trained artists was greatly inferior to that done in Europe.

Literature was different. There was plenty of it in New England, the one region with a high regard for literacy. The Puritan founders of Boston included quite a few college graduates who saw to it that Massachusetts, within a decade of their arrival, had a college of its own and a printing press.

What that press turned out in greatest volume was orthodox Puritan theology, but the Puritans also held classical writings in high esteem and applauded Anne Bradstreet for her long poems cast in conventional modes. More than a decade before fire destroyed her family home, she earned the reputation of being *The Tenth Muse Lately Sprung Up in America*—the title given, to her great embarrassment, to a collection of her poems published in 1650. Derivative style and stilted language did not bar acceptance in those days, as they would today. The simple, homely poems that she wrote later, expressing her private experience and emotions, now stand much higher in reader taste than her early formal poetry.

In 1937, a batch of poems by the Rev. Edward Taylor turned up at Yale and, when published, put him well ahead of Anne Bradstreet as America's finest poet before the Revolution. Taylor knew very well that his poems would not have appealed to taste in Puritan New England. To have published any of them would have been to risk strong censure and dismissal from his pulpit.

No Puritan in good standing was supposed to like the English metaphysical poets, Crashaw, Quarles, Herbert, or even Donne, who were of the Anglican persuasion; but Taylor liked them and wrote in their style. His devotionals, as he called them, were impeccably orthodox, completely in accord with Puritan doctrine, but they were full of elaborate figures of speech and symbols. So much has taste changed that today he is praised for just such poetizing as this stanza from "Upon a Spider Catching a Fly":

> Thou sorrow, venom Elfe.
> Is this thy play,
> To spin a web out of thyselfe,
> To Catch a Fly?
> For why?

Versified Calvinist doctrine in conventional ballad meter was quite all right, as Michael Wigglesworth, English-born and a Harvard graduate, discovered in 1662 when his *Day of Doom* was an instant best-seller. Its full title was *The Day of Doom, A Poetical Description of the Great and Last Judgment,* and its 224 doggerel stanzas, each of four lines with seven accents and consistent internal rhyming, are just that. Its appeal to reader taste was not limited to New England, for it was popular in the South and in England, and it sold steadily in one edition after another for more than a century. It is as low in artistic quality as Taylor's work is high. But this is a modern judgment, and it has no bearing on standards of taste three centuries ago. Puritans took their religion with deadly seriousness and had little sense of humor.

One form of literature, satire, if aimed at Calvinism, would have outraged Puritan taste; but satire did not come into general favor until after 1700. Satirical method applied to the Puritans had to wait until 1858, when Oliver Wendell Holmes demolished Calvinism in "The Deacon's Masterpiece."

The first American satire of note appeared in 1708, Ebenezer Cook's *The Sot-Weed Factor.* The fictional persona of this extended poem is an English merchant who arrives in Maryland with a shipload of goods, only to be cheated of the lot by a scheming sot-weed factor, the term for a tobacco middleman. But the main thrust of the poem is to satirize every facet of Maryland life, including the "Drunken Humours of the Inhabitants of that Part of America," as we learn from the subtitle. It is an amusing book, but neither Maryland nor any other part of the country was ready for satire. Most secular writing accepted as tasteful in that period took the opposite tack, of glorifying the new land and the people who were developing it.

All sections had their writers, but only in New England were there any to approach the popularity of British contemporaries. One small book with no author named on the title page won immense favor: the *New England Primer,* first issued in 1683. It taught the alphabet with a picture and a rhymed caption for each letter, for example, C—"the cat doth play, and then doth slay," which any cat owner knows to be true. It also provided rules for correct behavior, a catechism, Bible verses, assorted poetry, and prayers, including the famous one for bedtime:

> Now I lay me down to sleep.
> I pray the Lord my soul to keep.
> If I should die before I wake,
> I pray the Lord my soul to take.

This simple children's prayer, almost entirely in words of one syllable, may not be literature in any true sense, but it had as much emotional effect as any other poem, and it had unquestioned appeal to American taste then and later.

Right-minded New Englanders also had an insatiable appetite for printed sermons, theological treatises, and anything written by the great pedant Cotton Mather, who set a record for productive industry with 444 titles published between 1682 and 1727. It would no doubt be outrageous to suggest that the Puritans, monstrous in zeal as they seem to have been, held witch-burning in good taste. Their prompt revulsion from the hysteria of 1692 and their lessened regard for Cotton Mather for his labored defense of the prosecution better illustrate Puritan character. Yet New Englanders, church members or not, were as fond as any of their contemporaries in other colonies of attending public hangings and reading the broadsides on sale at the executions, usually containing the culprit's final confession and warning to the young.

Employers declared a holiday for a hanging, which supposedly had a sobering effect, but there were no holidays given for such entertainments as turkey shoots, horse races, cock fights, and the baiting of bulls or captured wolves by ferocious dogs. Authorities in most of the colonies frowned on these as distracting attention from work and, on Sunday, from worship. In Virginia, a law was passed in 1624 requiring church attendance, and ten years later Massachusetts passed another, even more stringent. So many unregenerate citizens walked out after the roll was called that the doors of some churches were padlocked until the service ended. But taste for entertaining sports held firm, and they flourished despite every effort to curb them.

In New Amsterdam, Governor Stuyvesant forbade horse racing in or near the city limits, but by the 1660s, residents could travel out to the Hempstead Plain on Long Island to watch their favorites compete for silver cups. Hunting and fishing were tolerated, as productive of edibles, but ball playing and dice were not. Blue laws, so named for the blue paper Massachusetts used for printing its first, were most restrictive in that colony. One in 1647 outlawed "shovel-board" in any house of "common entertaynment" after complaints of disorder, and the ban was extended in 1650 to cover bowling and "any other play or game." The continuing immigration was apparently swelling the ranks of the ungodly, for it is hard to equate the taste that made *The Day of Doom* a best-seller with the growing appetite for play and games.

Clothing and social rank

The blue laws were not invented in America, but in America they covered more than the English statutes they were based on. Massachusetts even tried to dictate what women should wear, specifically banning lace and any ornaments. But by 1651, enforcement was relaxed for the benefit of the well-to-do: certain costly materials and specified ornaments were permitted for wives and daughters of men with assets of at least two hundred pounds.

As in England, social status determined what people might wear. The range of choice was narrow for much of the population in the early decades, for without money enough for clothing made to order in England or by one of the very few custom tailors in the large port cities, the majority wore plain, rather drab clothing that looked homemade, as it almost invariably was. Manufactured textiles of all sorts were so expensive that only the well-to-do could afford any variety.

Homage to Sir Christopher

No government, however authoritarian, can impose arbitrary standards of taste and maintain them inviolate. Some nations have tried, notably France, with its dignified academies created to prevent corruption of the language and to keep artists within bounds. Linguistic change simply cannot be prevented; if it could, we might all still be speaking Old English—if not a more ancient Indo-European language. So also with general culture, and with standards of taste: change is the universal rule, and nothing can stop it.

But the rate of change can vary. In seventeenth-century America, taste changed so little as to seem stationary. If the very first settlers could have awakened from eternal sleep in 1694 to survey the colonial scene, they would have rejoiced. They had hoped to transplant the Old World, and their descendants had done so admirably. But within another twenty years, our hypothetical wakers from the dead would have found a strange New World, one that had at last thrown off its long indifference to the changes occurring abroad. The principal agent of this redirection of taste was an Oxford astronomer and amateur architect who was knighted in 1673—Sir Christopher Wren.

After the Great Fire of 1666 burned out the heart of London, Wren designed replacements for fifty-one churches. His flexible mind, uncluttered with the prescriptions of academic architecture, produced original and widely popular designs. The Gothic would not do as a base; it was too closely associated just then with French Catholicism. Following the lead of Inigo Jones, who designed the Banqueting House of Whitehall Palace (1619–22), Wren adapted his work to Renaissance neoclassicism but with numerous modifications. Two of the most obvious of these modifications were the use of brick for exterior walls and the virtual elimination of conventional baroque ornaments. The new St. Paul's Cathedral, begun in 1675 and completed in 1710, is no doubt Wren's masterpiece, but he also

Elizabeth and James Bowdoin, III, as Children, *by Joseph Blackburn;*
Boston, Mass.; ca.1760. Their father was John Hancock's
chief rival for political power in post-Revolution Massachusetts.

Above: *Virginia State
Capitol, designed by Thomas
Jefferson; Richmond, Va.;
1785–92. Modeled after Maison
Carrée, a Roman temple at Nîmes,
France.* Right: *Rolfe-Warren House
(Smith's Fort Plantation); Surry
Court House, Va.; 1652.* Opposite
top: *Two-drawer Empire work
table; ca. 1840.* Opposite bottom:
*Country Sheraton sofa; New England;
early 18th century.* Opposite
far right: *Federal grandfather
clock; Connecticut; ca. 1820.*

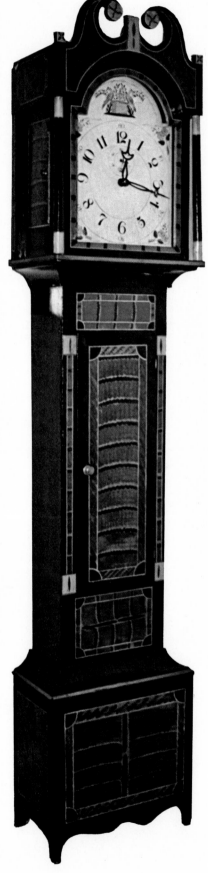

designed numerous secular buildings of great beauty, including the palaces at Kensington and Hampton Court, Greenwich Hospital, and the library at Trinity College, Cambridge. Few other tastemakers in history have had such an enormous influence on culture.

The style Wren originated went nameless or, when necessary, was referred to as "Wren's style" until after the first George ascended the throne, in 1714, whereupon people began calling it Georgian. It was so popular in England that its adoption in the colonies was inevitable. The break came in 1693 with the chartering of the second college in the colonies, at Williamsburg, and the need of a building to house its activities. The town itself, soon to replace Jamestown as Virginia's capital, was named in honor of King William III; but the college gave equal recognition to the queen, adopting as its name the College of William and Mary.

Construction of the main building, known as the Wren Building only since the 1930s, began in 1695. There is some evidence, not conclusive, that Wren himself sent over the original design; but whether he did or not, the structure is faithful to his style. The main entrance is an open arched passage that runs the depth of the building and has only a simple molding as decoration. Directly above it is an equally plain door fronted by a small balcony; and above that are a broad pediment and a six-sided clock tower surmounted by a weathervane.

The facade is completely symmetrical, with six windows on either side of the protruding central bay on all three floors. The third floor has dormers built out from the simple hipped roof. Two massive chimneys rise near each end and beyond the apex of the hipping. Slender wings equal in dimension extend from the rear at each end; one houses the chapel, in the firm tradition of English colleges, and the other is the refectory with its high table served by the kitchen in the basement below. The building has survived four fires, none serious enough to disrupt completely the academic process. It stands today as the oldest college building in the United States in continuous use, which is an enviable distinction. But for our purpose the building is more important as the pioneering Georgian structure, one that roused interest in all the colonies and prompted, within a few years, emulation everywhere for public buildings of every sort, and eventually for dwellings as well.

For the better part of a century, taste in America had looked backward, to the styles the immigrants had known before starting their one-way trip. Preoccupied as they were with transplanting the Old World in the New, they had no compelling reason to alter its forms and one good reason—limited money—to maintain them unchanged. Only after they had secured a firm hold on the new land, and the first American-born generations had achieved a degree of economic soundness, could the immigrants give much attention to changing their European culture.

Important as the college building in Williamsburg was in redirecting colonial architecture, its greater significance was the stimulus it gave to accepting other new forms from abroad. In what must be regarded as the first great shift in American taste, the transplanted Old World yielded, in the early 1700s, to the brave new world of the Georgian Age.

Sternboard of model of the Continental frigate Raleigh.
The actual Raleigh *was launched at Portsmouth, N.H.; 1776.*

The

Georgian Age

(1715–1775)

Preceding pages: *Sir Christopher Wren building, College of William and Mary; Williamsburg, Va.; 1695. The first major American building in the Georgian style.* Above: *Cliveden; Germantown, Pa.; 1767. Typical of the stone construction favored in the middle colonies.* Opposite top: *Detail of main stairway, Carter's Grove; near Williamsburg, Va.; 1750–55. One of the finest Georgian mansions in the Plantation South. Colonial Williamsburg Photograph.* Opposite bottom: *William Pepperrell House; Kittery Point, Maine; ca. 1683, given Georgian character 1720–23.*

For the better part of a century, the prevailing attitude in English America was one of respect for the Middle Ages and suspicion of the Renaissance. Not everyone knew the difference, by any means, or even the terms themselves, but for thinking men, in positions of authority and influence, the advance of Renaissance concepts in Europe was a cause for deep concern. In their view, it was a return to the irreligious practices, competing theologies, and sophisticated paganism of ancient Greece and Rome that triumphant Christianity had been able to keep stamped out

for almost a thousand years.

England, farthest from the source of Renaissance ideas in Italy and geographically isolated by the English Channel, was the last major country in Europe to respond to its influence. But although the English people were slow to abandon medievalism, they clung to it with varying degrees of fervor. The Church of England was split on the issue, with the Anglicans attracted to the love of beauty that marked the Renaissance and the Puritans rejecting it as distractive to purity of worship. Both views crossed the ocean but were separated in the New World by several hundred miles. Anglicans in the southern colonies could indulge their taste for formal worship in an attractive setting, and the Puritans in New England could follow their taste for simplicity. An objective observer aware of this regional difference in attitude might have predicted that Georgian symmetry would be welcomed first in the South.

Georgian foreshadowing

Even though recognizably Elizabethan, certain houses built in the South reflect an interest in formal design that predates Sir Christopher Wren. In Virginia, some of the oldest houses—Smith's Fort Plantation, the Adam Thoroughgood House, and others approaching Bacon's Castle in sophistication—were considerably closer to the Georgian style than they were to the dark, wooden dwellings of New England. Their chimneys, of the same brick as the walls, rose at both ends of pitched slate roofs that were broken in front by dormer windows. However, those windows and those on the ground floor were often irregularly placed, and the front door was not usually centered. Two building traditions, the ancient Elizabethan and the not yet born Georgian, could be said to be competing in such houses for the favor of regional taste.

Structures that approached the symmetrical Georgian style were not limited to Virginia. Middleburg, the South Carolina showplace with West Indian influence, had something of the "new look," as did Pennsbury, the country manor house built for William Penn on the 8,000-acre tract reserved for him as proprietor of Pennsylvania. Planned to resemble the kind of rural seat that wealthy Englishmen were favoring at just that time, the early 1680s, it had a hipped roof, three dormers in front, and a totally balanced five-bay facade.

From medieval to Georgian

The irregular outline of houses built in the medieval tradition gave them a dynamic quality, visually creating an illusion of movement, or restlessness, that may be taken as representing the character of the first two or three generations of Americans. But by the early 1700s, life was different: the wilderness had been subdued and made productive, villages that were strategically located had grown into cities, and people were confident that their new civilization would endure. Their achievement conditioned them to prefer a more formal architecture as being more indicative of stability and permanence. But Georgian architecture was never completely static in America; individual builders with ideas of their own kept changing it, with the full approval of the families they built for. It was not in the American character to settle for what Lewis Mumford later called "the prudent regularities of the later Georgian mode."

The transition in colonial taste from Elizabethan angularity to classical balance as Wren had revived it is admirably illustrated by the Hart House, which stood next door to the Whipple House in Ipswich, Massachusetts, until 1963. In that year it was taken apart, moved to Washington, D.C., and reassembled there in the Museum of History and Technology. The original section, built in 1698, showed no significant difference from other New England houses of the 1630s and 1640s. But by 1748, the dwelling had become roughly four times as large and was much more "finished," more reflective of a taste for beauty. The newer part has an open balustraded stairway, double-hung sash windows, paneled interior shutters, molded

cornices, wall paneling around the small fireplaces, and high ceilings plastered to conceal the beams. Except for absorbing intact the earlier Elizabethan rooms, the Hart House, at the age of fifty, had become typically Georgian.

The two period styles had so little in common that renovation of this sort was not always possible, or desirable. Families most concerned about keeping up with new fashions were more likely to discard their dark old houses and build on different sites, preferably in newly fashionable sections of town. If this was not feasible, they did their best to disguise the former design completely, to be rediscovered only in the twentieth century when some later owner tore the house down—or let historians study its past.

The alterations that Col. William Pepperrell made between 1720 and 1723 to his house at Kittery Point, said to be the finest in all of Maine, were no less extensive than those of the Hart House. Born in England, Pepperrell was first a fisherman after his move to America, then a trader, and finally a man of so many commercial interests that he needed his own countinghouse to keep track of his affairs. His home as he built it about 1682 was typically Elizabethan but larger than most in New England. It had two stories, a steep, pitched roof, and diamond-paned windows irregularly spaced. As altered, it acquired fifteen more feet at either end, a gambrel roof, fine paneling in the ground-floor rooms, a handsome stairway with three patterns of turned balusters, and an unusually large stair landing. The outside wall overlooking the busy family wharf on the ocean was completely rebuilt so that it included a centered door and sash windows placed in perfect Georgian symmetry.

Before he died, in 1732, the

colonel was granted the right to have a coat of arms, and for it he chose three pineapples, symbols of hospitality, particularly in colonial times. Another pineapple was carved over the front door. His namesake son added a fleur-de-lis to the coat of arms after leading the successful campaign to oust the French from Louisburg in Nova Scotia. For that feat in 1746, he was given a baronetcy, the first noble title granted to an American. As Sir William, he continued his father's hospitality, sharing with all comers the amenities of affluence—fine imported wine served in foreign-made crystal, equally fine Chippendale chairs and tables, beds with embroidered coverlets. His heirs lost all the family's wealth during the Revolution because they were Tories. The mansion survives, but most of the elegant furnishings, reflecting the highest taste of that period, including the richly ornamental silver pieces given by England to Sir William in gratitude for his services, are now dispersed.

The first Georgian town

It was the application of Wren's revived classicism to structures larger than dwellings, however, that brought it into general awareness; and the place where the new mode was first conspicuous was Williamsburg, designated in 1699 as Virginia's capital after the burning of Jamestown. A village of sorts, called Middle Plantation, was already on the chosen site, but the Virginia authorities saw fit to redesign the street layout and did so with the same commitment to formal symmetry that later marked the major buildings. No doubt the presence of the College of William and Mary, still under construction, influenced the choice of that site.

From the college, a broad street named for the Duke of Gloucester runs straight to the Capitol, a mile away, which was completed in 1705. Its east and west facades closely resemble the front of the college, with two stories and dormers above. But the shape is like an H, with deeply recessed north and south entries, each with a triple arch. The tower at the apex of the steep, pitched roof is almost a twin to that of the college. The most unusual features of the building are the rounded southern bays of the two longer sides. Wren would have been pleased with its look, but more important is that the details of design, for this and other buildings at Williamsburg, did much to establish taste for his style in all the colonies.

Opposite top: *Touro Synagogue, Congregation Jeshuat Israel, designed by Peter Harrison; Newport, R.I.; 1762.* Opposite bottom: *First Baptist Meeting House; Providence, R.I.; 1775.* Below left: *William and Mary side chair with leather seat; American; ca. 1700. Georgian desk box; English; early 18th century. Earthenware tankard with pewter and bronze decoration; German; ca. 1709.* Below: *William and Mary chest of drawers, Captain John Clarke House; Strawbery Banke, Portsmouth, N.H.; 1750.*

The Governor's Palace, begun in 1706 but not ready for occupancy until 1720, was first called merely the Governor's House, but its mounting cost prompted Virginia taxpayers to refer to it derisively as the "Palace," and the name stuck. Such lavishness, especially to a degree hitherto unknown in English America, was not universally approved, although the Palace did become a prototype for many private mansions, especially in Tidewater Virginia. Some of those mansions enclose more space under a single roof than does the Palace, but few approach it in elegance; in the number of *dependencies*—the architect's term for wings or outlying buildings; or in the extent of formal gardens and orchards. From the basement, with its storage bins for small beer, strong beer, rum, cider, Madeira, and cheese, to the two-storied cupola surrounded by a balustrade, from the ornamental front gate to the maze of English yew at the far end of the gardens on one side and the bowling green on another side, the whole estate amply deserved to be called a palace.

Fire gutted both the Capitol and the Palace in the late 1700s, but they have been restored to their former splendor with the aid of John D. Rockefeller, Jr. Some historic preservationists deprecate the restoration of Colonial Williamsburg, for they feel that it portrays an artificial degree of perfection. Yet the project, begun in the 1930s, was the leader of the entire modern effort to re-create the past *in situ* by patient research and exacting attention to detail.

Whatever its critics may contend, Williamsburg as restored gives a good idea of the taste for Georgian balance that it did so much to establish in the early eighteenth century. Of course, only the very wealthy could emulate its grandeur. In Virginia, the wealthiest of all the colonies because of its highly profitable tobacco exports, enough of that wealth was concentrated within few enough families that they could bring to reality the dream of creating an English gentry in America. The great houses they built near Williamsburg in the half century after 1700 demonstrate both that desire and the firm hold that the Georgian style had on regional taste.

Williamsburg's influence is evident on both banks of the nearby James River. One cluster, well upriver toward Richmond, includes Westover, built about 1730, and two houses dating from 1726: Berkeley, the ancestral home of two presidents named Harrison; and Shirley, one of several mansions built by Robert ("King") Carter and his descendants. Nearer Williamsburg and closer to the sea is Carter's Grove, built between 1750 and 1755 by Carter Burwell, grandson of the "King." In its present carefully restored condition, it represents the Southern Georgian style at its best. The front facade closely resembles that of Westover, with a seven-bay central block and two attached story-and-a-half dependencies, all perfectly symmetrical. But the great glory of Carter's Grove is the interior, with exquisite paneling that to produce took three years of expert work by an English woodworker, Richard Baylis, brought over with his family expressly for that assignment. At least six local carpenters assisted him.

Carpenters as architects

In England, Wren had overcome the opposition to brick and had demonstrated both its adaptability to buildings of varied purpose and its potential for beauty of facade when handled with imagination. The Dutch had been aware of both for a long time, and so were the earlier builders in the South, who had little trouble, after 1700, in shifting from the Elizabethan designs to those of Wren and his followers. In New England, however, where the builders were usually carpenters rather than masons, the changeover to Georgian took somewhat longer, until men familiar with wood could learn how to adapt it to designs intended for brick. Advice from architects might have been helpful, but the few professional architects in the colonies were preoccupied with designing churches and public buildings. Lacking their advice, master carpenters were free to design with a boldness that gives the Georgian in New England its regional distinctiveness.

Most independent-minded carpenters could not have drawn architects' plans if their lives depended on it, but they were fully competent to work from the type of detailed sketches that could be found in English handbooks published after 1720 and sold in colonial bookshops. The favorite was the *Book of Architecture,* by James Gibbs, a Wren disciple famous for several London churches, including St. Martin's-in-the-Field. In his preface, Gibbs insisted that he was writing for the benefit not of urban builders but of country builders with no professional architects nearby to consult. Almost as popular in the colonies were William and John Halfpenny's *Art of Sound Building* and Isaac Ware's *Complete Book of Architecture.*

Once such books were available, New England could begin to catch up with the South in the shift to Georgian. Men with mounting incomes from varied enterprises—fisheries and ocean commerce, shipbuilding and lumber operations, rents and mortgages—hired the best carpenters they could find to create town houses imposing enough to indicate their dignity as men of achievement. The relatively few who chose to build country mansions were presumably less eager for such acclaim. These rare individuals had more in common with the worthies of the previous century, who were respected for their public services, than with newly rich businessmen, and they felt no need to impress the common herd. In the country, there was ample room for dependencies, like those on southern estates, and for a broad frontage. In growing cities, there was seldom space for more than what would have been in a southern mansion the central block.

Rural and urban, most houses in New England built between 1715 and 1790 were unmistakably in the Georgian mode. But with the rapid growth of cities and the equally rapid growth of commercial enterprise, the regional Georgian departed markedly from what was standard in the agrarian South, and from what some historians of architecture consider the Georgian ideal.

In the process of adopting Georgian symmetry and elegance, successful New Englanders, even if still professing Puritanism, were in effect repudiating the Puritan theme of simplicity. It was one phase of a gradual drift toward secularism on several fronts. In doctrine, it led to the decline of stern Calvinist logic and the rise first of Congregationalism and then of Unitarianism. In dress, somber plainness yielded to bright and often gaudy attire. Instead of walking to Sunday worship, families rode in carriages, or chariots as the best of them were called, behind matched pairs of horses. Social calling changed from informal friendly visits to formal "at homes" for which written invitations were expected. What had been feared in the seventeenth cen-

tury became reality in the eighteenth: taste in almost everything was being dictated by Renaissance sophistication. The dominance of the Georgian style in housing everywhere, even in New England, was only one evidence of this great change.

If, in the Georgian Age, sophistication and secularism were forces reducing differences between regions, they did not eliminate them. In particular ways, indeed, the differences became greater. This was certainly true of domestic architecture. Construction with wood in New England continued as the most salient difference from the southern preference for brick, but other features not purely Georgian in style began to emerge. Some roofs were gambrel, as on the John Paul Jones House in Portsmouth and Nathaniel Hawthorne's modest birthplace in Salem. The railed "widow's walk" bestriding the peak of a roof was another design feature that grew in popularity in New England cities and villages. It had no such function as its name implies—a place from which a sea captain's wife could scan the ocean horizon for her husband's inbound ship—and it can be seen on Georgian houses far inland. It was actually a borrowing from England that happened to appeal to New England taste. Large glassed-in cupolas were also quite popular, and most of them were purely decorative.

Most wooden Georgian houses were painted in what are now called "colonial colors"—grayish bayberry green and a darker blue green; pale yellow and gold, both close to beige; soft gray; a blue like that of Wedgwood plates; and a dull red, often used for wooden coffins, called coffin red. Paint became so popular in New England that some of the stained or weathered seventeenth-century houses got belated baptisms in color,

usually dark red or brown.

The essence of Georgian

As in other regions of the country, all large Georgian dwellings in New England shared the basic qualities of what one cultural historian has called the Gentleman's Classic. The term has not been widely accepted, but it is an appropriate description of virtually every house built in America from about 1710 until well into the 1800s, whether Georgian, Federal, or Greek Revival, and whether of brick, stone, or wood. The essence of the type is a taste for formal symmetry and neoclassical design.

The symmetry was most immediately visible in the facade, with its large, perfectly centered front door framed by pilasters and often also by tall, very slender windows (known as lights), and topped by a low-relief pediment of varying elaborateness. Flanking the doorway were evenly spaced windows, usually two on each side but sometimes only one, with minimal decoration and large enough to admit copious light. Upper stories continued the rectilinear precision, both vertically and horizontally, with tiers of windows all the same size. In most parts of the country, houses had two full stories and a third, with dormer windows, under the roof. In the large port cities of New England, high land values encouraged three stories below the roof line and, especially in the Federal period, sometimes even four.

During the Georgian era, the corners of wooden houses were sometimes rusticated with squares of wood painted to look like stone blocks. More often a pilaster effect was achieved by incorporating wide boards that rose to classical capitals. Occasionally, all the exterior walls were painted to resemble stone. The rear facade usually matched the front and overlooked a flower garden as symmetrically

Above: *Queen Anne table and chairs.*
Right: *Japanned William and Mary highboy; 1720–30. Windsor writing chair with comb back (painted black); 1790–1810.* Below: *Kitchen, Captain John Clarke House; Strawbery Banke, Portsmouth, N.H.; ca. 1760.*

laid out as the house itself. The side walls, roughly the same length as the front and back walls, had somewhat smaller centered doors, giving access to lawns or more gardens, or to small annexes, attached or freestanding, one usually serving as the kitchen. As cities grew more crowded, these dependencies were often removed —a process just the reverse of the "add-on" habit of the previous century.

A broad central hall led from the front door to its twin at the rear. On one side was a banistered stairway, one of the few departures from perfect symmetry. Only a few of the grandest mansions had centered stairs that divided at a landing. Doorways directly opposite each other led from the hall to each of four rooms, all about the same size. Those in front were parlors, both formal. One, seldom used, was the place to entertain important visitors. Occasionally, one of the front rooms served as an office, as in the John Brown House in Providence, Rhode Island. The room opposite was the family sitting room and opened to the dining room behind it. The remaining ground-floor room might be the library unless it was needed as an inside kitchen. Each of the four rooms had a fireplace, the room's only source of heat, on the outer wall. The upper floors more or less duplicated the first, although the halls were progressively narrower and opened to more and smaller rooms. Flues led from the stacked fireplaces to four plain chimneys, one near each corner, that continued the symmetry above the roof line.

Individual houses varied from this general description in countless small ways because their builders were individualistic enough to deviate from whatever was thought to be standard. Collectively, however, these builders

were tastemakers, albeit with a heavy debt to the English authors of the handbooks they relied on.

Philadelphia Georgian

In the Philadelphia area, Georgian-style houses were usually built of local stone rather than wood. One is Cliveden, built between 1763 and 1767 by Benjamin Chew, later famous as chief justice of Pennsylvania. Deciding, as other men had before him, that the city was too warm in summer, and had too many flies, he bought eleven acres in what was then the "inhabited wilderness" of Germantown. He designed his house to resemble a sketch of Kew Palace that he had seen, hired a master carpenter and a skilled stone mason, and personally supervised the construction. As is characteristic of many Georgian houses in Virginia, the central bay projects slightly, accentuating the front door, the window above it, and the pediment at the edge of the roof line. Among other deviations from the standard Georgian, the central hall does not extend the depth of the house: instead, it is T-shaped, with the stairway, parallel to the front wall, rising behind a screen of Tuscan columns. The paneling and furnishings rival those of Carter's Grove.

The Pennsylvania Dutch

Germantown was one of the sites near Philadelphia settled by Germans, who by 1775 made up a good third of Pennsylvania's population. If there ever was a culture within a culture, successfully maintaining its distinctiveness, it was here in what outsiders called the Pennsylvania Dutch region, between the Delaware and Susquehanna rivers. Mennonites were the first to immigrate, in 1683. Other groups, each with a particular brand of religion, followed in the next half-century—Mora-

vians, Schwenkfelders, Dunkards, Amish—along with the more numerous Reformeds and Lutherans. They did not mingle, but they all had a common bond, the culture of their fatherland—architecture derived from the German baroque, the best farming methods anywhere (as good as in the Rhine valley and Bavaria), the most advanced industry, a peasant love for gay colors and designs based on birds and flowers, and an equally strong love of good music. They made no deference to fashionable taste in Germany, which was not yet a unified nation, and were indifferent to English taste, as set in London. Anglo-Americans left them alone—until the Revolution, when their manpower and enviable productivity were urgently needed if the rebel cause were to succeed.

The language barrier, which the German groups sedulously maintained, partly explains the cultural isolation. A few music-loving outsiders, George Washington among them, sometimes ventured into the region to attend concerts at Bethlehem, which they knew was the music capital of North America. But Anglo-American architects and carpenters never examined the strange buildings, silversmiths and pottery makers never looked to the Germans for fresh ideas about spoons or teapots, plates or pitchers, and homemakers knew nothing about the Germanic taste for brightly colored interiors. They had their own strong culture, and if they felt any need of guidance in matters of taste, it was more logical to seek it in England.

Ephrata Cloister, a few miles northeast of Lancaster, provides an excellent idea of what one small group could do in isolation. Founded in 1732 by Conrad Beissel, a German Pietist and somewhat of a mystic, Ephrata was a monastic settlement with three orders: a brotherhood and a sister-hood, both celibate, and married couples. All slept on board benches with wooden pillows, a custom unlikely to become wide-spread. All spent most of their waking hours at farming or mill-ing, to maintain the food supply, or at various other trades, includ-ing expert printing and bookmak-ing. They lived and worked in log and stone and wooden buildings in medieval German tradition, and at their services they sang hymns written by Beissel.

The Saal (or chapel) and the Sa-ron (the Sisters' house) are walled with wide boards, unpainted, and have tiers of dormer windows breaking the tall, pitched roofs. The nearby Almony (a combina-tion granary, bakehouse, and guest house) is of fieldstone. The Academy, built much later with white walls and a cupola, comes closest to English style. There is also a chinked log shed for farm purposes. All these buildings dis-play the beauty of undecorated simplicity that American archi-tects have rediscovered only in re-cent decades. Even the Elizabethan houses in seventeenth-century New England had more unfunc-tional decoration.

The Pennsylvania Germans were by and large highly skilled, hard-working, and as prosperous as any group in pre-Revolutionary America. But they had very little in common with the wealthy mer-chants, ship owners, and tobacco growers in other sections who, ac-cording to outdated history books, were the backbone of American development. They were closer in spirit to the untutored village workmen in New England and the ruggedly independent small farm-ers in the South, in ways that ur-banites could not have begun to appreciate. But theirs was a cul-ture apart, in a period of limited communications, and they had

neither the wish nor the chance to influence the taste of the English-speaking majority.

Anglo-American taste

That taste was not only dominant but shared almost everywhere, as the predictable result of expanding intercolonial trade. Josiah Quincy, the Boston lawyer who helped John Adams defend the British soldiers involved in the Boston Massacre of 1770, learned just how general co-lonial taste was during the course of a long trip he took through the southern and middle colonies, in 1773, in a vain effort to regain his health. In his journal, he recorded the very hospitable treatment ac-corded him everywhere, for as a gentleman he was welcome at the homes of other gentlemen with tastes as cultivated as his and the money to indulge them. In one Georgian mansion after another he relaxed on the same stiff Chippen-dale chairs, dined at the same long tables set with the same fine china, glassware, and silver, and slept on

the same carved beds with richly embroidered canopies. After din-ing at Miles Brewton's Charleston house, which he thought must have cost at least eight thousand pounds, he mentioned the magnifi-cent silver on the sideboard and re-ported that a pet bird gorged on crumbs under the chairs and then perched where it could watch the guests.

As he made his way northward, Quincy no doubt admired many a geometrically perfect garden, seen perhaps from a second-story Palla-dian window with its three sec-tions, the middle one arched; a Wren borrowing from the great Italian architect Andrea Palladio. On Sundays, he worshiped in churches similar to Boston's Old North Church, modeled after those Wren designed for London after the fire of 1666. The one place that disappointed Quincy was Wil-liamsburg: "It is inferior to my ex-pectations. Nothing of the popula-tion of the north, or of the splendor of the south." He admitted, how-

described as "country Georgian." Scholars call them "vernacular." Real estate agents call them "colonial" if large enough, "capes" if only one-story. Passersby, and many of the people who live in them, accept them for what they are—old houses—and feel no need to label them.

Georgian as veneer

None of these terms for such houses is wholly satisfactory, and neither is "country Georgian" itself. More of them were built after than before the Revolution and, speaking technically, are not really colonial. As for calling them capes, they did not originate on Cape Cod, where most older houses were shingled and unsymmetrical. "Georgian" is not inclusive enough, for after 1800, many of these houses exhibited Federal details. "Gentleman's Classic" might serve, but not for the smallest examples, and in any event the term has a very limited circulation. "Vernacular" smacks of academe and its learned jargon but is probably the most suitable. What matters more than terminology, however, is that taste for this style was strong and widespread and that it held firm longer than any other in our architectural history.

Country Georgian, or vernacular houses as they will henceforth be alternately referred to, combined familiar features of the Elizabethan style with basic elements of the newer Georgian. The most obvious change was from irregular to symmetrical facade, with essentially the same classical formalism as marked the urban Georgian mansions—a framed doorway pre-

ever, that the college made an agreeable impression and that its large garden was both ornamental and useful.

The taste for symmetry and decoration was no monopoly of men wealthy enough to install Palladian windows. In New England, at least, it extended far down the economic scale into rural areas remote from the style-conscious coast. Although taste may have been more highly developed among wealthy urbanites than in the less affluent hinterland, it does not follow that urban taste was necessarily superior to rural taste. What can and should be said is that urbanites with money not only could afford to live in houses that strictly accorded with the Georgian "ideal," but also chose to do so out of deference to standards set abroad. In what these privileged people viewed as backward rural areas, such blind deference to fixed style was rare, even among farmers with substantial incomes.

Country carpenters, the men

James Gibbs insisted he was writing for, had no difficulty creating facades as perfectly balanced as those of the finest houses on Salem's Chestnut Street, said (by Salem residents today) to be the most beautiful street in America. But rural taste in the eighteenth century was commonly satisfied with only partial adoption of Georgian standards. Two centuries later, when both the urban and the country Georgian exist only as relics, who can say whether one is better than the other, or represents better taste? Both styles appealed to the taste of the time but to different groups; and the group with a taste for modified rural Georgian was far and away the larger.

The transforming of the Hart House or the Pepperrell mansion was one way families could embrace the Georgian style without abandoning the cherished older elements. A different method was used for thousands of new dwellings built in villages and along back country roads that may be

Opposite: *Desk with reverse serpentine front; Essex County, Mass.; ca. 1760.* Above left: Lady Undressing for a Bath, *artist unknown; early 18th century.*

49

cisely centered and flanked by large sash windows with nine panes over six, molding around those windows and under the eaves, and corner upright boards suggesting pilasters. The door opened to a central hall or small entry. There were ordinarily only two chimneys, or just one in the center of the house serving fireplaces on inner rather than outer walls. Except for a formal parlor in one front corner, the ground floor was laid out with seventeenth-century irregularity, and the old add-on habit produced ells that violated book-standard symmetry.

Where winters are severe, and where farming is the principal occupation, the add-on ells destructive of symmetry were very practical, just as attached garages are today. Farmers had to be much more self-sufficient than people in cities, and close adherence to sophisticated taste would have jeopardized convenience and creature comfort. It could even be argued that taste for perfect classical balance was only superficial, to be modified or disregarded if it seemed unreasonable. Be that as it may, taste for classical balance and the awareness of practical needs in rural areas were, as Hegel might have put it, the thesis and antithesis that clashed and produced the synthesis of a distinctive new style.

James Gibbs had warned his readers not to let his designs be altered by "the Caprice of ignorant, assuming Pretenders." A more famous contemporary, Alexander Pope, expressed a similar fear in 1731, in a verse epistle to the Earl of Burlington, an ardent classicist who had recently published an English translation of Palladio's *Antiquities of Rome:*

> Yet shall, my lord, your just
>   and noble rules
> Fill half the land with imitative
>   fools;

Who random drawings from your
  sheets shall take
And of one beauty many blunders
  make.

These lines expressed well the derogatory attitude that was typical of educated, upper-class, native-born Englishmen toward modifications of standard modes by undisciplined builders and craftsmen—an attitude shared by the small, wealthy upper class in America that assumed the role of arbiters of taste. No doubt regrettably, this attitude laid the foundations for a pattern that persisted for almost two hundred years, in which indigenous forms and creative effort were considered inferior or worthless because they did not meet the standards set in Europe.

Taste for the comfortable Elizabethan way of life, quite clearly, could coexist with Georgian as a veneer, or with any other veneer of cultivated taste. The country Georgian, by its emphasis on such coexistence, was a bridge from past to present, keeping alive the old vernacular tradition and maintaining its hold on less sophisticated taste.

Cultivated taste kept shifting, producing changes in fashionable style. The vernacular tradition that flourished alongside it, even though deprecated by the urban arbiters of taste, could pay token attention to so-called standards and ignore most of the changes dictated from abroad. Shared by a large segment of the population, the taste for country Georgian succeeded in being a significant and enduring contribution to American culture.

Public architecture

Churches and public buildings, designed by architects with varying claims to professionalism, while generally closer to the Wren tradition, showed the same division between cultivated and indigenous taste. As was true of St. Luke's in the previous century, churches in the South showed the

Far left: The Copley Family, *by John Singleton Copley; 1776–77. Painted just after Copley went to London.* Top: Petticoat border, *crewel embroidery on linen; New England; 1740–60. Courtesy, Museum of Fine Arts, Boston.* Above left: Papermaker in smock, *from* The Book of Trades, *Part II; London; 3rd edition, 1806.* Above: Hartt Tea Set, *by Paul Revere; Boston, Mass.; 1799. Courtesy, Museum of Fine Arts, Boston.* Left: Kitchen equipment; *late 18th and early 19th centuries. Included are a scoop, strainer, ladle, spatula, skimmer.*

least deviation from contemporary English modes. When Alexander Spottswood arrived in Williamsburg as Virginia's new governor in 1710, he rejected the plans for a new church to serve Bruton Parish; he thought they were too old-fashioned and insisted upon classical details, including a Wren-type steeple. In 1775, when the First Baptist Meeting House in Providence, Rhode Island, was built, its steeple almost exactly followed a plate in Gibbs's *Book of Architecture,* published fifty-five years earlier.

Wren-style steeples continued to be built for many more years, but few were as close to textbook designs as the one in Providence. The general deviation of church design from imported standards, moreover, had the full approval of local taste. St. Michael's Church in Charleston, begun in 1732, is of brick, like most southern churches, but the brick is covered with stucco and painted white, the color that best repels the heat of the southern sun. Thomas McBean, who studied under Gibbs, ignored some of his teacher's precepts when he planned St. Paul's Chapel in New York, which was dedicated in 1766. For the exterior walls, he chose Manhattan mica and trimmed it with brownstone, a very intelligent use of local materials.

Well-trained men like McBean were encouraged to move to America by the growing taste for fine Georgian buildings. The century's most eminent architect, however, was native-born Peter Harrison. He spent several years studying in England and on the Continent, and on his return was soon in such demand that he could not accept all the commissions offered him. King's Chapel, which he designed in 1749 for Boston's Anglicans, was the first stone masonry church built in the colonies, and the most

consistently Georgian. Its spire was never added, but the interior is singularly impressive with its paired Corinthian columns and its huge Palladian window behind the altar. No less beautiful is the interior of the Touro Synagogue in Newport, which Harrison designed in 1762. The Ark of the Covenant is enclosed by a fine balustrade, and there are decorative details taken from Inigo Jones, Wren's English predecessor, who broke with Jacobean modes and redirected taste toward the classical.

Harrison also worked on many public buildings, including two in his native Newport, Rhode Island: a market with an arcaded ground floor open for the convenience of shoppers and the Redwood Library, notable for its wood made to resemble stone. He and a few other trained professionals represented the highest level of cultivated taste. No carpenter-builder, however talented, could approach Harrison in the emulation of genius, but Harrison, trained as he was, felt less impelled than the carpenters to redirect the Georgian away from foreign tradition.

The shift in taste from the casual irregularity of the seventeenth century to symmetry of outline and classical decoration in the eighteenth represented a wish to express in buildings the growing sense of dignity that the colonists were feeling. Even some of the religious bodies committed to simplicity of worship shared the impulse, creating handsome church buildings to replace their modest meetinghouses. Whereas religious attitudes had earlier influenced style of church structures, current taste was now a stronger force.

Lingering taste for Georgian

By mid-century, Georgian was on the wane in England, as cultivated taste turned to another neoclassical style, the Adamesque, or Federal,

as Americans preferred to call it. But the same cultural lag that had delayed adoption of the Georgian style in the colonies kept it uppermost in American taste for another quarter-century. To a certain extent, as in all artistic movements, American Georgian lost some of its daring after it had reached its peak, but even in its final plateau stage, it continued to grow in distinctiveness.

That process did not end with the Revolution, an event that might have halted all construction but instead only slowed it down. Some of the finest Georgian houses were still being erected in America after 1783, despite the fact that dominant taste was steadily shifting to the newer, Federal style.

The Peirce-Nichols House in Salem, begun in 1782, is one outstanding example if judged only by its exterior. Designed by Samuel McIntire, a native son who also won acclaim as a sculptor, its three stories are topped by a balustrade that hides its very low roof, a large deviation from the Georgian of Williamsburg early in the century. Corner pilasters capped by broad capitals, conspicuous cornices above the windows, and a heavy pediment over the front door betray an exuberance the earlier Georgian had minimized. Even the stable courtyard is elegant. But the interior tells a different story. The rooms that were decorated first are clearly Georgian in detail, but some, left unfinished until 1800, are just as clearly Federal. No stigma today is attached to furnishing rooms in the styles of different periods, but this was a form of eclecticism that arbiters of taste frowned on in those times.

A more consistent example of late Georgian is the Hamilton House in South Berwick, Maine, not far from the first sawmill built in the colonies. It was finished in 1788 for Col. Jonathan Hamilton, great-grandson of an indentured Scottish military prisoner, and it no doubt gave the colonel great pleasure to demonstrate with a fine mansion his family's rise, in three generations, from abject poverty to affluence. His wealth came from mercantile trade with the West Indies and, during the Revolution, from preying on British vessels along the Atlantic coast. A more immediate reason for building his mansion was the common one, among successful men, of simple vanity. Rivals downriver in Portsmouth—the Peirces and the Langdons—lived in great houses, and so could he.

Four-square with all four sides virtually identical, each with a centered door framed by Doric pilasters and topped by a simple pediment, the Hamilton House stands on a headland that affords a view of the river in two directions. The west windows gave a view of the colonel's wharf and private shipyard; to the east is a sunken formal garden. Four tall chimneys and dormer windows with broken pediments rise in perfect symmetry out of the hipped roof. The upper half of the interior walls, in the broad central hall from north door to south door and in all the rooms, is covered with wallpaper; that in the long dining room is a continuous scene portraying temples and other evocations of classical antiquity. The plastered fireplaces in the front parlor and master bedroom on the second floor are flanked by pilaster-supported elliptical arches with carved keyblocks, an unusual decorative device found in few other Georgian houses. There are inside shutters that fold back into the wall. The present furniture is not original to the house, but it generally reflects contemporary taste. American taste for the Georgian survived almost to the end of the eighteenth century, reaching in this house at least an apogee shortly before taste shifted once and for all to the Federal style.

Keeping up with English furniture

Like the furniture in the Hamilton House, most original pieces of American furniture were dispersed when families, for whatever reason, moved out of one home and into another; and Americans are noted for their mobility. In fact, the ancestry of thoroughbred horses is more precisely recorded than the provenance of most old furniture contained in museums and in houses open to public inspection. But knowing that this or that old chair supported the weight of John Adams or that a certain bombé desk now in Saco, Maine, represented the individual taste of Thomas Hutchinson, last royal governor of Massachusetts, little matters. What is more important, in a survey of changing taste in America, is to look for reasons why one style replaced another in prevailing taste. Part of this understanding comes from knowing particular facts of history.

In 1686, James II named Sir Edmund Andros governor of the consolidated northern provinces in America. A Catholic with no use for Puritans, Andros proved so offensive that a group of Bostonians led by Cotton Mather forced his recall in 1689, the year William and Mary became joint monarchs. Firm Protestants who supported the "Glorious Revolution" that forced King James into exile, this royal couple was so popular that not only was the second college in the colonies named for them but also the furniture introduced in England during their reign.

Changes in taste are seldom so easy to explain. Most styles in furniture rise and fall in favor like women's fashions, though not quite so fast. Women still obey the dictates of the fashion industry to some extent, but there is much greater leeway in choosing furniture now than there was in the past. For a good century and a half, after 1690, no status seeker in England or the colonies dared ignore the standards set in London. Heavy furniture gave way to light, in both weight and color, then light yielded to heavy, heavy to light again, and so on in a continuous sequence. A sure way to predict what the next style would be was to imagine the opposite of what was currently favored by cultivated taste. This is no doubt still true, but we no longer accept foreign dictation.

Stuart furniture that had satisfied colonists as long as they lived in Elizabethan houses was relatively simple, in both construction and design, and rather heavy. The William and Mary pieces that began to replace it in colonial taste about 1700 were neither. They were stronger than they seemed to be, made as they were to give the illusion of lightness. A tabletop was no longer a single thick plank, but a thin board inlaid with squares of veneer. Chair legs were mostly straight, but some were cabriole, describing elongated S-curves. Drawers multiplied, and their pulls were of bright metal. Honest plain wood gave way to burled ash or walnut and curly maple. Slats on chair backs were pierced in intricate designs. Almost every piece of William and Mary furniture, moreover, included a few solid round balls somewhere—at the feet of chair legs, suspended from crosspieces, or as bulges on horizontal tie bars. These balls were a borrowing from the Netherlands, like King William himself, but they remained in favor longer than he did (he developed a genius for infuriating his new subjects).

Mary died childless in 1694, and

when William joined her in 1702, the scepter passed to Mary's younger sister Anne. Almost at once a new furniture style emerged and was named for her. Transoceanic cultural lag being what it was, the colonies had by then barely caught up with William and Mary styles, and did not have time to adopt the new style before Anne herself died, in 1714. Once accepted, however, Queen Anne furniture dominated taste in America throughout the reign of George I and well into that of George II. It yielded in the 1750s to Chippendale, a style named not for a monarch but for a furniture designer—an advance, no doubt, in democratic egalitarianism. The two Georges, who already had a major architectural form bearing their name, could hardly complain.

The Queen Anne style, predictably, restored heaviness. It retained the curves and cabriole legs of William and Mary chairs, but it put them on almost every other kind of furniture, too. Secret drawers were all the rage, built into desks and highboys and secretaries. New forms appeared: card tables, tilt-top tables, and corner chairs with their legs set at a diagonal to the seat. The tops of mirrors and highboys, previously flat, acquired the broken pediments and corner urns common to Georgian architecture. Taste for all these increments of elegance, if not of comfort or utility, held firm until Thomas Chippendale came up with something radically different to replace it.

What he did about 1750—and what Englishmen first and then Americans welcomed with enthusiasm—was to alter the Queen Anne style only slightly while introducing fresh elements borrowed from the classical and the Gothic, and from France and China. Taste for Oriental styles, in fact, began with Chippendale. His book published in 1754, *A Gentleman and*

Cabinet-Maker's Director, had much the same effect on furniture design that the earlier handbooks by James Gibbs and other Wren disciples had had in redirecting architectural taste toward the Georgian. It pictured entire rooms with valanced French draperies, wallpaper showing Chinese gardens and odd pointed hillocks, and perhaps in one corner a folding Chinese screen. The framing of fireplaces was minimized, and the fire dogs were sometimes shaped like slender Chinese pagodas. For the wives of American mariners engaged in the China trade, these touches must have been irresistible, especially when viewed from the sofas and armchairs that made sitting, for once, a comfortable experience.

Stuart, William and Mary, Queen Anne, and now Chippendale—all in less than a century! The boon to London cabinetmakers was tremendous, but in the long run their colonial rivals had the better of the bargain. As their skill increased, imports declined. By 1730, furniture shops in Boston were shipping chairs hardly inferior to London's best to the South and the West Indies, and within a decade Boston had strong competi-

tion from Portsmouth and Newport, New York and Philadelphia. None of this industrial buildup could have happened without the majestic power of changing taste.

What explains the continuing deference to standards set three thousand miles away? It should be remembered that until 1765, when benign neglect by Parliament ended abruptly with the Stamp Act, people in all the colonies viewed themselves as overseas English subjects with all the rights and privileges of people living in England—including the freedom to share their tastes if they wished to and had money enough. If Londoners showed a sudden fondness

for Dutch claw feet on chairs or side tables with elaborate Chinese pedestals, these were certain to appear, in due time, in the parlors of American homes. It was no way to develop a distinctive native culture, but who in the colonies wanted one, or even—before the shock of the Stamp Act—thought of himself as an American?

Nevertheless there was partial repudiation of English taste at every social level. In parlors, formal dining rooms, and other parts of a house open to visitors, European taste dictated the furnishings. But for kitchens, work rooms, and servants' quarters, and for taverns and country inns and business of-

fices, simpler chairs and tables, outside the scope of fashionable taste, were both sufficient and preferred. Cabinetmakers catering to the carriage trade disdained the simpler pieces in principle but were not averse to making them for the mass market when the custom trade slackened. This was the kind of furniture found in all country Georgian rooms except the formal parlor.

Few American cabinetmakers were content with exactly reproducing imported pieces. Most were independent enough to alter small details, a practice that makes it possible for modern experts to ascribe particular pieces to a known master, or to his shop. Some can be known only to have been made in certain localities. Richly ornamented chests and desks, called bombé for their bulging or rounded front and sides, were made only in the Boston area, where they were much sought after. Another New England craftsman introduced "japanning"—the application of Oriental lacquer and motifs. Bostonians liked it so much that other cabinetmakers copied it, and it was soon high in regional taste.

An American chair

The now-famous Windsor chair

Opposite top: *Yellow earthenware bowl with seven-rayed sun, soapstone candlestick, and other utensils; late 18th and early 19th centuries.* Left: *Kitchen, or common room, Winslow-Crocker House; Yarmouthport, Mass.; ca. 1760 except Brewster armchair, which is 1660–70.*

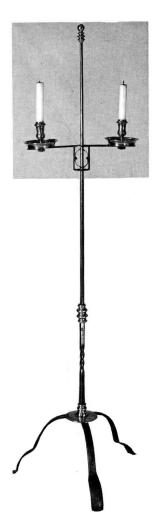

Above: *Iron and brass
candlestick, by B. Gerrish; 1736.
Courtesy, Museum of Fine Arts,
Boston.* Above right: *Stiegel-type
drinking glasses; 1770–75. Courtesy,
Museum of Fine Arts, Boston.*
Right: *Sir William Pepperrell,
by John Smibert; 1746. Courtesy,
Essex Institute, Salem, Mass.*

developed out of somewhat comparable circumstances. Chairs like it had been made in England in the late seventeenth century, but their legs were perpendicular, or nearly so, whereas the legs of the American Windsor are conspicuously splayed. This design combined medieval simplicity with the lightness of William and Mary pieces. It had to be sturdy, like the foot-worked spinning wheel it somewhat resembled, but being outside the range of sophisticated taste, it could be—and was—made in a great variety of sizes and shapes. For overweight adults, it could be made very large; for small children, minute; for babies, there were Windsor high chairs. It could be made with or without arms; high-backed or low, as in what is now called the captain's chair; with back-rest spindles all vertical or fanning out like a comb. Whatever form it took, the Windsor chair was always very simple, with a solid plank seat and no decoration. These were plain chairs for daily use by ordinary people, and they were made to last. Windsor styling could also be applied to settees, for several people together, up to ten feet long; or to chairs with one arm broadened to make a writing surface, with a small drawer tucked under it for pen and paper.

This last piece, the Windsor writing armchair, was original to America, and for decades proved extremely practical. Emerson owned one and used it when writing his famous essays in the 1830s. And it had multitudinous progeny —all the later classroom chairs with writing arms that replaced the old built-in desks and benches. As for the ordinary Windsor armchair, it gained enough respectability to seat the delegates to the first and second Continental Congresses, in 1774 and 1775.

Durable, spare in design, utili-tarian, and ignored by fashionable taste, the Windsor chair retained its popularity while fashionable taste shifted from one foreign style to another. It was one of the earliest genuinely native products, a major break with tradition that became, eventually, a tradition of its own and an unsung herald of modern taste for undecorated functional furniture.

Nobody drank water

Whatever chairs colonials sat on at mealtime, in mansions, farmhouses, or taverns, Londoners had little influence on what was served at the tables. At stately dinners, one course might be British game birds imported at considerable expense, accompanied by sherry and Madeira from Spain and Portugal. While in the Carolinas, however, Josiah Quincy noticed that port and claret were preferred to Madeira and Lisbon wine. Furthermore, many plantation owners, he learned, were propagating grapes with success and, in Virginia, were making brandy from their own peaches.

Of the numerous indigenous foods the colonists had learned to enjoy, Indian corn, or maize, had probably the widest range of uses. It was easy to grow and harvest, and friendly Indians had shown the early settlers many ways to cook it. It appeared as hominy, mixed with beans as succotash, as cornpone or johnnycake, as porridge or pudding.

Mush, the simplest of all cooked dishes, was dignified in New England by the name "hasty pudding." The recipe for it in *The Frugal Housewife* is hardly more than a lesson in how to add cornmeal to boiling water: "Stand over the kettle, and sprinkle in meal, handful after handful, stirring it very thoroughly all the time. When it is so thick you stir with great difficulty, it is about right." Simple though it was to prepare, however, it had its epic poet, Joel Barlow, one of the group known as the Connecticut Wits. His enduring fame, indeed, rests chiefly on "The Hasty Pudding; A Poem in Three Cantos," which he wrote in 1793 while abroad and feeling homesick. The very name he thought was

> . . . significant and clear,
> A name, a sound to every Yankee dear,

and considerably better than names given it elsewhere:

> . . . how I blush
> To hear the Pennsylvanians call thee
> *Mush!*

Here, with a vengeance, was regional chauvinism; but it was also a tribute to a native dish held high in gustatory taste.

Enterprising men, meanwhile, had found quite a different important use for corn. Fermented and aged in special barrels, it proved the most suitable grain for making a whiskey to rival Scotland's major export. But corn whiskey, later called bourbon after a county in Kentucky that produced it in quantity, was not ready before the Revolution to compete with rum at any social level.

The distilled, fermented by-product of sugarmaking, rum flowed freely on election days, at weddings and wakes, and at the installation of clergymen. It was the one ingredient always present in the numerous concoctions that today we call "mixed drinks." Some were the devil's own brew— "stone-wall," for example, with equal amounts of rum and hard cider and nothing else. Others, considerably less deadly, were varied forms of flips and punches, some favored only in waterfront dives, others served to guests at the most elegant mansions. The recipe for one widely popular punch called for sugar, spice, brandy, lemon peel, porter—and Jamaica rum. Drinking was an almost universal colonial habit, and not even pious citizens considered it poor taste.

Almost nobody drank water. In Europe's crowded cities, it was not safe to drink, and prejudice against it was in the cultural baggage of immigrants early and late. It lost its power to intimidate, though, if it were boiled, as for tea, the closest thing to a national drink. Cider was a mealtime favorite of all but the most aristocratic families. Milk was seldom served as a beverage, but was used in cooking and fed to pigs and to calves after weaning. It was an ingredient, however, of one well-known delicacy, syllabub. A 1742 syllabub recipe from Williamsburg called for cream rather than milk, two kinds of wine, sugar, and lemon juice, all beaten together with a whisk for half an hour. Called "everlasting syllabub" because it would keep several days, it was spooned into glasses for serving.

The red horse of famine, from all the evidence, rode nowhere in the land. The sheer abundance and variety of native foods, grown in kitchen gardens or bought at the numerous farmers' markets, helped confirm the sense of independence and self-sufficiency. Beyond that, foods and spices from distant places, brought into colonial ports in quantity by far-ranging ships, made it possible even for middle- and lower-income families to indulge a taste for good dining that relatively few Europeans could share.

Homespun variety versus urban uniforms

Clothing was another matter. Of the three basics of survival—food, clothing, and shelter—it was far and away the most expensive. A few wealthy families ordered theirs from France or England, the surest way to keep up with the latest fashions. Other urbanites had clothes made by tailors and dressmakers, who varied in skill and in the fees they exacted. In rural areas, where families had learned to produce most of what they needed, maintaining a decent wardrobe cost less but meant hard work for the women of the household. The homespun clothing country people wore was the end product of a long series of necessary steps. First came the shearing of sheep, followed by carding the wool to remove impurities, spinning it on a wheel to thread of the desired thickness, weaving the threads together on a loom, cutting the resulting woven fabric, and sewing the pieces together in an approximation of fashionable design. To make the common linsey-woolsey fabric, linen thread, or cotton in the South, was interwoven with the wool; and both were usually home-produced, from flax or cotton plants.

Shoes and leather jackets, caps, and work aprons were made from skins of animals, wild or domestic, that had to be tanned and cut and pieced together by strong hands. Here the men contributed labor. Even the children helped, using tape looms to produce shoestrings and cording and trim for edging. It would have been far beyond the ability of even talented families to make clothing that would escape notice as country wear in any city. But urban clothing was just as conspicuous in the country. The difference was comparable to that between a city house built in strict conformity to standard Georgian style and one in vernacular style with just a few concessions to that standard. Country clothing conformed to country taste, out of necessity; and country taste had as much right to exist as did the urban insistence on foreign fashions.

If country clothing was rather drab compared to that worn by urban sophisticates, it was largely because of limited available colors. Wool from black sheep could be used for black accents, and white wool could be dyed before the thread was spun. But dyes with strong hues were costly. Natural dyes, made at home from nutshells and berries, commonly yielded soft or dull colors, and these tended to fade with time. Surviving examples of rural colonial clothing are commonly so faded that they give no idea of even the little variety of color they once had.

Country clothing had some variety because it was made by individuals using their own ingenuity. It was easy in a village to keep up with local fashion because it was limited. It was considered poor taste to dress above one's station in society, and rural Americans were all pretty much of the same social class.

Variety in apparel was much greater in cities, where class distinctions were evident, fixed by occupations, and where for almost every kind of work there was a particular way of dressing. The eighteenth century has with justice been called an age of uniforms. Drovers worked in smocks conveniently loose. Servant girls and saleswomen in shops wore simple, ample skirts and low-cut bodices. Tradesmen wore leather aprons cut in whatever way best suited their work. Male servants in wealthy households wore liveries, especially coachmen, who were most often seen in public and represented, by the lavishness of what they wore, the family's social ranking. Unskilled laborers went about in cheap clothes too varied to describe and wore trousers instead of the breeches and stockings worn by most males. After all, men at that level had no time or reason for vain display of their calves.

Skilled urban craftsmen who

had won favor with the mercantile aristocracy gained the privilege, as they approached affluence, to dress when not at work like the merchants themselves, with buckled shoes, white stockings, breeches ending just below the knees, and an open jacket over a waistcoat. But as long as they remained in trade, affecting the elegant attire reserved for the very rich would have been a serious breach of taste.

Not every man of wealth and high social standing habitually wore an extravagant ensemble, however. Some never did. But they had the right to. Such clothing might include an enormous cocked hat with a bright feather or two, a scarlet cloak lined with velvet of a contrasting color, a richly embroidered waistcoat with deep pockets, a shirt heavily ruffed in front and at the wrists, silk knee breeches and stockings, low shoes with silver buckles, and gloves of doeskin or beaver. All such clothing was symbolic, in the colonies as well as in England, of the topmost rank in society.

John Hancock, in his early years as heir apparent to his uncle's immense fortune, sometimes dressed that way. His friend Josiah Quincy, much less interested in public admiration, was very conservative in his dress. The difference was one of degree, for the pieces of clothing and their cut were much the same whether conspicuous or modest. At a concert in Charleston, Quincy noticed that most of the gentlemen dressed more richly and elegantly than was common in Boston, and many of them had dress swords at their sides. But when overdressed dandies appeared, just back from London, there were murmurs of disapproval. "See the macaroni!" went the rounds of the hall. The term was popular just then for a fop or a dandy preoccupied with putting himself on exhibit by affected

dress and fastidious manners.

Male attire in Philadelphia, where sober habits were the rule, was more to Quincy's liking. There, men commonly wore more subdued colors, probably in accord with Quaker tradition. But it made it rather difficult to distinguish solid citizens from upstarts. In any event, nobody there had been rich very long. One resident pointed this out in a letter to the editor of a local newspaper: "Is not half the property in the city of Philadelphia owned by men in LEATHER APRONS? Does not the other half belong to men whose fathers or grandfathers wore LEATHER APRONS?"

He was right, for by the middle of the eighteenth century, urban crafts were so highly developed that numerous men, in that city and others, had been able to rise from the trades to the status of gentlemen. And for gentlemen, fine clothes, whether modest or elaborate in ornament, were not only a prerogative but a necessity for showing their rank.

The wives of gentlemen, in all the colonies, wore gowns of expensive fabric and assorted jewelry, but they left the flamboyant plumage to the males of the species who chose to display it. One custom that seems rather curious today was the partial exposure of petticoats, which were actually part of the costume. It was the counterpart to the male practice of showing the waistcoat under the jacket—much more of it than is shown of vests under modern jackets.

After about 1750, stylish women took to wearing stays, which account in part for the stiff carriage and straight bodies shown in contemporary portraits. Of more than two hundred fifty Charleston ladies presented to him at a St. Cecilia Society concert, Quincy wrote that they stooped to the daughters

of the North "in loftiness of headdress; in richness of dress, surpass them; in flirtation after the music on a par with them." Hair piled high, in "towers" held up by metal rolls, was uncomfortable; but comfort is a common sacrifice to fashion. The loftiness that some of the towers acquired, especially in the North about the time of the Revolution, made them targets of ridicule and caricature in magazines. Doves could nest in them, one Boston editor insisted, and another called them miniature Bunker Hills.

A few sensible women turned to wearing wigs for social occasions. Men had been wearing them for decades, but these declined in size by the 1770s and then gave way to powdered natural hair, shoulder-length with a queue down the back.

Silver, pewter, pottery, and glass

At the leather-apron level, silversmiths were the aristocracy of tradesmen and were accorded some of the social privileges of the ruling caste. Silver in any form was the material possession most highly prized by those who could afford to own it, not only for its durable beauty but as an investment, for in hard times it could be melted down and converted to currency. Then, as prosperity returned, it could be reconverted, especially for "coin silver" spoons. There were no banks in those days for investment of savings.

By the 1770s, American silversmiths were closing the gap that had long given their London rivals a marked advantage. Established wealthy families continued to prefer imported silver, or already owned so much of it, as heirlooms, that they had no need to acquire more. Fine English silver had been a status symbol on both sides of the Atlantic since the seventeenth century, and continued to be, but

American-made pieces steadily gained in favor. As they did, taste began to diverge. Pieces made abroad were almost always elaborately designed, like those given to Sir William Pepperrell for his conquest of Louisburg. A skilled American artisan could turn out such pieces, but his clients increasingly showed a preference for greater plainness, of the sort that Paul Revere carried to perfection in the years after the Revolution. Whether this shift in taste represented a conscious repudiation of the styles of the former ruling nation or a move in the direction of less ornament and stress on the functional is hard to determine.

Many of the same articles made in silver were produced also in pewter, which cost less and was easier to work. It had, however, two weaknesses—it dented easily and, with its low melting point, was subject to destruction if inadvertently placed too near a hot fire. Pewter craftsmen, especially in Connecticut, for generation after generation improved their wares, adding decoration that made them competitive with silver. Porringers acquired pierced side tabs, and designs were etched on teapots and tankards.

There were advances also in other crafts. Native pottery bowls

Above right: Mrs. Isaac Winslow, by Robert Feke; 1748. Right: Detail, tombstone of Rev. Nathaniel Rogers; Ipswich, Mass.; 1775. Far right: Wooden ship's figurehead; Massachusetts; late 18th century.

and plates increasingly bore attractive designs. Most ironstone and glazed stoneware dishes, as well as fine porcelain, though, were still imported from England.

Glassmaking, earlier limited to producing bottles and other containers, and to small window-panes, began to include other objects. Finer glass pieces were at first copied from one or another home country in Europe, but as more skilled glass workers immigrated, indigenous design increased. A pioneer in this expansion was Caspar Wistar, who had his own glass factory in New Jersey in the 1740s. A quarter-century later, Henry William Stiegel, a German immigrant, set up shop in Pennsylvania. It did not last long, but it wielded considerable influence on glassmaking, especially on the making of colored glass with enameled designs and etched glass. Stiegel pieces quickly attracted attention, and, together with others made the same way, held a high place in taste for several decades. Without alternatives to choose from, taste has no meaning. The growing variety of articles made by American craftsmen multiplied the alternatives and at the same time cut into the advantage long held by foreign rivals.

More and better painters

Fresh immigration brought not only gifted craftsmen but better painters than the colonies had known before 1700. The colonists had always liked to have their portraits painted, and with increasing prosperity there arose a demand for better talents than those of the early limners. Gustav Hesselius, from Sweden, was among the first of the new breed. A Scot named John Smibert crossed the ocean in 1729, at the age of forty-one, with enough of a reputation to gain him numerous commissions. He painted Bishop Berkeley, his fellow passenger on the Atlantic crossing, and such New England worthies as Jonathan Edwards, Peter Faneuil, Sir William Pepperrell, and Chief Justice Samuel Sewall. An exhibit of his work at Yale in 1730 prompted an extraordinary poem by Mather Byles. "To Pictorio, on the Sight of his Pictures" addresses Smibert as a kindred soul, doing in his art what Byles himself sought to do in verse: "I the Description touch, the Picture you."

Byles was a fighter, ahead of his time in pointing out the value that the fine arts could have in a new, still raw civilization. Puritan leaders had condemned painting; in 1701, the popular Samuel Willard had called it a violation of the Second Commandment, forbidding graven images. Byles recognized Smibert as an ally in his effort to free the arts from the negative aesthetic attitudes that in New England, at least, were retarding a healthy development of taste.

There were encouraging signs, however, in the number of painters, and in the quality of their work. Of several native-born artists who advanced portraiture as the century grew older, two may be cited here—Robert Feke and Joseph Blackburn.

Robert Feke, a New Yorker who became a favorite in Boston, immortalized the family of Isaac Royall and idealized Mrs. Isaac Winslow. His adult subjects often look as though they had assumed unnaturally stiff postures for the paintings.

Colonial taste in portraiture was somewhat unusual in preferring full-length to head-and-shoulder renderings and also in demanding realism. Joseph Blackburn, who dominated portraiture from 1754 to 1763, carried the realism almost too far by committing to canvas the small eyes, large weak chins, and simpering smiles of Isaac Winslow's entire family. Conversely, he could and did capture the rugged strength of Col. Theodore Atkinson's face, and his portraits of James Bowdoin's children are delightful.

Rich colonials from the South often crossed the ocean to sit for the master artists of England until good native portrait painters began to migrate south. By the mid-1700s, Charleston was an important center of portraiture, and artists also worked in Baltimore, Richmond, and Savannah. New Orleans could boast of a few good Spanish and more French portrait painters. Quality everywhere steadily improved, in response to the growing demand, to the point where John Singleton Copley's *Boy with a Squirrel,* when exhibited in London in 1766, won the unstinted praise of artists there. *The Copley Family* and other portraits by this master stand comparison with the best by contemporary Europeans.

The laggard—sculpture

There was little demand for three-dimensional portraiture, in stone or metal or even in wood, the preferred material for what passed as sculpture before the Revolution. As ocean trade expanded, carved figureheads on ships became popular. Many were female figures, most often fully clothed, although a few were bare-breasted. Many more were male—Indian chieftains, nattily dressed young sailors, political heroes, and men in business attire, presumably the owners of the ships. Sternboards, wide and flat in the current nautical mode, were often painted and sometimes exhibited low-relief carving. So did some tavern signs, but the artistic level was low. The lettering and designs of gravestones showed little advance from a century earlier, but there were some exceptions—incised work so excellent that an occasional carver proudly signed his work.

The only statues in the colonies were of English notables, and they were all made in England. Quincy in 1773 described the colossal statue of Mr. Pitt in Charleston: the draped garments were well done, he thought, but the attitude, air, and expression of the piece "to me was bad." In New York on his way home, he wrote that "The equestrian statue of his Majesty, near the fort is a very great ornament to the city of New York." But the statue of Mr. Pitt in New York, in his opinion, "had all the defects of that in Charleston."

Most of these statues succumbed, during the Revolutionary ferment, to mob violence against anything to do with royalty. One statue that survived was the marble likeness of Lord Botetourt, the very popular royal governor of Virginia from 1768 until his sudden death in 1770. The "best of governors and best of men," as his obituary in the *Virginia Gazette* described him, was honored by burial in the crypt under the chapel at the Wren Building, and the next year the House of Burgesses voted funds for a suitable statue. It arrived in Williamsburg in 1773, a ton in weight, and stands today in the Swem Library at William and Mary College, one of the oldest statues in the country, if not the very oldest.

A limited taste for music

As the Georgian era opened, music was almost entirely under foreign influence. By far the best-known composer was Isaac Watts, whose *Psalms of David Imitated,* issued in 1719, was welcome in colonial churches that did not bar music from their services. Like lesser rivals, Watts assigned the melody to the tenor rather than to the soprano in four-part metrical settings of hymns and Psalms.

Before 1760, no more than seventy-five tunes were known, including those of Watts, but after that year the number grew rapidly to about four hundred. Even so, texts greatly outnumbered tunes until William Billings of Boston boldly identified each text with a particular tune in his 1770 *The New-England Psalm Singer.* What is more, he broke with tradition by using texts written by American poets, or by himself, rather than depending entirely on English talent. Unfortunately for the cause of indigenous taste, he stood alone, and nobody followed his lead for many more years.

He had more success in introducing the pitch pipe, that boon to choirmasters ever since for unaccompanied music, and in composing vigorous songs filled with patriotic sentiments, such as his ringing hymn "Chester":

> Let tyrants shake their iron rod,
> And slavr'y clank her galling chains.

Billings strengthened his status as America's first professional composer by issuing his *Singing Master's Assistant* in 1772. For most secular music, however, colonists relied on what crossed the Atlantic. It might have been otherwise if a versatile Philadephian, Francis Hopkinson, had chosen to give more attention to music. He is credited with composing in 1759 the first native secular song, "My Days Have Been So Wondrous Free," and with other works for voice and instruments, but his fame rests on other activities. He was author of propagandistic wartime poems, signer of the Declaration of Independence, designer of the Great Seal of the Republic, and holder of varied appointive offices of importance. But even if he had confined himself to music, as did Billings, what must be called cultural provincialism retarded, as it

was to do until the present century, full recognition of native composition.

Charleston and Annapolis, and of course Bethlehem, Pennsylvania, were noted for their interest in serious music. There was no scarcity anywhere of popular music, for parades and musters, rural frolics and stately dances, most of it borrowed or adapted from familiar English tunes. It may seem ironic that the Acton fifer, on the march toward the North Bridge in Concord early on April 19, 1775, set the pace with an old English song, "The White Cockade"; but he had little choice. In the long period of good relations with England, and even later, nobody was unhappy about the reliance, for every purpose, on music from abroad. At the folk level especially, English tunes were part of the popular culture, and their use was not questioned. When people are enjoying themselves, they seldom pause to question whether the music accompanying their recreation is native or borrowed.

Good performers were scarce, but in Charleston, at least, where fortunes were quickly made and as promptly spent, there was enough interest to hire Europe's best. Quincy reported a St. Patrick's Day event he attended there: "While at dinner, six violins, two hautboys, etc. After dinner six French horns in concert—most surpassing music. Two solos on the French horn, by one who is said to blow the finest horn in the world. He has fifty guineas for the season from the St. Cecilia Society." At another concert that Quincy attended, a Frenchman just arrived played the violin "better than anyone I ever heard." Charlestonians may not have had better taste than people in other colonial cities, but they could afford the best playing, and were unwilling to settle for anything less.

Time for recreation

By all accounts, in their last decades as overseas subjects, the colonists welcomed every chance they had to relax from their labors. Horse racing drew the largest crowds and attracted men at every social level. Class distinctions were recognized in other sports, however; riding to hounds was for the wealthy, and shooting at targets or at live turkeys was for the yeomanry.

The taste for such blood-lust spectacles as baiting animals had declined—wolves were nearly extinct in civilized areas, and bulls were becoming too valuable for farm work. Hunting continued to be popular, but with diminishing returns as men killed wildlife increasingly for sport instead of for food. Gambling at cards, despite prohibitory blue laws, approached a mania, whether played on inlaid tables in luxurious drawing rooms or on barrel heads in low dives. Weddings were social occasions, and, as in the previous century, there were always large crowds at such public entertainments as orations, hangings, and the funerals of celebrities. Attendance at some of these was still required of employees, a fact that roused little resentment, because it meant time off from work.

Guides to heaven and to horticulture

The books most eagerly bought and read in this enviable age reflected its diverse values and aspirations. Wherever hope of heaven —and fear of eternal hellfire—ran strong, titles like Lewis Bayly's pocket-size *The Practice of Piety* and *An Alarm to Unconverted Sinners,* by Joseph Alleine, an English clergyman, sold rapidly in urban bookstores. The first was a practical handbook with specific suggestions and even a procedure for warding off witchcraft. The other,

under its later title *The Sure Guide to Heaven,* so impressed Samuel Sewall that in 1717 he gave a copy to each member of the General Court, the elected legislature of Massachusetts. Most households throughout the colonies owned Bibles, whether or not everyone in the family could read them, and only Catholics lacked *Pilgrim's Progress.*

Books like Bacon's *Advancement of Learning* and Raleigh's *History of the World,* popular in the previous century, lost ground in the eighteenth century to practical "how-to-do-it" books on such subjects as shipbuilding and seamanship, cooking, carpentry, accounting, home medical care, and horticulture. Eagerness to acquire the means for rising in the world had replaced the earlier stress on mere survival, and a growing taste for practicality complemented the steady advance of secularism. With rising economic status, moreover, came a need for knowing how to behave properly on social occasions, and books on etiquette sold readily—as they were to do increasingly in the nineteenth century.

Unlike Benjamin Franklin, not everybody could amass money enough to retire early, but the ambition to do so was approved by taste. This attitude resulted in a steady growth of middle-class respectability. Franklin himself was both living proof of the potential in every citizen and, through his many writings, virtually the patron saint of the "getting ahead" philosophy. The so-called better class in Philadelphia, meaning those few families enjoying wealth earned by industrious forebears, took their time about recognizing Franklin. After all, he had arrived in their city at seventeen, almost penniless, and for years had been one of the "leather-apron" crowd that held him in great esteem. On

the other hand, he could write in a simple, always interesting way about almost any subject—deism or paper money, education or a witch trial in Mount Holly across the Delaware, the efficient stove he had invented or the notion of street lighting, *Advice to a Young Man on Choosing a Mistress,* or *Meditation on a Quart Mugg.*

There were men of greater intellect in eighteenth-century America, but none gained the lofty ranking Franklin did among his compatriots. One contemporary who might have been a rival in some other age was the Rev. Jonathan Edwards, a firm champion of Calvinism, whose *Freedom of the Will* is now considered, by the few who have read it, an American masterpiece of philosophical writing. By 1754, though, the year it was published, taste for Calvinist logic was in decline, even though Wigglesworth's *Day of Doom* was still being reissued and read after more than eighty years. The secular, open-minded view of life that Franklin helped to confirm was definitely in the ascendant.

Another contemporary of Franklin's (and one of his few enemies) was a fellow Philadelphian, John Dickinson, whose *Letters from a Farmer in Pennsylvania,* carefully stating the conservative position regarding relations with England, was a best-seller in 1768. If this term sounds like an anachronism, it may help to know that best-seller status for every year in American history is based on reliable figures of print orders and actual sales. But Dickinson was one of only three Americans to have best-selling books during the period from 1714 to 1775, the other two being Franklin and another almanac publisher, Nathaniel Ames. The French philosopher Jean Jacques Rousseau won best-seller status in 1761 with *La Nouvelle Héloise,* but all the rest who did

Right: Francis Hopkinson Conversing with a Lady, *from sketchbook of Benjamin West.* Below: The End of the Hunt, *by an unknown artist; ca. 1800.* Bottom left: Grand Rehearsal of the Anniversary Ode *(of the Tuesday Club), sketch by Dr. Alexander Hamilton; Annapolis, Md.; 1751. Dr. Hamilton was founder and historian of the club.* Bottom right: *Embroidered picture of a New England wedding; New England; 1756. Courtesy, American Antiquarian Society.*

were British poets, essayists, novelists: Addison, Steele, Pope, Defoe, Swift, Richardson, Fielding, Goldsmith. In a way, this colonial preference for what are acknowledged classics of English literature bespeaks of very sound taste. But it also indicates an almost total deference to foreign judgment that delayed the emergence of a national literature.

Spotty education

In the New England colonies, literacy was general, thanks to the Puritan regard for education, but elsewhere, especially in the South, it was very spotty. Sons of the tobacco aristocrats were tutored by college graduates in preparation for Oxford or Cambridge, Harvard or William and Mary. Philip Fithian, a Princeton graduate who was a tutor from 1773 to 1774 at Nomini Hall, one of the Carter plantations, concluded that the educational "basics" in the South were "Dancing, Boxing, playing the fiddle, & Small-sword, & Cards." He may have been biased; when he left, it was to become a clergyman.

Not all wealthy Virginians lived for pleasure and indolence by any means. William Byrd of Westover spent several years of his youth in England, where he came to understand his obligation, as a rich and cultivated gentleman, to patronize the arts and contribute to the public good. He owned about four thousand books, the largest private library in America, and what is more, he read them. An entry in his secret diary for March 12, 1712, is typical: "I rose about 6 o'clock and read two chapters in Hebrew and some Greek in Lucian. I said my prayers devoutly and ate boiled milk for breakfast." Byrd is remembered as the founder of Richmond and director of the survey establishing the line between Virginia and North Carolina, which he called "Lubberland" in his journal account of the expedition. Like Edward Taylor's metaphysical poems, the journal was not published until after 1900, and his contemporaries had no chance to savor his fine prose or to judge it on the scale of taste.

Poetry and drama

One evening in 1767, Philadelphians attended a theater just beyond the city limits to see *The Prince of Parthia.* Its author, Thomas Godfrey, had died four years before, and it had taken that long to secure its staging. The play was a blank-verse hodgepodge of passages derived from Shakespeare and other old dramatists, but the audience hailed it because, as they knew, it was the first play by an American to be professionally produced. Philadelphia was unique in barring theaters within the city limits, for taste for drama was strong in all the colonies. Most of the fare was imported, however, and would be for another century.

An even greater sensation than *The Prince of Parthia* was created by the publication in 1773 of *Poems on Various Subjects.* The poet was Phillis Wheatley, a black girl born in Africa who belonged to a Boston merchant. Here is the opening quatrain of "An Hymn to the Morning":

> Attend my lays, ye ever honour'd nine,
> Assist my labours, and my strains refine;
> In smoothest numbers pour the notes along,
> For bright Aurora now demands my song.

Lines of this sort when written by Anne Bradstreet more than a century earlier had a strong appeal to reader taste, but by 1773, they were old-fashioned. The very fact that a black could compose poetry at all ran counter to the general notion of racial inferiority that was among the justifications for slavery. Intellectuals throughout the colonies were impressed, however. One was Thomas Jefferson, who went out of his way to vouch for Wheatley's originality when English friends questioned it.

Most of the poetry of the period appeared not in collected volumes but in almanacs, newspapers, and magazines, and as broadsides. All these were widely read, but magazines published in the colonies had a curious habit of dying early. Prior to 1776, sixteen had been launched only to expire within a few months. British magazines, like British furniture, had a grip on colonial taste that seemed unbreakable, even by canny Isaiah Thomas of Worcester, whose *Massachusetts Spy,* violently rebel in tone, was the most respected newspaper in the colonies. Taste favored the staid, solid *Gentleman's Magazine,* published in London, the very first periodical to be called a magazine.

News traveled slowly, and newspaper reports of events were often weeks late. This accounts for the great popularity of broadsides, single sheets printed on one side only that could be issued quickly and distributed by runners throughout a city and its close environs. They sold for a penny, but this was enough to yield a welcome profit. Political news was only one of their topics. Dying confessions of convicted criminals were common. So were lugubrious funereal verses and, just before and during the Revolution, wartime ballads, propagandistic verse, and declarations by colonial officials.

The war brought to an abrupt halt the virtual monopoly that English literature held on colonial taste. The leading best-seller of 1775 was the first part of *M'Fingal,* a political satire by John Trumbull, best of the Connecticut Wits. Its short lines in rhymed couplets made it easier to read and enjoy than most poems of the period. Canto I opens with:

> When Yankees, skill'd in martial rule,
> First put the British troops to school;
> Instructed them in warlike trade,
> And new manoeuvres of parade;
> And true war-dance of Yankee reels,
> And manual exercise of heels . . .

These allusions to the battles of Lexington and Concord, and to guerilla tactics confusing to the redcoats, no patriot could have missed.

Again in 1776, the top best-seller was American, Thomas Paine's *Common Sense,* with its immortal justification for rebellion. Two best-sellers back to back! That was indeed the "seedtime," as Paine put it, and as rebels all agreed, "of continental union, faith, and honor."

Or was it? John Adams said years later that the Revolution was over, in the minds and hearts of the people, before a single shot was fired. He no doubt meant that they were already independent in all but name. The seeds had sprouted years before and the harvest was at hand, though it took a dozen hard years of war and argument to tally it up and form "a more perfect union."

But that was political. Cultural independence was quite another matter. Patriots demanded it at once, but did not know how to go about creating it. Viewed in long perspective, the effort got off on the wrong foot. Nobody saw the importance of departing from cultivated foreign taste or the futility of stepping up the reliance on foreign methods and models. How much longer would it be before the vernacular could exert its influence and form the basis of an indigenous culture?

The

Federal Decades

(1776–1825)

Enthusiasm for the Constitution was hardly universal. Having enjoyed state autonomy for the dozen years since independence was declared, a good many Americans were reluctant to lose it to a new authority, even one of their own creation. Who could be sure it would not become, in time, as oppressive as the English government had been in the decade after 1765? Distaste for centralized power has lingered ever since. It is one reason why the Fourth of July is annually celebrated with gusto, and why few of us even know the day and month when the Constitution was adopted.

The first freedom

Ratification might not have been possible without the promise of a Bill of Rights, now the first ten amendments. The priority given in the first of these to religious freedom suggests how very strongly the majority of people opposed established churches that were accorded special status and such privileges as taxing all citizens for their support. But there were other grounds for such opposition. Most of the population belonged to no church at all and suspected, often with good reason, that whatever church dominated in a given state represented a minority intent on maintaining its political and social control. Distasteful as this was to individuals of an independent turn

of mind, there was also the fear that theologies already in decline, Calvinist Puritanism among them, would survive if established and in a position to be forced upon everybody. Not even the prompt action taken by the Anglican Church after the Revolution to cut loose from the Church of England, reorganizing itself as the Protestant Episcopal Church, could mollify the freethinking majority.

As it turned out, newer denominations benefited most from the First Amendment freedom. Using aggressive tactics distasteful to the staid old churches, they grew rapidly in membership, influence and wealth. With success, however, they lost much of their enthusiasm for the crude proselyting their fire-and-brimstone spellbinders indulged in, and with their coffers filling, they considered the wisdom of holding worship in edifices in whatever style was currently favored by cultivated taste—Georgian, Federal, Greek Revival, Gothic. Refined ritual in a sanctuary as handsome as any the conservative denominations worshiped in was attractive as a means of gaining respectability and the reputation for exercising good taste.

Churches without belfries

Church architecture, in the half-century after the Declaration, was not closely tied to any one style,

Preceding pages: Federal room, Stephen Chase House; Strawbery Banke, Portsmouth, N.H. Furnished as would befit a well-to-do merchant of 1800. Opposite: Nancy Lawson, by William Matthew Prior; 1843. Wife of Rev. William Lawson, a popular abolitionist preacher.

Nancy Lawso
1843.
W. M. Pr

Right: *Painted wood* retablo;
San Jose, Calif.; 1783. Below:
*Pennsylvania German Fraktur
certificate; Northampton County,
Pa.; 1779.* Opposite: *Cigar-store
Indian of the type popular between
the 1850s and the 1880s.*

but the trend was definitely in the direction of symmetry and elegance. One of the most beautiful churches built during the Federal period is the Alna Meeting House in Lincoln County, Maine, constructed in 1789. The group taste of the congregation is reflected in the partitioned booths and the second-story gallery on three sides. But the floor plan was not in the Anglican tradition, for the raised pulpit is against the longer wall instead of being at the end of the nave. The worshipers faced each other across the center aisle instead of looking directly at the preacher. The exterior of the building, moreover, resembles a barn more than a typical church; and there is no belfry.

Numerous other churches built about the same time lacked belfries, although some were added later as money became more plentiful. By what may seem an odd transposition, belfries were standard on courthouses, like that in Wiscasset not far from Alna, and on banks and mills and business blocks, where they were more decorative than functional—working hours were from sunup to sunset and not set by clocks until employers agreed to a 72-hour week, late in the nineteenth century.

If humble churches had no belfries, they increasingly had balanced facades, with either one centrally placed main door or one near each corner. Windows on the side walls were usually quite large, in the Georgian tradition of designing so that interiors would be flooded with daylight. Despite the steady increase of neoclassical elements, however, some people thought that church architecture should revert to the Gothic, as being more symbolic of religious sincerity. In 1816, Ithiel Town's Trinity Church in New Haven boldly asserted the Gothic preference, and two years later the Rev. Samuel Jarvis, son of

the Episcopal bishop of Connecticut, designed a church like it in Gardiner, Maine. Jarvis was later active in the New York Ecclesiological Society, a high-church group committed to the Gothic. Their cause faltered during the Greek Revival era but eventually triumphed after the craze for Doric columns and pediments ran its course.

"One God and no more"

Ecclesiastic architecture might have been in constant flux, but doctrinal differences remained constant. Quaker distaste for proselyting new members kept the Society of Friends small, and also regional. But where they were strong, in Philadelphia and its environs, for example, their influence was great. Their rejection of structured ritual and salaried preachers, their refusal to bear arms or to take oaths, their espousal of total equality of the sexes, and their unwillingness to remove their hats before alleged superiors made them repugnant in other sections. In New England, with its time-honored militia service and its lofty respect for clergymen and magistrates, Quakers were not only unwelcome but sometimes victims of humiliating persecutions. What eventually dissipated antagonism was their ability to prosper materially. Even for Puritans, that was evidence of divine favor.

What seemed to outsiders to be the peculiarities of Quakers, and of smaller religious bodies scattered about the country, posed no serious challenge to major denominations, or to the standards of cultivated taste. But quite a different set of beliefs, held by deists, was generally regarded as a serious threat. Not a formal religion but an outgrowth of advancing science and eighteenth-century rationalism, deism completely rejected the tenets of all organized churches.

The few Americans who shared deistic views were usually discreet enough to keep their interest from becoming public knowledge. Franklin touched upon deistic principles in a few essays that were couched in oblique language, and expressed his complete endorsement only in private letters, notably one he wrote to Ezra Stiles in 1790, shortly before he died. Ethan Allen was less cautious: his *Reason the Only Oracle of Man*, published in 1784, compromised his reputation as the hero of Ticonderoga. But the boldest of all was Thomas Paine, who in 1795 attacked all formal religion in *The Age of Reason.* "I believe in one God and no more," he wrote, and went on to insist that "All national institutions of churches, whether Jewish, Christian, or Turkish, appear to me no other than human inventions, set up to terrify and enslave mankind, and monopolize power and profit." That was too much. It so outraged taste in America that it canceled out his immense fame as the author, nineteen years earlier, of *Common Sense.*

"The worst of trades"

No matter what he wrote, Paine's kind of writing would not have been considered literature despite its great eloquence. It might have been a century earlier, when New England sermons were admired for their careful composition and for their liberal use of classical allusions. But by the time of the Revolution, the definition of literature had narrowed to include only the conventions of English taste. The satirical approach was acceptable; the head-on attack was not. Paine was not the kind of man for whom satire was attractive. On the other hand, his poetic contemporary John Trumbull could accept the rules. Even when blasting the Tories in his *M'Fingal,* he adopted

Typical advertising chromolithographs of the late 19th century.

the conventions of English satire and a verse form, the octosyllabic couplet, that had been long honored in English poetry.

Trumbull's protégé, Timothy Dwight, a grandson of Jonathan Edwards, carried obeisance to English literary taste even further in *Greenfield Hill*, written in 1794 to glorify a typical village in Connecticut. A nostalgic pastoral, it is transparently imitative of Oliver Goldsmith's *The Deserted Village*, famous in America since 1770. Goldsmith opened with these lines:

> Sweet Auburn, loveliest village
> of the plain,
> Where health and plenty cheered
> the laboring swain,

and Dwight with these:

> Fair Verna! loveliest village
> of the west,
> Of every joy, and every charm,
> possessed.

Dwight was more successful when

he became president of Yale College; that post was ideal for a man as serious and unpoetical as he seems to have been.

A better poet of the period was Joel Barlow, who shared the dream of creating a distinctive national culture but, like Dwight and too many others with the same ambition, adopted the wrong course. In a misguided effort to emulate Virgil, whose *Aeneid* was a paean to all-powerful Rome, Barlow sought to glorify America's past in an epic he titled *The Vision of Columbus*. It was well enough received in 1787 to encourage him to enlarge it twenty years later and to give it an even more classical title, *The Columbiad*. More applause. But such are the vagaries of taste that it is now considered a "tin-plated" epic and one of America's monumental failures.

At least the poets tried. And, being poets, they were better able than most people to verbalize the

dreams of having a great native literature. John Trumbull put it this way in 1770:

> This land her Steele and Addison
> shall view
> The former glories equall'd by
> the new;
> Here shall some Shakespeare
> charm the rising age,
> And hold in magic chains the
> listening stage.

Two years later, in their commencement poem at the College of New Jersey (Princeton), Hugh Henry Brackenridge and Philip Freneau hailed *The Rising Glory of America* with equal optimism:

> I see a Homer and a Milton rise
> In all the pomp and majesty of
> song,
> A second Pope . . .

Freneau tried as hard as any of the other writers to fulfill the prophecy. Two impudent ballads in 1775 and 1776, *General Gage's Soliloquy* and *General Gage's Con-*

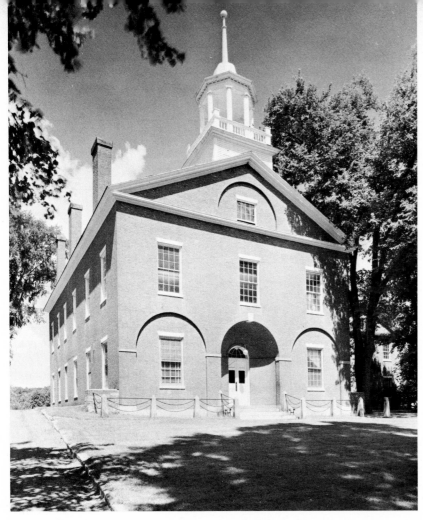

Opposite: *Interior, Alna Meeting House; Alna Center, Maine; 1789. The building was used for public meetings as well as religious services.* Above left: *Lincoln County Courthouse; Wiscasset, Maine; 1818–24.* Top: *Detail of stairway, Capt. Keyran Walsh House; Strawbery Banke, Portsmouth, N.H.; ca. 1800. Wooden steps were painted to resemble marble.* Above: *Door with painted graining, front sitting room, Capt. Keyran Walsh House.*

fessions, won the praise of patriots; but nobody much cared for his numerous poems with Romantic themes. "The Wild Honeysuckle" is now regarded in some quarters as one of the finest nature poems, and "The House of Night" (1779) as perhaps the best poem in English written during the Revolutionary period. Frustrated as a poet, Freneau turned to journalism and succeeded so well as Jefferson's henchman that Washington, whose presidential actions he attacked, called him "that rascal Freneau." In old age, aware that he was considered not quite respectable, Freneau summed up his career wryly:

> To write was my sad destiny,
> The worst of trades, we all agree.

Poets were not alone in trying to promote cultural independence— or in falling short of that goal. In 1789, the year the new nation began to function, its first novel appeared: *The Power of Sympathy* (written by William Hill Brown and published anonymously). Nation proved more durable than novel. The next decade saw two others, *Charlotte Temple* by Susanna Rowson, and Hannah Foster's *The Coquette.* All three used the seduction theme of Richardson's *Pamela,* published in England in 1740 and still in favor with readers there and in America after fifty years. Why it took Americans so long to produce a novel is hard to understand, especially when the *Pamela* formula was so easy to adopt and so certain to gain the approval of taste. *Charlotte Temple* had a special popularity because it was allegedly based on an actual case in New York. It spawned the rumor, which still persists, that the actual Charlotte lies buried in Trinity churchyard— and perhaps she does.

Seduction as a theme waned in literary fashion by the end of the century, to be replaced by gothic horror. Its chief exponent was a Philadelphian, Charles Brockden Brown, but not even his best effort, *Wieland,* issued in 1798, approached the success of its English rivals, from Horace Walpole's *The Castle of Otranto* in 1764 to Mary Shelley's *Frankenstein* in 1818. Nor was the nation ready to put its stamp of approval on *Modern Chivalry,* a satirical novel on politics and social behavior by Freneau's old college friend Brackenridge. Satire was acceptable enough, but Americans were too sensitive about their image to laugh at their own foibles in print. They had been amused by *M'Fingal,* but in that work the satire had been aimed at hated English agents. It takes a certain maturity to support a taste for satire on one's character and behavior.

Trumbull came closest of all his contemporaries to being a professional writer. Most had to earn their living in other professions. Brackenridge was a lawyer, Freneau a journalist, Barlow a diplomat. Charles Brockden Brown's heroic effort (six books in four years) to live by his pen ended in failure. Only when English readers and critics hailed an American writer could there be any hope of achieving professional status and success. That happened for the first time in 1820, when Washington Irving's *The Sketch Book* was so great a success in England, where Romanticism was further advanced, that Americans could no longer view their writers as second-rate. Authorship has been a recognized profession in America ever since.

Establishing a mother *tung*
Lexicography is hardly literature by anybody's definition unless, like some of the crotchety definitions in Samuel Johnson's dictionary, it acquires a literary patina with passing time. No such fame has accrued to the definitions proposed by Noah Webster, but his early campaign to convince his countrymen that their language differed from that of England put him in the forefront of our cultural nationalists. In the preface of his *Spelling Book,* first issued in 1783, he boldly announced his intention to make America "as independent in *literature* as she is in *politics,* as famous in *arts* as for *arms.*" Native writing, he must have believed, would improve and rise in reader taste if English spelling and pronunciation yielded to American spelling and pronunciation.

Webster, a Connecticut Yankee and a Yale graduate, sought to impose his own personal and regional standards on the entire population. The language habits of the South and the mid-Atlantic states, and even of remote parts of New England, were by his reasoning simply wrong. Like Joel Barlow in *Hasty Pudding,* he was a regional chauvinist, once writing in his diary, "O New England! how superior are thy inhabitants in morals, literature, civility, and industry!" He reveled in controversy, knowing its value in drawing attention to any subject. Much that he advocated never caught on; if it had, we would all be pronouncing *ask* as *ax, nature* as *nater, deaf* as *deef,* and we would use such spellings as *soe* for *sew, tung* for *tongue,* and *fether, groop, crum,* and *iland.* Webster had his successes, too, as in the dropping of *u* in such words as *labor* and *honor* and in the pronouncing of every syllable in *secretary, laboratory,* and the like. We are still arguing, however, about *it is me,* a construction he favored over the grammatical *it is I.* But in general Noah Webster is a towering figure in the select company of tastemakers, for we all, to one degree or another, conform to linguistic standards he did his best to establish and promote.

"Who looks at an American picture?"
The champions of cultural nationalism may have been distressed by the virtual monopoly on American reader taste held by Lord Byron and Sir Walter Scott in the quarter-century following 1800. Year after year these great Romantics dominated sales in America as in England except for 1820, the year of Irving's *Sketch Book.* Why had the strong impulse to develop a native literature waned after the good start in the 1790s? Was the effort too great to maintain?

The Rev. Sydney Smith, astringent critic for the *Edinburgh Review,* was contemptuous of American aspirations. "In the four quarters of the globe," he asked in 1820, "who reads an American book? or goes to an American play? or looks at an American picture or statue?" It was no way to win friends this side of the Atlantic, yet what he said had some basis in fact and would continue to as long as Americans deferred to taste in literature set abroad. Scott and Byron deserved their great fame, but what Smith did not mention was the unfair copyright situation of that era. Any foreign book could be pirated and sold in America with no royalty paid to its author; the resulting flood of cheap editions of popular English books in America put American authors at a great disadvantage. Economics can influence taste.

Smith was on firm ground regarding other facets of American culture. Nobody outside the United States, and not too many there, looked at American sculpture or attended American plays for the simple reason that both were almost nonexistent in that age of continuing imitation of foreign, mostly English, models. Despite the loud demands by American journalists, politicians, orators, and scholars for cultural independence, cultivated taste still followed the foreign lead. The shift from Georgian to Federal architecture is an eloquent example. Had American architects and builders, and their clients, really wanted to break away from English domination, they might have chosen that time to do so. But they did not.

Federal mansions

Prime mover of the new Federal style was a Scottish architect working in England, Robert Adam, aided in varying degrees by his three younger brothers. In 1748, they shared the enthusiastic interest of all Europeans in the excavations at Pompeii and Herculaneum, buried by volcanic ash since A.D. 79. What came to light was ample evidence of the Roman love for bright domestic colors, rooms in varied shapes, and delicate decoration. Adam set about duplicating such effects in a style of house design, and that style was soon named for him. Some thirty years later, when American preoccupation with the Georgian style was waning, the style crossed the Atlantic and was given a new name, Federal, more appropriate than Adamesque to the pretensions of the emerging nation. It dominated American architectural taste for four decades, roughly from 1780 to 1820, reaching its climax in New England at the hands of Charles Bulfinch and Samuel McIntire.

Like the Georgian it replaced in favor, the Federal style was clearly neoclassical. Externally, a fine Federal building differs only slightly from one in the Georgian mode. In general, the decoration is flatter, thinner, and less emphatic and gives the impression of greater delicacy. Corner pilasters are usually narrower, moldings less conspicuous, rounded forms more common—as in the use of semicir-

Top left: *Peirce Mansion; Portsmouth, N.H.; 1799. A key example of Federal domestic architecture in New England.*
Top right: *Octagon House, designed by William Thornton; Washington, D.C.; 1800. Photographed 1904.*

Center: *Blair House; Washington, D.C.; 1827. A Federal-style town house.* Above: *Daguerreotype of U.S. Capitol with dome designed by Charles Bulfinch and installed in 1825; Washington, D.C.; ca. 1846.*

cular windows with radiating sash bars, or fanlights, over doorways instead of Doric pediments.

There are greater differences indoors. For centuries, rooms had been square or rectangular; now many of them were round or oval, like the only room in the unfinished White House that Abigail Adams, its first mistress, thought well of. It was "very handsome," she wrote on November 21, 1800, adding that when completed, it would be beautiful—as the Oval Office indeed is.

Whatever the shape of its rooms, the ceilings of a typical Federal house were likely to be decorated with molded plaster rosettes, urns, and bulging festoons known as swags. Sunbursts sprouted on cornices, window frames, and mantels. Nothing was inexpensive about a fine Federal house, one that won the awe and admiration of visitors; its perfection was proof of the owner's impeccable taste and his willingness to pay for it. Unlike the Georgian, the Federal could not easily be imitated by those far down the economic scale. Even the fences enclosing the grounds were elaborate. Despite their cost, for forty years Federal houses were generally recognized as the most desirable.

The Federal in New England

In New England communities that reached their economic peak during the early years of the Republic, fine Federal houses survive in some quantity. Perhaps the greatest concentration of them is in Portsmouth, New Hampshire—in 1800, a major port and the commercial gateway to all of northern New England. Because three serious fires—in 1802, 1806, and 1813—destroyed many of Portsmouth's older buildings, an opportunity was provided for wealthy families to build anew in the currently fashionable style. Although the records

for the Peirce Mansion, built in 1799, were consumed in one of these fires, its design is traditionally credited to Bulfinch or McIntire. In fact, the structure so admirably illustrated the Federal style that it served as model for many later houses in New England, including those in Portsmouth built after the fires. The Nathan Parker House, on a dead-end street, dates from 1814. Built of brick rather than wood, it has, like the Peirce Mansion, five bays, and a centered front door topped by a flat-arched fanlight, but it

lacks the Peirce Mansion's conspicuous pilasters with their Ionic capitals and the balustrade that surrounds the entire flat roof. Such omissions exemplify the growing local taste for exercising greater restraint in exterior decoration.

Interest in historic preservation, pioneered by Colonial Williamsburg in the 1930s, prompted the effort in the late 1950s to restore Strawbery Banke, the original settlement that developed into Portsmouth. Thanks to enlightened federal policy, local citizens were able to incorporate in order to acquire

the site with its surviving buildings, most of them derelict, that would otherwise have been bulldozed for urban renewal. Thirtyodd structures have now been returned to their former condition in whole or in part. The oldest dates from 1695, the youngest from the Federal period. A great advantage of this and similar projects involving restoration of an integral community rather than individual buildings is that more historic continuity is provided, which, in turn, enables the results of shifting taste to be better observed.

The Strawbery Banke district had begun its decline in the Georgian years, and the most impressive Federal houses of Portsmouth are elsewhere, in sections that had become more fashionable. Yet the relatively modest house built in the district about 1796 and redecorated four years later for Capt. Keyran Walsh shows the influence of the Federal ideal. Of special interest are the panels skillfully painted to look like grained wood, and the fireplace hearth and the stair treads and risers, to look like marble. The more impressive Gov. Goodwin Mansion nearby, built in 1811, also displays Federal tradition with its balustraded main roof and one ground-floor room with a conspicuous rounded bay window.

In Kittery just across the Piscataqua River and in one old village after another on down the Maine coast toward Canada, there are numerous Federal houses, some so huge that it is hard to believe that they once housed single families. The yellow Capt. Lord mansion in Kennebunkport, fronted by a spacious lawn sloping down toward the Kennebunk River, has a main entrance hall and another, on one side, that is a hardly less elegant entrance hall. One of the marvels of the house is an elliptical freestanding staircase. The mansion, built by unemployed ships' carpenters during the English blockade in the War of 1812, has twenty-three rooms on its three floors and a large octagonal cupola atop the nearly flat roof.

There are Federal houses along the main street of industrial Saco, and more of them in Portland, some of brick, others wooden. Yarmouth and Brunswick, Thomaston and Camden and Belfast—all have what may seem more than their rightful share; but Maine seaports were busy and prosperous during the Federal era, producing the wealth needed for full compliance with Federal standards. South of Portsmouth also, many survive in all their glory—in Newburyport and Salem, in the comfortable Middlesex villages near Boston, as neighbors of Brown University in Providence, in towns facing Long Island Sound in Connecticut, and inland as well—wherever men had the knack of making fortunes and sought the reputation of being men of sound taste.

A selectman and a woodcarver

Charles Bulfinch and Samuel McIntire designed few of the Federal houses in New England, but they were the acknowledged leaders in interpreting the style throughout the region. In 1793, Bulfinch designed Franklin Crescent in Boston, a long, curving row of attached residences inspired by similar blocks built by Robert Adam in London. It was the statehouses he provided for Connecticut and Massachusetts, however, that brought Bulfinch to the forefront of public attention. He was very active in politics, serving as Boston's

Opposite: *Fireplace mantel, front parlor, Gardner-Pingree House, designed by Samuel McIntire; Salem, Mass.; 1804. Courtesy, Essex Institute, Salem, Mass. Above left: Empire bedroom; ca. 1815. Above right: Hepplewhite tambour washstand; early 19th century.*

79

head selectman (the equivalent of mayor) from 1799 until 1818, yet he found time to design numerous other buildings, including University Hall at Harvard and the Massachusetts General Hospital. In 1818, he was summoned to Washington to help complete the Capitol, which had been burned by the British in 1814. His dome, built in 1825, stood for twenty-six years, being replaced by the present tiered dome after the Federal style lost its grip on taste.

Whether Bulfinch confirmed the taste for Federal architecture in America or merely rode it to its crest, he put his unmistakable brand upon it. The contribution of McIntire was almost as great. A Salem native for whom architecture was only one of many interests, McIntire began as a woodcarver. His skillfully worked ship figureheads and decorated signs attracted the attention of the shipping aristocracy, who wanted proper mansions in the latest style and felt that he could design them. As a result, McIntire was responsible for several of the finest residences in Salem, including the Peirce-Nichols, the Peabody-Silsbee, and the Gardner-Pingree. With each new commission, he moved further from the Georgian and closer to the standards of Robert Adam. Being a woodworker, he was particularly interested in interiors, and under his hand cornices and mantels became more and more delicate and restrained. His son and other relatives skilled in the various decorative arts assisted him, for no one man working alone could have handled all the commissions—for both public and private buildings—offered him at the peak of his reputation.

Outside of New England, the Federal style fell off markedly, probably for lack of architects and decorators as adept as Bulfinch and McIntire. Good examples exist, however, in many parts of the country. The Octagon in Washington, D.C., a mansion built in 1799 to accommodate the acute angle formed by an unusual pattern of converging streets, is a marvel of adaptation unlike anything the New Englanders ever had to attempt. Woodlawn in Fairfax County, Virginia, built in 1802, conforms in general to the Federal mode but is closer to the Georgian features favored so long in that state. Bremo (1815–19), in Fluvanna County, deviates from standard Federal even further; its touches suggesting the style of Palladio betray the personal bias of its architect, Thomas Jefferson. The Gadsden House in Charleston, dating from about 1800, follows local Georgian tradition by fronting a garden instead of the street, which rather obscures its Federal elements. And the 1803 home of William Henry Harrison in Vincennes, Indiana, has only one conspicuously Federal touch, a great rounded bay at one end. The more remote from New England a given Federal house was, the less likely it was to conform completely to Federal standards.

Federal interiors

Federal interiors varied from house to house and from one individual decorator to another. As with exteriors, the Federal standard not only permitted but virtually demanded individualism of design and execution. Even the work of McIntire shows variation, for he was not the kind of man who was ever quite satisfied. A skilled cabinetmaker might be proud of being able to make a hundred fine chairs exactly alike; but houses and rooms are not chairs, to be multiplied indefinitely. The fireplace and mantel he carved for the front parlor of the Gardner-Pingree House may be his finest work. Sheaves of wheat, vines ascending the border columns, and garlands looping from the sides to a centered basket of grapes are all worked with exquisite delicacy.

The walls of the son's bedroom on the third floor of that house show a continuous scene, setting human figures against buildings and streams and trees native to widely scattered parts of the world —typical of the French scenic wallpaper currently very high in taste. Most Federal rooms of the period, if they were papered at all, had wallpaper printed with simple repetitive patterns, which was less costly than the scenic, and a few had designs stenciled directly upon the plaster.

Good taste required such elaborate interior decoration to be complemented by furniture of equal delicacy. Neither the heavy Queen Anne style favored before 1750 nor the ornamented Chippendale that dominated taste for the next quarter-century would have been right in a Federal house. Pieces that would be appropriate had to be provided, and they were—by followers of George Hepplewhite, just then the most fashionable London designer. His book *The Cabinet Maker and Upholsterer's Guide,* issued in 1788, two years after his death, was an instant success, and occasioned a stylistic revolution. Out went cabriole legs and bulging claw-and-ball feet. They were replaced by slender legs, usually straight and tapering to no feet at all. Wide chair arms with deeply carved molding yielded to arms so thin as to seem fragile, and with barely visible carving. And all the Chinese fretwork beloved by Chippendale vanished, for it was hardly compatible with Pompeiian motifs.

By 1800, designs by yet another Londoner, Thomas Sheraton, gained the acme of fashionable taste, holding it for another twenty years. His major innovation was replacing the curving lines of chair backs that Hepplewhite had popularized with right angles and straight-line geometric designs. Sheraton published two books, more than a decade apart, to explain and illustrate his style, and he changed his mind in that short period. The second book, issued in 1803, introduced the French Directoire style, distinguished by its lyre-shaped chair backs, acanthus-leaf carving, paw feet of brass or carved wood, and by such new pieces as the fancy painted chair and the chest of drawers with mirror attached.

Aside from the turn to France for inspiration, what gives the French

Top: *Boy's room, Gardner-Pingree House; Salem, Mass. French scenic wallpaper; early 19th century. Sheraton work table; ca. 1810. Field-type Federal bedstead with white net canopy; 1785–1800. Chippendale dressing table, or lowboy; 1760–80. Courtesy, Essex Institute, Salem, Mass.* **Left:** *Duncan Phyfe table and rocking chair; early 19th century.* **Above:** *Sheraton side chairs; New York; 1790–95. Chippendale pole fire screen with needlework panel; New York; 1760–75. Queen Anne wingchair; New England; ca. 1730.*

Directoire style its significance for our purpose is that, for the first time, the name of an American furnituremaker, Duncan Phyfe, became a household word because of his distinctive interpretation of the style. Like Sheraton's chairs, Phyfe's were usually square-backed, but he was less committed than Sheraton to straight-line designs. Produced between 1810 and 1820, his lyre-backs are famous today; at the time they were made, his turned-leg, curule (X-frame), and saber-leg chairs were held in equal esteem by his affluent contemporaries. He had his own workshop, but such was his reputation that it could not keep up with the demand for his design, and he could not prevent the multiplication of rival shops, in several cities, that copied his chairs and rode to prosperity on his coattails.

What Phyfe proved was that an American furnituremaker could produce pieces as high in quality as any made abroad, and as appealing to taste. For decades, there had been Americans as expert as he was and as painstaking in their choice of wood and method of construction, but he had the luck to be the first to win recognition. He was hardly a tastemaker, though, for he worked in styles other men created and willingly accommodated his designs to every shift in foreign taste. After 1820, he lost clients through his inability to do well with the Empire style that

Top left: *Lithograph of Shaker Village; Alfred, Maine; 1880. The village was organized in 1793.* Above left: *Sisters' shop and workroom; Shaker Village, Hancock, Mass.; 1790.* Left: *Built-in storage units in the main dwelling house; Shaker Village, Hancock, Mass.; 1792–93.*

next came into fashion.

It meant something, of course, that the work of an individual American, for the first time, stood high in cultivated taste. Deference to foreign taste continued, however, which was a rather ironic position for a nation that prided itself on its independence to be in. It was not for lack of alternatives, for they existed and could easily have been noticed and perhaps adopted, if anybody had made the effort. Nobody did. Nobody, that is, who shared the overweening desire to be considered tasteful.

Other forms

Windsor chairs were in continuous demand, as they had been for more than half a century, for use everywhere except in the formal parlors, where visitors, who formed the all-important judgments that determined social standing, could see them. By the standards of cultivated taste, the suitability of furniture was judged not by the comfort, durability, or practicality it offered but only by how closely it conformed to currently approved style. Consequently, furniture such as the Windsor chair, which was in use by people at the lower economic levels, could be ignored by sophisticated Anglo-Americans. So could the furniture used among the diverse population groups scattered across the country, such as the radically simple styles developed by an English-speaking group that called itself "The United Society of Believers in Christ's Second Appearing." Other people knew them as Shakers.

The Shakers

A 1747 offshoot of the Quakers, the Shakers suffered so from persecution in England that merely being ignored there might have been heavenly. Ann Lee, their great leader, spent eight years in prison before she was able to lead a handful of followers to America in 1774. Once settled, they gained new converts and by the end of the century had communes, which they called families, from Maine to Indiana.

Accepting Mother Lee's strictures against ornament of any sort as both unnecessary and sinful, Shaker workmen built plain, very practical buildings, some of them in unusual shapes, such as the great round barn at Hancock, Massachusetts. They developed implements and furniture on wholly functional principles. They made round and oval boxes, assorted tinware, small and very large baskets, and the best brooms anybody could buy. They did not invent the common ladder-back chair, more widely used than even the Windsor, but they elevated it and other ordinary furniture to the ultimate of utility and simplicity. More perhaps than any other group in America, they created indigenous forms that but for the power of sophisticated taste might have hastened the advent of a distinctive national culture. As it was, Shaker furniture had a greater impact on the development of modern functionalism than the Queen Anne, the Chippendale, the Hepplewhite, and the Sheraton styles combined, each of them rising quickly to the peak of taste only to be rejected in short order.

The Shakers insisted on the presence of both "logic and beauty" in their designs and were indifferent to shifting styles dictated by taste in Europe and urban America. Indeed, logic and beauty ought to be related, but in the early 1800s, as in the previous century, the relationship was something most Americans were unprepared to understand. Nor were they ready to see much of cultural value in the folk art that flourished in America for the century from 1776 to 1876, after which it began to succumb to the machine-made products that told of the beginning of the modern age of industry.

Art from untrained hands

The dates 1776 to 1876 are somewhat arbitrary, but there is fairly sound evidence to support the fact that the break from subservience to England, on the first Fourth of July, stimulated ordinary citizens all up and down the eastern seaboard to express their new sense of independence with original artistic efforts that were in no way tied to formal tradition. In other, older countries, folk art has been a seedbed of the fine arts, but in America, the colonial psychology —the awareness of having a transplanted culture, and the strong desire not to appear provincial—gave the spontaneous creativity of common people no chance to provide a base upon which a genuine national art could be built. With the signing of the Declaration, however, this mass of creativity was liberated.

Once folk art began to flourish in America, it exhibited a variety that was unusually rich because of America's ethnic mix, which blended together the old traditions of many countries—Germany, France, Spain, the Netherlands, and Scandinavia among others. It was also, as the output of a confident, aggressive population, marked by a high level of vigor, inventiveness, realism, and sense of design. Like all folk art, it was often crude, with distortions that professionally trained artists would have known how to avoid or correct. But its very ineptitude, as judged by academic standards, gave it an emotional intensity that was lacking in the work of urbane masters, and lacking also in the machine-made products that superseded handwork. By definition, these creators of folk art had no formal training, but many of them showed genuine talent. None were anonymous in the way that the originators of ancient ballads were, but the few names that are known are known because of descendants or the work of local historians. In their magnificent volume *The Flowering of American Folk Art,* Jean Lipman and Alice Winchester were able to name sixty-two painters, sixteen sculptors, and thirty men and women active in decoration and furnishings during the century after 1776. These are only the elite—famous enough that their names have survived—among thousands, the most talented and active, but, like all the others, they were unrestrained by exposure to academic tradition. As the great collector Maxim Karolik once said of them, "Fortunately, they had no academic training." That fact alone would have condemned America's folk artists among the early arbiters of taste, who no doubt never dreamed that one day taste would make another of its inevitable shifts and find folk art more intrinsically tasteful than a great deal of what those arbiters prized.

Portraiture, the kind of painting most in demand until photography reduced the need for it, was the principal work of folk artists, as it was for their trained professional cousins. Old houses, particularly in rural areas where having good taste never required adherence to formal conventions, were commonly graced with ancestral portraits that range from very crude to quite masterful. Individuals who may first have shown talent in the painting of tavern signs or weathervanes were likely, sooner or later, to be importuned to try portraits, and if they were at all successful, they were glad to join the ranks of limners. The best of them could hardly match the polish and sophistication of Charles Willson Peale or Gilbert Stuart;

but men of such talent were rare and, furthermore, had all the commissions they wanted or could handle from the nation's famous and wealthy.

Like the "great names" in art, many of the country painters sooner or later tired of portraiture and turned to other subjects. Perhaps what they tired of was the constant travel required of them, for they were usually, of necessity, itinerants who accepted board and lodging with one family after another as partial payment for their work. In any event, some tried painting views of homesteads or villages and found that proud local people would buy them. There was also a good market for copies, usually in watercolor, of foreign scenes and buildings—the gorge at Toledo in Spain or perhaps an onion-dome church in Russia. Famous sailing ships and race horses were always popular, as were renderings of Fourth of July and other celebrations and scenes from the Bible.

As mentioned earlier, one reason for abandoning portraiture for other kinds of painting was that the latter could be done at home, or in a studio. The career of William Matthew Prior was typical. Born in 1806 in Bath, Maine, he began by advertising "fancy, sign, and ornamental painting" before taking to the road as a painter of portraits and landscapes. Later, in company with in-laws, he opened a studio in Boston, named it "The Painting Garret," and made a fair living from the paintings he did on canvas, cardboard, and glass, with the price of each being determined by the size. He was particularly adept at "reverse painting," a technique in which the image is painted in reverse on the back of a piece of glass and is then looked at through the front of the glass.

Less typical but better known today was the painter Edward

Hicks (1780–1849), who spent most of his life in Bucks County, Pennsylvania. His career began with coach and sign work and ended with oil paintings of local farms, landscapes, and historical scenes. An active Quaker preacher, Hicks dabbled in allegory, especially in his numerous versions of *The Peaceable Kingdom* showing assorted wild animals living together in perfect harmony.

Ruth Henshaw Bascom of Massachusetts also stayed at home; her specialty was profile portraits in pastel tints, sometimes ornamented with tinfoil or gold paper details. She is said to have consistently refused pay for her profiles.

These and all the other talented folk artists differed as individuals and in their interests, but each had a definite standing in local or regional taste even though they seldom won wider fame. A taste existed for their kind of art, and that taste was no less strong or important than the taste for what highly trained professionals sold to sophisticated patrons.

With steadily advancing prosperity, interrupted only by periodic financial slumps, women were freed from much of the former drudgery of housekeeping and found an outlet for their energy in folk art, not for income but for the pleasure of making it and owning it afterward. Daughters in well-to-do families, until college doors began to open to them about 1830, were encouraged to study art and such other related skills as needlework. Others learned stenciling, or made designs with cut pieces of paper. Samplers—most often linen blanks worked into scenes or designs with embroidery thread and containing a simple poem above the maker's name and age: "Nabby Dexter's work done in her 16th year, 1800"—multiplied at their hands. In German communities, penmanship was a form of art. What is called *Fraktur,* with all the lettering and the complete design made with pen and ink, comes closest to the traditional concept of folk art, having been brought to America after centuries of development in Germany. *Fraktur* certificates bore decorative motifs drawn from flowers or animal figures or from geometry. These designs and the calligraphy were part of the regular curriculum in German-language schools until all states decreed that instruction had to be in English.

Stenciling was one of the commoner outlets for the folk art impulse, perhaps because it was such a useful technique, particularly for the decorating of walls. Cutting out the design of the stencil itself was tedious work but well worth it because it could be used over and over. For large, flat surfaces, fruit, flower, and leaf motifs were especially popular—particularly the pineapple, the now nearly forgotten symbol of hospitality. Pieces of furniture were often stenciled with the outline of an eagle or some other patriotic emblem. These were also commonly applied to tin utensils and pottery, and the same emblems could be woven into bedspreads.

Most decorated gravestones were pieces of folk art, being the work of carvers with no formal training, and so were carved wood pieces, woodcarving being another skill slow to attract professional artists. In the Spanish missions in California, the folk art impulse produced a distinctive style marked by religious imagery, especially saints. To this day, *un santo* is a term used to describe any of these indigenous folk images, and one who makes or repairs them is called a *santero.* Religious figures painted on wood, *retablos,* highly valued in Far West areas with a Spanish heritage, are

the legacy of unknown folk painters. The same folk heritage also influenced the punched-out designs of saddles and other leather work and the carving and decoration of the heavy square chairs in the old mission tradition.

Washington as Caesar

Folk art, however much a later age would cherish it, had obvious limitations. No untrained sculptor, for example, could have met the level of sophistication needed to immortalize national heroes in the new Capitol. But there were no trained native sculptors to consider for such commissions. Samuel McIntire had carved adequate figureheads, but his foot-high wooden bust of John Winthrop reveals no real capacity for carving major figures. William Rush of Philadelphia had turned out better pieces, including a charming *Nymph of the Schuylkill* in 1812. But for monumental statues to place in the Capitol rotunda and in the niches Benjamin Latrobe had designed for the main corridor, the decisionmakers in Washington thought it best to employ Europe's finest talent, no doubt a justifiable decision. Latrobe himself had, in fact, shown a certain competence in sculptural designing: his columns for the east front entry are fluted to resemble cornstalks and they rise to capitals of ears of corn; elsewhere there are Corinthian capitals showing tobacco leaves and blossoms.

The two leading European sculptors in the early 1800s were an Italian, Antonio Canova, and a Frenchman, Jean Antoine Houdon. Both were classicists. Canova was renowned for the polished perfection of his marble figures, including a virtually nude Napoleon in the guise of a Roman emperor. In 1820, he provided North Carolina with a statue of George Washington, which was placed at the statehouse in Raleigh. Now destroyed,

it showed the Father of His Country dressed in Roman armor.

Canova's French rival had a decided advantage. As a houseguest at Mount Vernon in 1785, he had been able to make life masks of Washington and such other leading figures as Jefferson, Franklin, and John Paul Jones. These masks assured that a reasonable resemblance could be achieved in a carved face that would have been difficult to create from two-dimensional sketches or paintings alone, and of course there was value in having studied these men in person. Houdon got the commissions. The several statues he provided, set in conspicuous places, qualify him as a genuine tastemaker, for they confirmed the style for a whole generation of American sculptors and the standard by which Americans were to judge sculpture even longer. That style was a strongly classical one, emphasizing smooth features, dignity, and a static nobility.

Enough painters to export them

If good native sculptors were in short supply in the early decades of the Republic, there was no dearth of trained painters. When the eighteenth century opened, the demand in America for portraits was attracting professional painters born abroad, but before it closed, America was exporting native-born painters without depleting the ranks of sound talent. Benjamin West left for Europe as early as 1760, and earned fame enough to succeed Sir Joshua Reynolds as president of the Royal Academy in 1792. John Singleton Copley, born the same year as West, 1738, joined him in England in 1775 after winning acclaim as the foremost American artist. The rank he vacated was shared, in the final years of the century, by two younger men, Charles Willson Peale and Gilbert Stuart.

Peale had been a militia colonel in the Revolutionary War and was later active in politics. About 1780, he transferred his considerable energy to painting and was soon hailed as the nation's best at portraits. Not surprisingly, he concentrated on portraying Revolutionary leaders, working unrivaled until 1792 when Stuart returned from a long stay in Europe. In the ensuing years, Stuart produced well over a thousand portraits, more than a hundred of which were of George Washington. In that first decade of the new nation, citizens were especially conscious of the importance of preserving the memory of the men who had led in the nation's creation. There could not be too many likenesses of the one man who towered above the others in the popular mind as commander in chief during the war and as the first chief executive. He had to be pictured as noble, and Stuart was able to make him seem so on canvas. In so doing, he created a distinctive style of classical portraiture that was comparable to Houdon's statuary in the qualities of dignity and static evenness it expressed. More realistic portraits were left for the future. American taste just then was for idealized heroes in the spirit of Greek and Roman grandeur.

Patrons for art were more numerous than ever in the late 1700s —men with fortunes made during the war from privateering, government contracts, and speculation in real estate and paper money. There were commissions enough not only for Peale and Stuart but also for talented aspirants. Peale fathered seventeen children, many of them named for great artists of the past. Four of these eventually approached their father's stature in painting. Rubens and Raphaelle specialized in still life, Rembrandt in portraits and historical subjects, and Titian, who lived until 1885, in

animals. Of the four, Rembrandt had the most talent. It reached its peak in his 1805 portrait of Thomas Jefferson, perhaps the best ever painted of the great Virginian.

Peale Senior, meanwhile, was not a man to bask in the rising glory of his sons. In 1784, he opened a museum of art and natural history, and in 1805, he was prime mover in organizing the Pennsylvania Academy of the Fine Arts. Both reflected his compelling desire to educate the public. His numerous inventions included a velocipede, new styles of eyeglasses and false teeth, and, in collaboration with Jefferson, a device called the polygraph for reproducing pictures or writing. His most unusual painting, a departure from anything known to current conventions, was *Exhuming the Mastodon.* Learning in 1801 that a farm worker in Newburgh, New York, had uncovered a thighbone thirty-nine inches long, Peale, with his customary energy, organized an excavation that took three months and uncovered skeletal remains of not one but two prehistoric monsters. One of these he put on exhibit in his museum; the other he sent to London for display in Pall Mall. His painting, with its realistic details of the excavation method, was one of the first and among the best of American genre pieces. But viewers of the finished canvas were troubled. The subject was interesting, but was it Art?

"Genre painting" in those days was understood to refer to scenes taken from everyday life, as Dutch artists had painted so extensively and so well in the seventeenth century. Digging up the bones of a mastodon was hardly an everyday event, and Peale's taste in putting it on canvas was openly challenged by many viewers.

Peale did not worry about the adverse criticism. Like many other

artists of the period, at both folk art and higher levels, he was in a mood to ignore the limits on subject matter set by convention. John Vanderlyn, branded a genius by no less an authority than Aaron Burr, learned in 1814 that exceeding those limits was risky. He painted a reclining *Ariadne,* quite nude, that outraged conventional taste. Nudity on canvas was acceptable in that period only if the work was of one of the old masters, long dead. Raphaelle Peale was more discreet: his *After the Bath* showed only the bare arms and feet of a girl who was presumably no more fully clothed.

People acquainted with mythology knew that Ariadne gave Theseus the thread that enabled him to find his way out of the Minotaur's labyrinth. Vanderlyn's painting gave no hint of that act of friendliness. But Greek and Roman myths were gaining favor in popular taste as it gradually broadened. Samuel F. B. Morse, before abandoning art for electrical experimentation, produced a *Dying Hercules* and a *Judgment of Jupiter,* both of which were generally admired.

Great scenes in American history were even more in demand. Portraits of men eminent in winning independence abounded by 1800, and the public welcomed paintings that showed such men in action. John Trumbull, remote cousin of the poet with the same name, had been one of General Washington's first aides-de-camp and could paint the battle at Bunker Hill from memory. For the death of Montgomery at Quebec, he had to rely on eyewitness accounts, but for his most famous work, *The Signing of the Declaration,* he was able to paint thirty-six of the signers from life. When the Capitol was being rebuilt, Trumbull offered to paint for it a series of twelve great events related to the nation's founding, and was some-

what miffed when Congress commissioned only four: *The Signing, The Surrender of Burgoyne, The Surrender of Cornwallis,* and *The Resignation of General Washington.* Four were more, however, than any other artist ever painted for the Capitol.

The neoclassical temperament that had made Georgian symmetry welcome a century earlier and that now was sustaining taste for Federal architecture could hardly be expected to condone realism. Yet a substantial minority of the population, perhaps those who chafed at the long hold of classical forms, took pleasure from the local-color brand of realism that began to appear. John Neagle of Philadelphia painted the aging Gilbert Stuart in a way that revealed the lined old face and bleary eyes; and his *Pat Lyon at the Forge* was one of the very first paintings of a manual laborer at work. Francis Guy caught

the bustle and color of New York's harbor district in his *Tontine Coffee House.* William Bennett drew Fulton Market with almost photographic precision and left for posterity a view of neat houses that once lined Broadway just north of Bowling Green.

Realism: the beginning of Romanticism

Landscapes were just beginning to attract attention. They were often called "views"—W. G. Wall's *View near Fishkill,* Neagle's *View on the Schuylkill.* But in the first two decades of the nineteenth century, nature was not a subject of much interest—and it would not be until Romanticism pushed classicism aside. Nature in America had for too long meant the wilderness, which was considered as being hostile to people's hopes, something to be tamed for survival, or perhaps exploited for profit, but

hardly to be loved. Freneau had extolled its beauties but with little success. He had been born too soon—or in the wrong country, for nature poetry like his was being well received in England during the very years that his own best efforts were ignored. From the beginning, there had been curiosity about native flora and fauna, especially among scholarly naturalists. As early as 1672, John Josselyn reported his observations in *New Englands Rarities Discovered,* a book marred by references to mermen and to Indians who talked in perfect hexameters. More scientifically reliable was John Bartram, who traveled widely and not long before the Revolution reported his findings. After his death, in 1777, his son William kept up the good work of collecting species for the botanical garden, the first in the nation, at their home beside the Schuylkill near Philadelphia. For

Oil portraits of Deacon Daniel Appleton and Sarah Brown Appleton, by Jona Tredwell, an itinerant limner; Buxton, Maine; ca. 1838.

Top: Ariadne Asleep on the Island
of Naxos, *by John Vanderlyn; 1814.*
Above: *Wall stenciling of pineapple;
from a house in Alewive, Maine;
1820–40.* Right: Lady with Red
Book, *by John Brewster, Jr.; 1830.*

the admiring public, visiting the garden was a popular holiday excursion. But that same public showed no more interest in the Bartram *Travels,* when published in 1791, than in the poems Freneau wrote in that decade. In England, by way of contrast, the *Travels* attracted considerable attention. Two avid readers were Coleridge and Wordsworth; it encouraged them, in fact, to proceed with their plans to issue *Lyrical Ballads* in 1798, a move that ushered in the "High Romantic" period of English literature. Credit America with an assist.

The Bartrams' interest in roaming about the country in search of native species was shared by two foreign-born artists. One of them, John James Audubon, a Haitian, wandered for twenty years, observing birds and painting them in their native habitats. When money ran low, he returned to civilization only long enough to paint a few portraits—the unfailing resource of every artist in those days. Not until the late 1830s could he find a publisher willing to risk money on an edition of his accumulated watercolors, so large that they had to be printed in "elephant folios." By then, though, the Romantic Movement had taken root and was dominating American taste.

The other artist with itchy feet was French-born Charles Balthazar Julien Févret de Saint-Mémin. He too depended on portraiture to support himself, turning out almost eight hundred portrait engravings during those times when he was not visiting Indian encampments in the upper Missouri valley. For his profile drawings of chieftains and other warriors, easterners showed little enthusiasm. Saint-Mémin was ahead of his time. The Noble Savage, like wilderness scenery and indigenous birds, had to wait for his turn in the spotlight of taste.

Bryant and Irving and the move from neoclassicism

Nature as a suitable subject was accepted somewhat earlier for poetry than for painting, thanks to William Cullen Bryant. In 1808, his book *The Embargo* was published in Boston as the work of a "Youth of Thirteen." A satirical attack on the policies of President Jefferson, it was as neoclassical in style as it was conservative in its politics. But he soon discovered Thomas Gray and other early English Romantic poets and began to turn out verse in the same mode. In 1817, the *North American Review* printed his "Thanatopsis," a somber, dignified "view of death" that established his reputation and has never completely lost its appeal to reader taste. It did not quite raise the curtain on Romanticism in America, but it helped to create a potential audience that was sympathetic.

Washington Irving underwent a similar conversion. His first writings were as firmly neoclassical as *The Embargo,* especially his burlesque *History of New York from the Beginning of the World to the End of the Dutch Dynasty* (1809). With his *Sketch Book,* which made him famous in 1820, he did an about-face, turning from satire to sentiment, nostalgia, gentle humor, and melancholy. Perhaps it was easier for writers than for people in other fields to change their style and to break free of neoclassical restraints. Static in its very essence, stressing permanence and resisting change, neoclassicism did not easily yield to the continuous restless questing of its antithesis, Romanticism.

"Toward the skies/What columns rise!"

Architecture, the most substantial of the arts and the one with the greatest impact on human awareness, could be expected to be slow to respond to the challenge of an ideology that was in every way different from neoclassicism. Even when the Romantic temper forced a major shift in the 1820s, the first effect on building style was still within the neoclassical range—the Greek Revival. And earlier, just at the turn of the century, the one great challenge to the dominant Federal style was also one stemming from revived classicism, the Roman style to be used for government structures.

The "Federal City," as it was usually called until George Washington died in 1799 and "Washington City" came into favor, was from the outset intended to be different from any other city in the nation. From the time its site was selected in 1790, it was conceived as a place of splendor rivaling that of imperial Rome. The street plan designed by Pierre Charles L'Enfant, and only slightly changed in the laying out, was in strict accord with the classical principle of symmetry, but the generous dimensions exceeded anything the Romans had ever known. Unfortunately, the site was low and much of it so flat that the wide dirt streets were quagmires for days after a hard rain. This, coupled with the city's general emptiness and rawness, offended the taste of all newcomers and visitors. Abigail Adams, arriving in November 1800, liked the vistas from the unfinished "President's House" but little else, and she was glad that her husband did not have to serve a second term. It was not easy to share the vision of future glory. One who could was Thomas Jefferson, who had been active in the planning of the city as secretary of state under Washington.

In his own two terms as president, Jefferson paid close attention to the designing of new federal buildings, and appointed men amenable to his ideas to superin-

89

tend their construction. As a recognized architect, Jefferson could speak with authority. One of his most distinctive early designs, for the Virginia capitol in Richmond in 1784, closely followed the Maison Carrée, a Roman temple built in France in 16 B.C., that he had admired when serving as ambassador to France, and anyone seeing it could have predicted his recommendations for the national capitol. Ideal democracy, he had come to believe, deserved a style of architecture as durable and as dignified as that of the only great democracy of the past. No more recent style would do. As the principal force in making official Washington a "white city" of Greco-Roman splendor, Jefferson was one of the most effective of American tastemakers.

Not all his contemporaries applauded his efforts. His good friend Philip Freneau, steeped in Romanticism as he was, saluted the trend with heavy sarcasm:

> Toward the skies
> What columns rise
> In Roman style, profusely great!
> What lamps ascend,
> What arches bend
> And swell with more than Roman state!

But such mockery had no effect, for most people accepted the Roman Revival (or Jeffersonian style, as some prefer to call it) as the most appropriate. What is more, it became a standard style for governmental buildings all across the nation for another century—state capitols, customhouses, courthouses, large post offices, city halls. The only difference was superficial; most were of stone or brick and were not painted.

Whether or not ordinary citizens think of ancient Greece or Rome when they have business in a Roman Revival building, its massive stone walls and columns and arches are reassuring evidence of governmental soundness and permanence. If this thought does cross their minds, they should recall Mr. Jefferson and be grateful that one president understood the symbolic nature of architecture—and that he did something about it.

James and Dolley

The same population that approved of Roman Revival architecture for government buildings in Washington was more aware, in the early years of the nation as always since, of life in the White House, a mansion in the Federal style. When James Madison was inaugurated in 1809, the crowd in attendance was the greatest yet, no doubt because he was the first president to give an inaugural ball. Later he and his wife Dolley held weekly levees that were less stiffly formal than the Washingtons' had been, if not as casual as the widower Jefferson's. Hostesses in every city took note. Individuals who dropped in at odd times were invariably treated with courtesy and offered refreshments. Formal state dinners were hearty meals served not in courses but with all the food put on the table at once. Dolley's desserts were famous, especially her layer cakes. She took snuff, like many other fashionable ladies at the time; and she played cards. Loo, a game now forgotten, was her favorite, and because it was, it became the most popular among women who gathered on afternoons to ward off boredom.

What Dolley wore was also widely imitated; all it took to own a wardrobe as extensive as hers was enough money. She was fond of turbans and evening slippers. For the inaugural ball, she chose a buff-colored gown with a long train, a turban of the same velvet and satin with two bird-of-paradise plumes, and pearl earrings, necklace, and bracelet. Even women with no real hope of ever dressing in such style recognized in Dolley Madison a lady of excellent taste in clothes. In her way, she was a tastemaker; but nobody, not even a beloved First Lady, can exert enduring influence on feminine fashions.

The major White House social occasions, then as always since, were New Year's and Independence Day. For the New Year's reception in 1817, their last, Madison upstaged Dolley by wearing a suit of cloth made in America from the wool of merino sheep raised in America. The gesture was applauded by patriots, for whom it symbolized being one step closer to total independence from England. It capped eight presidential years that set welcome new standards of official and private behavior.

New clothes

Most clothing was still either homemade or provided by professional dressmakers or tailors. Some of the homemade clothing showed considerable talent. A man's dressing gown worn in Stonington, Connecticut, in the late eighteenth century was of wool in plain weave with brown, gray, blue, and white stripes, and had a brown wool lining. A woman's short gown from the same period, worn in Germantown, Pennsylvania, was of plain-weave cotton with a flower-sprig print and was shaped from one length of fabric. With it was worn a petticoat of beige cotton. A professionally made petticoat was of quilted blue satin. Homemade waistcoats were likely to be of colored cotton with white cotton lining; one made by a tailor might be of cream-colored satin ornamented with an embroidered chain stitch in several colors and lined with silk twill. The embroidery on the most expensive waistcoats was often added to the flat fabric by skilled workmen in China.

Before 1800, professional tailors worked alone, but increasingly in the early nineteenth century, they joined forces in firms to produce clothing made to individual order. One result was a greater variety in cut, material, color, and ornamentation. Gentlemen were still wearing breeches in 1810, but soon thereafter trousers were favored at every social level. By 1820, taste favored double-breasted greatcoats for men, with high collars and artificially shaped shoulders and chest. Some ready-made clothing was becoming available, requiring only the same minor fitting adjustments that are needed today. Tailoring firms with imagination increased their trade and their profits by introducing new forms of clothing—the dress shirt for men was one, and another was the mantle for women, a loose cloak that needed no fitting.

Leaving the formal garden

The increasing variety of clothing available and readily accepted by the public was one small indication of a rebellion that was brewing against the tyranny of narrow taste that had, up to this point, governed many aspects of people's lives. Interest in broadened subjects for painting was another. More telling, however, was the welcome given to Bryant's nature poems, especially his "Thanatopsis," and soon after to Irving's *Sketch Book,* for both revealed an incipient taste for Romanticism.

There was something artificial about neoclassicism, something alien to a society made up of people as dynamic and diverse as Americans have always been. That it maintained its hold on taste as long as it did is cause for wonder.

But did it? We have seen numerous instances of deviation from accepted neoclassical standards and also an introduction of forms that were created with no regard at all for the neoclassical tradition. Contemporary arbiters could ignore the latter as being outside the range of cultivated taste, but they could not overlook the many deviations. Nor have later critics altogether abandoned the old habit of deploring the deviations as evidence of failure to grasp the accepted rules or as the result of clumsiness of execution. This is not done by all modern critics, but it is done by those who subscribe to the notion of an ideal form for every object. American builders and cabinetmakers modified patterns they found in books by English authorities, thereby producing divergence from established standards. It seems reasonable to suggest that they were exercising independence and creating new variants no less worthy of approval by taste—new, and distinctly American. To disparage the deviations as being low in taste is to deny Americans the right to choose from available alternatives —the right to determine their own taste. Neoclassicism, by whatever momentary term it goes by, is by its very nature imbued with this spirit of denial.

Lest this be mistaken as a general expression of hostility aimed at any form of neoclassicism, it may be pointed out that neoclassicism had been welcomed, after 1700, as being symbolic of the victory over a hostile wilderness that seventeenth-century Americans had hoped for and worked hard to achieve. But by 1800, that victory was historic and no longer a reason

for continued adherence to such static formalism. Nor did it seem necessary, by 1825, to prove the country's civilized status by mindless adoption of every new style approved by cultivated taste in Europe. As for nature, was wildness really the enemy that neoclassicists insisted it was? In the eighteenth-century view, it was thought to be unnatural to live without rules; and "natural man" was condemned as brutish, loutish, and unforgivably sensual. But by 1825, with the frontier open toward the West, Cooper's Natty Bumppo became a hero, a white Noble Savage uncorrupted by man-made civilization, which itself was being viewed as evil.

Having conquered the first frontier on the fringe of the continent, the American people were restlessly looking to others, beyond the eastern mountains, and for new heroes, able to live close to nature and not in fear of it. The neoclassical world was a formal garden, tame and regular, where everything was measured precisely and protected from change. Now the dream of another world was forming, a world of new venturing, less subject to restrictive rules, more varied and interesting, more dynamic, democratic, individualistic—more American.

The new America began as a dream, the shadow of poetry. But the dream had substance; it was reality just beyond reach and then, when reached for, it proved not a dream at all but the stuff of actuality. The repudiation of static neoclassicism was a turning point in the nation's history, one of immense importance to the people's culture and to their standards of taste.

IV

The
People's Choice

(1826–1875)

Preceding pages: A Disputed Heat, Claiming a Foul; *lithograph by Currier & Ives; 1878.* Above: *Mark Twain House, designed by Edward T. Potter; Hartford, Conn.; 1874. The house has 19 rooms, 5 baths, 18 fireplaces.*

The willingness of most Americans to accept cultural dictation from abroad for two centuries is, indeed, hard to square with the proverbial American drive and ingenuity. Those traits existed in Americans from the outset, but whatever divergent styles they produced were ignored or disparaged by cultivated individuals as being outside the range of taste. Simple furniture and utensils lacking any trace of "style" didn't seem to pose a challenge to culti-

vated standards. They were what the poor had to make do with. Families breaking out of poverty and advancing to affluence no longer needed to rely on homemade objects, and they commonly made an effort to live according to what was currently fashionable. Some of those fashions, meanwhile, sifted steadily down to lower economic levels. Symmetrical facades and formal parlors were no longer limited to urban mansions, appearing also in rural houses that were otherwise in the vernacular.

America looks on Greece

The first great break from the tyranny of taste was the introduction of the Greek Revival style, a style that was essentially American as measured by its enthusiastic reception at every income level. Greek-style architecture had long been familiar to Americans, but in a form that was combined with Roman and then further modified by Renaissance designers. Recreating forms as they actually existed in ancient Greece—as the Greek Revival did—was another story, for it was a redirection of the long history of neoclassical adaptation, beginning with Palladio in the sixteenth century and continuing to the Adam brothers in the eighteenth. On American soil, Greek Revival flourished and acquired a distinctive American character. In the second quarter of the nineteenth century, it dominated building taste as no other style had ever done earlier, or was likely ever to do again.

Benjamin Latrobe is credited with introducing pure Greek forms to America with his design for the Bank of Pennsylvania, completed in 1800. It was basically Ionic, with its columns rising to capitals with paired scrolls. A few other buildings imitating the Greek, most commonly the simpler Doric, with wholly unornamented capitals, were erected over the next few years, but widespread interest in Greece developed only—and suddenly—in 1821, when news came of the Greek rebellion against Turkish rule. Incipient Romanticism, with its stress on democratic freedom, was a conditioning factor. So was the memory of the Revolutionary War, for here was another small country trying to get out from under a strong foreign oppressor. The French Revolution had stirred similar emotions in 1789, but American ardor had cooled with the reported beheadings and other excesses of that war, as well as the subsequent rise of Napoleon to dictatorial power. The Greek effort, as viewed from America, was a much nobler cause.

Lord Byron, long a favorite with American readers, further stimulated sympathy for Greece with his *Don Juan* (1819–24). One quatrain in the third canto was especially memorable:

> The mountains look on Marathon,
> And Marathon looks on the
> sea;
> And musing there an hour alone,
> I dreamed that Greece might
> still be free.

Marathon, as every college boy knew in that era when Greek was central to the curriculum, was the site of a Greek repulse of a huge Persian army in 490 B.C. Byron's hour of musing was atop the mound, still there, that covers the Greek soldiers killed in that battle. His personal commitment to the cause, and his death at Missolonghi, further excited young Americans. Some joined the struggle, and a few are buried at Missolonghi. Aid for the rebel cause was organized by Samuel Gridley Howe of Boston, a move that was the beginning of his long career in philanthropy. Pro-Greek editorials and poems multiplied, and so did Greek-letter fraternities on college campuses. Gen. William Henry Harrison announced that "the Star-Spangled Banner must wave in the Aegean," and the navy ordered its Mediterranean Squadron to Greek waters. It would be hard to name another foreign event that has stirred the entire nation so profoundly.

Temple fronts everywhere

American response in the adoption of Greek style was immediate, for the first time not delayed by the familiar cultural lag. Alexander Pope's couplet in his *Essay on Criticism,*

> Be not the first by whom the new
> are tried,
> Nor yet the last to lay the old
> aside,

was forgotten, and so was the habit of waiting for guidance from the upper economic echelons of society. Thousands of modest new homes were built with Greek details, and many older houses, whatever their original style, acquired new doorways with classical Greek framing or Greek temple fronts. Most of these were made of wood despite the fact that the ancient Greeks, who had more surface rock than forests and for whom marble was abundant, had never used wood for exteriors. But Americans were accustomed to using materials readily at hand and were already experienced in adapting classical forms to wood; they had been doing it for a century.

The Greek Revival influenced home construction everywhere but most extensively in the developing parts of the country such as the Midwest, where new construction could hardly keep up with the rapid migration westward. It has been stated that during the 1840s and 1850s, the temple-form house directly replaced the log cabin as the common type of midwestern dwelling, repeating the process two centuries later that had been initiated by the very first settlers who had lived in crude shelters only until they could build in what was then the current style. It is tempting to suggest that the midwesterners eagerly adopted old Greek forms for their houses because of their greater commitment to democracy and their more pervasive sense of Americans being the spiritual heirs of the ancient Greeks, who invented democracy.

Plantation Greek

Remoteness from the settled East made it easy if not inevitable for regional variants of the Greek Revival to develop. The most familiar is no doubt the "Plantation Greek" that was built in the newer parts of the Deep South. The plantation house Seven Oaks in Westwego, Louisiana, is not only completely surrounded by a Greek-columned porch but it also has a second-floor balcony, for it was built in an area where summer heat makes deep shade valuable. Chretien Point Plantation, also in Louisiana, has a two-story verandah only in front, and the Grove in Tallahassee, Florida, has no upper porch at all to break its columned facade.

In Ohio, a less pronounced variant appeared first in Connecticut's former Western Reserve along Lake Erie. Known, appropriately enough, as the Western Reserve style, its minor differences show up in towns settled later in the state's interior. One such is Granville, close to the exact center of Ohio. Because a college, now Denison University, is its only "industry," the town has been spared the all-too-common fate of unplanned growth. It survives, as do other fortunate towns centered around a college from Brunswick, Maine, to McMinnville, Oregon, as an attractive museum of architectural history.

The Granville story

Granville was settled in 1805 by New Englanders who built, as immigrants have always done, in the style they were familiar with. The prototype of the Levi Hayes 1810 House was the two-story vernacular Denison Homestead near the seaport town of Mystic, Connecticut, dating from 1717. A second Granville house, built in 1820, is also vernacular, but with its regular spacing of five bays along the front and a fine fanlight over the

door, it suggests a greater awareness of cultivated standards. Closer to the Federal is the Lucius Mower House, built in 1824 with a modified Palladian doorway, which, with the flat-arched window above it, forms a bay not centered in the facade but at one end.

In 1838, a Greek Revival church was completed in Granville—St. Luke's. Its builder, Benjamin Morgan, drew heavily from Asher Benjamin's 1830 handbook *The Practical House Carpenter,* which was one of several popular guides to Greek styles that Americans had written to accommodate the new enthusiasm. Morgan also had help from drawings that he requested from Minard Lafever, a leading New York architectural designer. The siding of St. Luke's is of boards, the edges of which were rounded to resemble stone blocks. The church entrance, recessed into the facade, has two freestanding Doric columns, and the corners are Doric pilasters. The one deviation of the facade from pure Doric style is the small belfry at the gable end over the entrance.

A wealthy local merchant, Alfred Avery, was so taken with the church that, in 1842, he hired Morgan to erect what has been ever since Granville's most distinctive dwelling. The two-story front portico, derived from the design of the north porch of the Erechtheum on the Athens acropolis, has four two-story Ionic columns that enclose a balcony with a richly ornamented iron railing. One-story side porches are Doric, each with four columns. The siding, like that of St. Luke's Church, is of wood cut to resemble stone. Other Greek buildings in Granville still in use include two houses and the opera house (originally the Baptist Church), all built between 1842 and 1849. By that time, the Greek Revival was beginning to ebb and about to yield to its Gothic successor. The two styles overlapped, as a matter of fact, and a Granville house built in 1848 is unmistakably Gothic.

Greek for schools, churches, and banks

Although the Greek Revival had its greatest impact on dwellings, it was not limited to them. The largest and most conspicuous examples were built to be used for religious, commercial, and educational purposes. Greek Revival buildings appeared in most American cities. Philadelphia still has the Second Bank of the United States with its Doric porches, the classi-

Opposite top: Phoenix Line, "Safety Coaches"; *lithograph by Moses Swett; New York; 1830–40. The coach made the Washington-Baltimore run in 5 hours.* Opposite center: *Clipper ship* Tropic; *built at Kennebunk Landing, Maine; 1857.* Opposite bottom: Central Park, The Lake; *lithograph by Currier & Ives; 1862.* Above left: Funeral Car used at the Obsequies of the late Pres. A. Lincoln; *lithograph by J.H. Studer, Columbus, Ohio; 1865. The car is passing Ohio's neoclassical capitol.* Above: Ralph Waldo Emerson, *by Daniel Chester French; 1914.*

cal Fairmount Water Works, and Girard College with columns in the Corinthian style, the most ornate of the three Greek orders. In Boston, the block-long Quincy Market built next to Faneuil Hall in 1825 proclaims the glory of ancient Greece. Designing these buildings and many others with varied functions were architects of varying competence, most of them native-born, a great change from a century earlier when the few professional architects were born abroad.

Churches in the Greek Revival tradition have their own history. A few, including Beth Elohim Synagogue in Charleston and the Swedenborgian Church in the coastal Maine town of Bath, have the usual Doric porch with columns and pediment but no steeple or cupola. Others, however, are hybrids, combining a Greek porch with a belfry or, especially for the largest, a soaring steeple in the Wren tradition. This mixing of styles might seem like an early example of Victorian eclecticism, and in a way it is. But steeples had so greatly appealed to taste in both England and America all through the Georgian and Federal periods that they were not about to be abandoned with the advent of a new style. Cupolas were regarded just as fondly, and many factories, even though built with Greek details, sport them. But almost every temple-front Greek Revival building violated one ancient practice, the enclosure of the sacred precinct by windowless walls.

Nevertheless, the Greek details adopted were faithful to those of antiquity, and the sentiment that made the temple front popular for a quarter-century was genuine. What the deviations reveal is the old American habit of modifying foreign forms, thereby creating distinctive variants. Although some art historians deplore this tendency, the Greek Revival did indeed make a unique and enduring contribution to the American landscape.

Architects lost their interest in the Greek Revival long before the public did, for the simple reason that it posed no real challenge to their creativity. For most of the population, however, it symbolized the moral commitment Americans had made to Greece as the fountainhead of democracy. For once, academic tradition was ignored. The American people had become their own tastemakers.

A passion for speed

But Americans had become tastemakers only in architecture and, to a lesser extent, in the use of ornamental details with Greek motifs on furniture and utensils. Nobody felt any impulse to revive Attic fashions in dress or in dining or, until the 1890s, to suggest that the Olympic Games with its twenty-six-mile foot race should be resumed. What interest there was in racing centered on horses, as it always had. Hardly a village of any size was without a racetrack, and any kind of celebration was likely to climax with a full slate of thoroughbred racing. Horses that had set track records for speed were so highly regarded that their portraits, multiplied by the new technique of lithography, were more often hung on walls than those of any human beings except George and Martha Washington.

Fast horses of a different breed were valued as motive power for stagecoaches, the common means of travel by land until after 1830. A few of the coaches were elegant, but beauty as such counted less than speed, which was a matter of growing concern in an era of expanding commerce. The Concord and Conestoga wagons that were used for carrying freight had to be strongly built in order to survive on the poor roads, meaning that

both speed and elegance had to be sacrificed to sturdiness. Canalboats, drawn by mules, were slower yet and comparably clumsy in design. Railroads, encouraging the hope of faster travel and transportation, were still a curiosity in 1828 when the Baltimore and Ohio began operating with cars drawn by horses. Two years later Peter Cooper's small locomotive, the *Tom Thumb,* proved the feasibility of steam power, and the Railroad Age was born. But it took many years for it to outgrow its infancy.

If canalboats, freight wagons, and the primitive rolling stock of railroads were all low in aesthetic appeal, the clipper ships of the 1830s were not. The *Ann McKim,* launched in Baltimore in 1833, was the first—long, slender, and carrying a mass of sail. In short order, Donald McKay of Boston improved the type with his *Flying Cloud* and *Glory of the Sea,* so fast that they could easily overtake the sailing ships of any other country. Built for speed and profit, and stripped of decoration and anything else that had no function, the clippers won instant admiration for their grace and unadorned beauty. They demonstrated a concept that would be both unvoiced and ignored for another half-century—the concept that form dictated by function can produce a beauty of its own and a new standard of taste.

Shipyards everywhere, especially in New England, were hard-pressed to keep up with the demand for clippers. For one thing, they stimulated a new sport, one that only rich men could afford—yachting. In 1851, when the Royal Yacht Squadron in England offered a silver cup to the winner of a race around the Isle of Wight, the New York Yacht Club, just seven years old, ordered a yacht built, named it *America,* and sailed it across the Atlantic to enter the

competition. The same skill in ship design and construction that had won ocean trade supremacy for the clippers gave the *America* its winning edge. The prize, still sought today by foreign challengers, is the America's Cup, symbol of an enduring fascination with speed as such and of the aesthetic appeal of efficient design.

A second revolution

The success of the clippers and the *America* was a source of general satisfaction, even among citizens too poor to own canoes or rowboats. Let Englishmen sneer, as Sydney Smith so offensively did in 1820, at America's minimal contributions to the arts and technology, let English visitors write what they wished to in derogation; by now it was meaningless. The nation was making giant steps in every endeavor and was rapidly overtaking "tired old Europe." Such thinking could lead to complacency—and it did, by the Centennial Year of 1876. But the forward strides were real, and impressive. It has been suggested that the nation owed much of its progress to the steady flow of immigrants arriving from countries that had not contributed significantly to the population in earlier years. Whether or not this notion is valid, the ethnic mix steadily increased, giving support to Walt Whitman's term for America as a "nation of nations."

The election of Andrew Jackson in 1828 as seventh president gave the White House its first occupant not a member of a long-established Virginia or Massachusetts family. The son of an Irish immigrant, Jackson owed his victory to his reputation as a successful general, but more directly to his popularity among small farmers and businessmen who had had enough of rule by eastern seaboard aristocrats. Jackson's liberal land policies alone would have alienated the

Opposite top: *Avery-Hunter House, designed by Benjamin Morgan; Granville, Ohio; 1842.* Opposite center: *Lyndhurst, designed by Alexander Jackson Davis; Tarrytown, N.Y.; 1838.* Opposite bottom: *Wedding Cake House; Kennebunk, Maine; 1826. Scrollwork added 1855.*

Above: *P. T. Barnum's Iranistan; Bridgeport, Conn.; 1848, destroyed by fire in 1857. Inspired by England's Brighton Pavilion.* Above right: *Masonic Temple; Philadelphia, Pa.; 1837. A mixture of Oriental, Ionic, Norman, and Egyptian styles.* Above far right: *Jefferson Market Courthouse, designed by Calvert Vaux and Frederick Withers; New York, N.Y.; 1877.* Opposite: *Victorian parlor, King House; Virginia City, Nev.; late 19th century. Complete with harp.*

properties class, but his record as a sharp-tongued debater, a duelist, a man who married a woman who had not yet been divorced, and an advocate of the spoils system earned him not only the distaste but the total loathing of prim conservatives. They viewed him as an upstart who brought the rabble into the White House and overstepped the bounds of democracy. His eight years in office were marked by partisan rancor far worse than that of any earlier administration. In the perspective of time, however, it is clear that what was occurring was a veritable revolution not only in politics but in standards of behavior and taste. Never again would ordinary Americans be as willing as they once were to defer to a small ruling caste.

A novelist defends the old order

The Jacksonian Revolution, as historians now call it, or the democratic ferment that supported it, may be thought of as a phase of the Romantic Movement. It was strongly resented, naturally enough, by everyone whose privileges it threatened. One who was both conscious of what might be lost and able to express it force-

fully in writing was James Fenimore Cooper. Although his novels pitting noble white and red men against villains of both skin colors, in settings of wild nature, helped advance Romantic thinking, such other Romantic themes as democratic egalitarianism and free exercise of individualism repelled him. A wealthy man with vast land holdings in upper New York State, he was, quite naturally, the friend and defender of the rich.

On his return from Europe in 1833 after seven years abroad, Cooper was horrified by the social changes he found and, in 1838, wrote *The American Democrat* to vent his disapproval. In it, he dismissed social equality as being contrary to nature and Holy Writ and argued that the propertied class was best suited, by breeding and education, to direct the nation's affairs. All citizens, he felt, should have the same chance to become wealthy and join that class, but if they could not, or chose not to try, they should not expect to enjoy the privileges that go with position and property.

Men of assured position, he added, should set the standards of taste and behavior; letting those standards be set by less advantaged people, he firmly believed, would only assure mediocrity. His book, not published until after the Jacksonian Revolution had succeeded, had something of the ring of a postmortem on his own class. A century earlier, it would not have been necessary to spell out the duty of lower economic groups to defer to the privileged minority in matters of taste. Upward social mobility existed as a possibility in the eighteenth century, but the great majority of the population stayed at the level they were born to and accepted the limitations that went with it. One of these limitations made acceptance tolerable: only the well-to-do were expected to keep up with cultivated taste as it was dictated from abroad.

"But do your work, and I shall know you."

But the Romantic Movement changed general thinking. Classical restraint and fixed order yielded to individual freedom and democratic egalitarianism. Men dressed as they pleased, no longer forced to reveal their occupations by their clothing. Whether ready-made clothing abetted this freedom or gained in popularity because of it, the result was the same— greater personal freedom from conformity. Ralph Waldo Emerson, arch champion of individual-

ism, provided the slogan, a virtual commandment: "Whoso would be a man, must be a nonconformist." He wrote that in 1841, in "Self-Reliance," an essay that caught the spirit of the era and did much to nourish it. Conformity to outmoded practices was no longer a mark of good taste, he insisted. "But do your work, and I shall know you." Not what a man wore, or who his grandfather was, but what he did in his life was what really counted.

Cooper and Emerson, both Romantics, were in total disagreement on this issue. The nation's enterprise, in any event, was increasingly in the hands of individuals whom Cooper would not have considered qualified for the ruling elite. One thinks of Mary Lyon, who founded Mount Holyoke Female Seminary in 1837 in defiance of the tradition limiting higher education to men; Joseph Henry, who discovered induced electrical current and in 1846 was named the first director of the Smithsonian Institution; Maria Mitchell, born on Nantucket Island, who won fame as an astronomer; and James Buchanan Eads, whose jetties tamed the lower Mississippi River enough for navigation. Not one of these people came from a family of assured position; not one of them had had the advantage of attending college. Would the country have been better served in education and science and engineering if opportunity had been restricted to sons and daughters of wealth and privilege?

Cooper might have viewed the rise of social nobodies to eminence as exceptions, just as Emerson admitted that scions of honored old families—the Lees and Byrds, Schuylers and Winthrops and Adamses—could be reasonably confident of recognition and respect. Walt Whitman, somewhat later in the century, carried egalitarianism

much further; he scorned the First Families of Virginia and their like everywhere else, and insisted that leadership potential was greatest in the lowest stratum of society. Abraham Lincoln was his Exhibit A. But individual merit was apparently not always easy to recognize, whatever the source. For writers, there existed a palpable hurdle on the path to fame—reader taste, which is seldom entirely reliable as a measure of greatness.

Outcasts, household poets, and scribbling women

Nathaniel Hawthorne, whose forebears had enjoyed status in the upper ranks of privilege, had to wait for years until society was ready to acknowledge his genius. Several of his equally gifted contemporaries were never approved in reader taste, for reasons having nothing to do with literary standards. The new, Romantic freedom did not extend to behavior considered immoral or to the expression of opinions too far out of line with prevailing attitudes. Writers were as free as other people to act as individuals, but what they wrote was weighed on Victorian scales. Edgar Allan Poe, a genius if there ever was one in America, was widely reputed to be a hard drinker who could not hold a job. As a result, never in his lifetime was he honored at home, although he earned great respect in France. Henry Thoreau's espousal of anarchy and his animosity toward churches and churchmen was also offensive; his rise in reader taste is a twentieth-century phenomenon.

The same holds true for Herman Melville and Walt Whitman. After a good start with adventurous South Seas fiction, Melville compromised his reputation by turning to ever darker, more obscure, and more pessimistic themes that ran counter to the general optimism of the period. Whitman lacked a sin-

gle redeeming feature in the opinion of the upper crust of society, and was commonly misunderstood by the common people with whom he identified. His worst fault, frankness about sex, was a sin against Victorian morality. These four writers fell afoul of the rather odd belief that no artist of questionable character could produce work that would meet the standards of good taste.

The authors who did win and keep high ranking in taste in the Victorian years were the "household poets," Bryant, Long-

fellow, Holmes, and Whittier, whose writings were never obscure or offensive and, as a result, were welcome in virtually every home. Taste also approved, on a slightly lower level, the witty fluff of *Fern Leaves from Fanny's Portfolio* (by Fanny Fern) and sentimental novels bearing such titles as *The Fatal Marriage, The Gates Ajar, The Lamplighter,* and *The Country Minister's Wife*—all written by what Hawthorne once called "a d—d mob of scribbling women." There were also first-rate women writers, notably Harriet Beecher

Opposite: *Grand Stairway, Morse-Libby House; Portland, Maine; 1859–63. A supreme example of the Italianate.* Above far left: *Etta Swallow, age 16; ca. 1865.* Above left: *Daguerreotype of Dr. and Mrs. James Hamilton Peirce; ca. 1843.* Above: *Daguerreotype of Rebecca Jane Hosmer, age 8, and Nathan Davis Hosmer, age 10; 1855.* Far left: *Daniel Peirce and his daughter Ida; ca. 1874.* Left: *Plaid taffeta dress of 1860s modeled by Sandra Armentrout; Kennebunk, Maine.*

Stowe and Rebecca Harding Davis. But Mrs. Stowe's *Uncle Tom's Cabin,* one of the most widely read books of all time, polarized taste when it was published in 1852. It was regarded as excellent by liberal northerners and cordially hated by defenders of slavery—a prime example of conflicting regional tastes. Mrs. Davis, best known for "Life in the Iron Mills," a story printed in the *Atlantic Monthly* in 1861, was not highly regarded anywhere; she was a realist in a Romantic age, as Freneau had been a romantic when

neoclassical writing alone was highly favored.

A taste for the Gothic

Although Romanticism, like neoclassicism, turned to the past for models and inspiration, it was to the medieval period instead of the classical. Examples of Romantic thinking occurred in England as early as 1747 with the building of Strawberry Hill, Horace Walpole's medieval castle, but it took much longer for such interest to develop in America. In fact, almost a century passed before Americans in

any number built in this style, a style that became known as Gothic. First used in derision to describe any medieval style deliberately revived in the nineteenth century, the term *Gothic* eventually came into general use with the rise in popularity of the medieval look. Today, the word describes any style characteristic of the thousand-year period known, without good reason, as the Dark Ages, even though the Gothic was dominant for only about two of those ten centuries.

In 1799, the year before he antic-

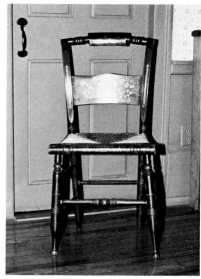

ipated the Greek Revival in America with his Bank of Pennsylvania, Benjamin Latrobe designed a house with Gothic elements—Sedgeley, near Philadelphia. Nobody was much interested, then or for the next forty years, although architects did design a few churches that had Gothic towers, buttresses, and pointed arches. Among those few were St. Mary's Chapel in Baltimore (1806), Trinity Church in New Haven (1814), and Christ Church in Gardiner, Maine (1818). But taste for the style did not develop, and this minor Gothic boom had subsided by 1820, when the Greek Revival began to sweep the nation.

As for dwellings, the immense popularity of Sir Walter Scott's medieval romances might have been expected to encourage private builders to imitate his own castellated Abbotsford, built in 1816 and enlarged in 1823. But taste moves in mysterious ways and with no logical timetable. It often needs prodding by some electrifying event or by an aggressive and persuasive tastemaker. The Greek War of Independence had been just such an event, producing the Greek Revival; now Alexander Jackson Davis and Andrew Jackson Downing were just such taste-

makers, pioneering the taste for Gothic buildings.

Plain houses to Gothic cottages

The architect Davis won fame and fortune early in life for inventing a lattice truss that proved helpful in bridge building. He was an expert in the practical uses of iron, and, in 1835, he designed a storefront of cast iron. Working alone or with such other architects as Ithiel Town, he had his share in designing many neoclassical public buildings, including the New York Custom House—now called Federal Hall—and the U.S. Patent Office in Washington, an enormous building that now houses the National Portrait Gallery and the National Collection of Fine Arts. Davis was also responsible, in whole or in part, for several state capitol buildings. But by 1838, his allegiance turned to Gothic, as evidenced by Lyndhurst, near Tarrytown, New York, which he designed that year and later—in 1864 —greatly enlarged for a new owner. Some of the furnishings were also of his designing. Lyndhurst is a veritable castle, complete with battlements, foliated windows, finials, a massive square tower, and even a small rose window, all with fine disregard for

classical symmetry. But castles did not exhaust his interest, for Davis planned numerous "Gothic cottages" that would be within the means of middle-income families.

Downing shared Davis's preference. A horticulturist first and then a landscape gardener, Downing wrote several books in which he emphasized picturesqueness, detailing how a house should harmonize with its setting. He asked Davis to provide sketches for the books, which he did. It is clear, however, that the two men did not always see eye to eye, for some of the sketches appearing in *Cottage Residences,* published in 1842, differ in detail from Downing's text. Even so, the book was widely read and engendered a taste for houses vaguely medieval in design and set on grounds deliberately landscaped to appear natural.

Downing reminded his readers that local carpenters, using scroll saws, could easily turn a plain house into a Gothic cottage by adding finials, filigree, scrolls, and brackets. And by the thousands, his readers followed his suggestions. A simple two-story brick house in Kennebunk, Maine, built in 1826 with classical symmetry, was transformed in the 1850s by just such work and has been fa-

mous ever since as the Wedding Cake House. It illustrates a very practical point made by Downing, for its very elaborate "improvements" can be removed whenever the original brick surface needs a fresh coat of yellow paint. Such added doodads were strictly decorative and bore no relation at all to function, not even the brackets, which hung from the beams they appeared to support.

Wilderness created

Taste for natural settings, whether they were genuine or fabricated, soon extended to include urban parks and, in the process, boosted Frederick Law Olmsted to national prominence. When New York City decided it needed a large park, Olmsted and Calvert Vaux, a Downing protégé, were commissioned to plan it. They did so well in creating Central Park that other cities—Chicago, Washington, Brooklyn, and Montreal among them—clamored for Olmsted's services, keeping him busy the rest of his life. Nature as found was not good enough; current taste demanded a special kind of artistry. It produced, at the cost of many man-hours and dollars, lakes and lawns and wooded hills that seem closer to wilderness than real wilderness itself—this despite miles of drives, footways, and bridle paths, arbors and benches, and

Opposite left: *Detail of stairway, Lockwood-Mathews Mansion; Norwalk, Conn.; 1868.* Opposite right: *Hitchcock chair; ca. 1850. The stencil decoration is typical.* Above left: *Victorian dining room, Durgin House: Willowbrook at Newfield, Maine; mid-19th century.* Left: *Cottage furniture with painted graining, Durgin House.*

Two views of a bedroom in the Governor Goodwin Mansion; Strawbery Banke, Portsmouth, N.H.; ca. 1811, furnished in the style of the 1850s. Room is distinctive because of its Chinese pieces. Above: Tilt-top table. Above right: Lacquered sewing table outfitted with ivory thimbles, thread winders, and spools.

playgrounds. It would be hard to overrate Olmsted's achievement, for it was close to transcending nature. With the true spirit of the Romantic, he changed the entire concept of urban parks, and in doing so created something immediately high in taste.

The same Romantic taste for wildness also altered the design of cemeteries. For centuries, it had never occurred to anyone that a graveyard should look like a pleasant park, or that it was in any way distasteful to lay out graves on rectangular plots in straight lines, on level ground cleared of all trees and shrubs. Romantic thinking changed all that. It prompted the laying out of new cemeteries—among them Mt. Auburn in Cambridge, Mt. Hope in Bangor, Laurel Hill in Philadelphia, and Greenwood in New York—on wooded, rolling terrain with odd-shaped lots. Simple headstones might still do, but interest in markers and monuments of varying size and ornateness was growing. The main entrance of these new cemeteries almost invariably acquired an impressive arch or something resembling the Egyptian temple at Luxor. To a true Romantic, it must have been good to know, with Bryant, that when the

time came to "mix forever with the elements," it would not be in some flat, treeless field but where "the oak shall send his roots abroad and pierce thy mould."

The wilder image

Bryant had risen in life since he wrote those words in "Thanatopsis." After graduating from Williams College, he studied law but, in 1825, took up journalism. Within four years, he was editor of the New York *Evening Post,* a position he was to hold for the rest of his life. He continued writing poetry as an avocation, and his subjects continued to be Romantic—such things as mankind in nature and natural religion. Yet in 1826, he gave several lectures on poetry, defending the conventional forms and urging poets to innovate with caution. This advice, along with the example of his own works, served to maintain the conservative reading taste that was outraged in 1855 when Whitman broke all the rules in *Leaves of Grass.*

Almost single-handedly, Bryant had guided readers—who were much more devoted then than they now are to belletristic writing, to accept nature as a fit subject for poetry. As a friend of many artists, moreover, he had a consider-

106

able influence on their gradual shift to wild nature as a theme and on the development of the Hudson River School of painting that glorified rough scenery. When one promising young friend, English-born Thomas Cole, went abroad for further training, Bryant published this sonnet:

To Cole, The Painter, Departing
for Europe

Thine eyes shall see the light of
distant skies;
Yet COLE! thy heart shall bear
to Europe's strand
A living image of our own
bright land,
Such as upon thy glorious canvas
lies;
Lone lakes—savannas where the
bison roves—
Rocks rich with summer garlands—solemn streams—
Skies, where the desert eagle
wheels and screams—
Spring bloom and autumn blaze
of boundless groves.
Fair scenes shall greet thee where
thou goest—fair;
But different—everywhere the
trace of men,
Paths, homes, graves, ruins,
from the lowest glen
To where life shrinks from the
fierce Alpine air.
Gaze on them, till the tears
shall dim thy sight,
But keep that earlier, wilder image bright.

In the days of neoclassical restraint, so public a statement of personal feeling would have been as offensive to good taste as Whitman's poetry was in the 1850s. But expressing regret at a friend's departure was not the real purpose of the sonnet. Bryant was addressing two groups: young artists, to remind them of the "wilder image" awaiting their brushes, and the general public, to make them aware that impressive scenery was

not far beyond New York's boundaries, to be admired there or in galleries when captured in oils and watercolors. He did not organize the Hudson River School of painting, but he was unquestionably its foremost advocate and publicist.

Cole was not yet a leading member of this group when he left for Europe. He returned in 1832 more American than when he left, and gave a lyceum lecture—a popular form of entertainment in that era—to express his thoughts. In Europe, he said, nature had been tamed by man, but in America it was still uncorrupted, with "no ruined tower to tell of outrage, no gorgeous temple to speak of ostentation." He may have forgotten momentarily that ruins were part of the Romantic canon. To practice what he now believed in, he proceeded to roam the countryside in search of subjects, painting numerous scenes in the Catskills, an oxbow of the Connecticut River, and Crawford Notch in New Hampshire's White Mountains. In his absence, his colleagues had been active. Thomas Doughty, self-taught, settled in Newburgh, on the Hudson River near the Catskills, just to be close to wild scenery. He specialized in wilderness rivers. Asher Durand also exploited the Catskills. His painting *Kindred Spirits,* probably considered his best at the time, makes it very explicit that he at least appreciated Bryant's encouragement, for it shows the poet and Thomas Cole on a ledge overlooking a wild Catskill gorge.

Popular views

By 1849, when Durand completed *Kindred Spirits,* wild scenery as an artistic theme was firmly established in taste, and literally dozens of artists lived well by satisfying the demands of galleries and individual patrons. Many of them no doubt looked on the scenes they

painted with the same awe and wonder of ordinary visitors, but they were as subject to the profit motive as anybody else and, in effect, they painted what they knew would interest buyers. If they failed to do so, it was at the risk that would-be authors often took—of producing something that had no appeal to taste and yielded little if any income.

So many Hudson River and Catskill vistas were painted that they saturated the market. In an effort to avoid hackneyed subjects, artists went further afield in search of fresh areas. For a time, Mt. Chocorua, south of the Presidential Range in New Hampshire, was a favorite subject. One result was the conversion of the nearby Conway area to the popular resort region it has been ever since. John Kensett, whose *Chocorua* is perhaps the best rendering of that jagged peak, went on to discover New England's rocky coastline. His *Newport Harbor* and other paintings of the old seaport in Rhode Island made it look most attractive. Later, as a summer resort, Newport was to have some of the costliest "cottages" in all the world, built in styles far removed from the "Gothic cottage" design of Alexander Davis.

Other artists discovered winter. It was hardly a popular season until John Greenleaf Whittier's nostalgic "Snow-Bound," an idyllic description of a self-sufficient farm family's life during a protracted blizzard, became a best-selling poem in 1866. Artists tried snow scenes with some success, and FitzHugh Lane did very well with ships locked in the ice near Gloucester. But George Durrie, a man of modest talent, did best of all with roughly a hundred large pictures of snowbound farmyards. A New York lithographer and printmaker, Nathaniel Currier, who in 1857 formed a partnership with an artist named James Merritt Ives, smelled profit. He made the necessary arrangements with Durrie and turned out his paintings, with minimal tinting by hand, in prints that were immediately in great demand. The method of reproduction has long since been improved upon, but Currier and Ives prints have never completely lost favor in popular taste. In those days, they sold at retail for fifteen or twenty-five cents, or three dollars for the large folio size. Eventually, the firm offered more than a thousand separate titles. The project, appealing to people of limited means, pioneered "art for the masses" in America.

Western grandeur

Meanwhile a few artists, not content with the eastern version of wilderness, were venturing into the Far West. Scenery there was so awesome, and so abundant, that preserving tiny bits of it as urban parks would have seemed amusing. Surveying and reporting it were more pressing needs. Shortly after the Civil War, the federal government sent out two expeditions, one in 1871 to explore the Yellowstone region, the other by boat down the Colorado River in 1873. Thomas Moran went along on both, and his paintings made a profound impression in the East, especially *Chasm of the Colorado* and *The Grand Canyon of the Yellowstone.* The latter, backed by photographs taken by his friend William Henry Jackson, prompted Congress in 1872 to establish the first national park, a nature preserve larger than Rhode Island and Delaware combined.

Writers had tried to capture the western grandeur, but with limited success. Painters did better. The Hudson River School had conditioned viewers to admire "the wilder image," and now they could thrill to that image at its spectacu-

lar wildest. Moran's chief rival in painting it, German-born Albert Bierstadt, did not restrict himself to scenery. His *Indian Encampment* and *The Last of the Buffalo* appealed to other facets of Romantic taste. But what won the most applause were his huge paintings of scenes in the Rocky Mountains and Yosemite valley. It might be hard to find the equal, for sheer overwhelming effect, of *A Storm in the Rocky Mountains—Mount Rosalie,* completed in 1866 on a canvas twelve feet long and seven feet high.

Indians had their special artist in George Catlin, who happened to see an Indian in Philadelphia in 1832 and decided at once to visit the western tribes and paint them before whites could destroy their integrity. Five years later, he returned with a substantial portfolio, put it on exhibition, and attracted far more attention than was given earlier to Saint-Mémin's Indian profiles. In one pen and pencil sketch, Catlin showed himself painting a Mandan chief while the rest of the tribe watched. Other painters had sometimes produced self-portraits but none in quite such exotic settings.

Catlin's numerous books, especially *Catlin's North American Indian Portfolio,* established his reputation for painstaking accuracy of detail. People who liked his work, and they were numerous, were most taken by such dramatic scenes as a prairie fire and a buffalo hunt on snowshoes. Catlin's full-length paintings of individual Indians were in the tradition of "warts and all" realism that had long been favored for portraits by some Americans, even in the neoclassical era of idealization. Daguerreotypes, available by the 1840s, could hardly idealize human features, and more or less forced acceptance of realistic likenesses. Photography, in any event,

steadily reduced the demand for hand-painted portraits, thinning the ranks of itinerant artists.

Romantic nationalism

Despite the strong interest in western scenes and people, paintings by the Hudson River School retained their popularity well into the 1870s. By then, the favored member of that group was George Inness, whose later work shows a distinct foray into mysticism. The taste of average art lovers was steadily becoming more sophisticated, and gallery visitors were becoming more discriminating. Bierstadt could overwhelm, but Inness could convince, even with such common subjects as *Millpond* and *Autumn Oaks* and *Rainbow after a Storm.* Some of the older landscape painters felt it necessary to instruct, or to moralize; Inness merely painted what he saw, with the hand of a genius, and the public was alert enough to appreciate the difference. After 1870, when realism was superseding Romanticism, taste for awesome scenery receded, and discriminating people began to respond more to atmospheric effects as Inness ably put them on canvas and as Sarah Orne Jewett, in her quiet stories about rural Maine, was beginning to do in fiction.

But the Jewett brand of realism, highly respected today, had far less popular appeal just after the Civil War than did the sensational mining camp fiction of Bret Harte. He exploited, in such vivid stories as "The Luck of Roaring Camp" and "The Outcasts of Poker Flat," the public fascination with the Far West, the region most symbolic of Romantic nationalism. That it was all now part of the United States was a gratifying fulfillment of the dream of "Manifest Destiny." It was a new Eden, one last Promised Land, vast and empty, innocent of the problems that plagued the East

—or so most easterners thought. The difficulty of getting there only made it more alluring. The brief great vogue of Bret Harte measured the readiness of readers to believe anything that was written about it no matter how distorted it was in both facts and values. Reality was something different, but taste, if romantic enough, can make people indifferent to prosaic actualities.

Prefab Gothic

Even facts can be romantic. It was certainly a fact that in January of 1848 gold was found in a millrace at Coloma, in foothill country northeast of Sacramento, and that its announcement to a startled world by Sam Brannan, California's first millionaire, caused a stampede to the region. Few of the gold-seekers found enough to make them rich. It was men like Brannan who profited most, and by methods then generally approved by taste.

The Gold Rush created an acute housing shortage and made it highly profitable to ship precut frame houses from eastern cities all the way around Cape Horn. Sam Brannan ordered as many as he could get, unloaded them on his own wharf in San Francisco, transported them on his own vessels upriver to Sacramento, and sold them at outrageous prices to be assembled on lots he had for sale for equally outrageous sums. Once erected, they were the first of a type later known as "Gold Rush Gothic." Local carpenters with access to sawmills added others like them throughout that central part of California. Most were cheap imitations of houses in the style made popular by Davis and Downing, Gothic only in their few scroll-saw ornaments and occasional pointed arches over the windows.

A more elaborate house built in 1851 for Gen. Mariano Vallejo, in Sonoma, is a striking example of this West Coast version of the Gothic. Others survive in the Napa valley, in the environs of Hangtown, later renamed Placerville, and in such hill towns as Grass Valley, where the notorious Lola Montez lived for a while in one of them. A small prefabricated house had no attraction for Brannan himself. For a ranch he owned on the Feather River, he combined several of the precut frames to create an eight-room mansion with a winding staircase. It was a house as similar as he could make it to the fine Federal houses he had envied as a boy in Saco, Maine. Later he bought land at the head of the Napa valley and began developing a resort around natural hot springs. He named it Calistoga, for he intended it to be the Saratoga of California. When it opened in 1862, it had one central hotel and numerous small guesthouses in the California Gothic style.

Brannan was a very aggressive man, always alert to any new opportunity to increase his fortune. Had he, or one of the other entrepreneurs who pioneered California's development, given full attention to housing, it might have revolutionized the building industry on both coasts, through a determined effort to create a vogue for prefabrication. That development had to wait, however, until the twentieth century. It was not that taste in that time disapproved of prefab houses, for where they were assembled, they were considered quite attractive. What deferred their wider popularity was the strong opposition of the construction industry, for it was feared that prefabs would eliminate too many jobs.

Gothic variety

As an architectural style, Gothic was whatever passed as Gothic in different parts of the country.

Greystone, in Missouri, is quite unlike the Afton Villa in Louisiana. In remote Nevada, silver kings did their best to build in Gothic style, but they were more successful in furnishing their parlors, which were as lavishly Victorian as any in eastern cities. They also lavished money on their saloons. In Salt Lake, even more isolated, the huge Mormon Temple is the ultimate expression of what is called "Mormon Gothic," a variant first developed for the original Temple in Kirtland, Ohio. Most of the Latter-Day Saints lived in modest frame houses as neat and clean as their dedicated lives. Brigham Young's Beehive House, of necessity a "house of many mansions," has few Gothic touches but does have a carved wooden beehive, symbol of both Mormon industry and the State of Utah, atop the square cupola on the roof.

A few architects began to bring order to the style by studying the original Gothic as it had been constructed in the Middle Ages. Among the first in this effort was Richard Upjohn, a transplanted English cabinetmaker. He was intelligent and ambitious enough to study books by the great French authority on Gothic architecture, Augustus Pugin, and to apply what he learned. One of his first and most interesting productions was Oaklands, a large country home for the Gardiner family of Gardiner, Maine, completed in 1836. Compared with Lyndhurst overlooking the Hudson, finished two years later, Oaklands overlooking the Kennebec is quite plain. But its castellated gray stone walls, its slender corner turret, and its irregular lines made it equally "medieval."

Upjohn is best known as a church architect. His masterpiece is Trinity Church in New York, built in 1847 on Broadway at the head of Wall Street. Its quiet mag-

nificence lowered the barrier of disdain for Gothic that had long been manned by religious conservatives and academic architects. In 1832 one British visitor described New York's churches as plain, neat, and kept in perfect repair but "without the least pretensions of splendour." With his Trinity, Upjohn supplied the missing splendor and guided taste to appreciate the Gothic. For decades thereafter, it was the preferred style for new places of worship.

Upjohn also designed wooden churches for New England congregations, some of them with the vertical exterior boarding known as "board and batten." Admirers built numerous others in close imitation, and it is hard today to be certain, without inquiry, whether a given "Upjohn church" was built by the master or one of his disciples. All, however, were held high in taste.

Cathedrals, too

Architectural education on a formal level was available nowhere in the United States until 1868, when the Massachusetts Institute of Technology inaugurated the first collegiate program. Until then, architects got their training abroad or under the tutelage of men who had studied abroad. Far more numerous were the carpenter-builders who sometimes called themselves architects but whose knowledge of the art came straight out of handbooks. There were also gifted amateurs like Thomas Jefferson and men like Upjohn who, by assiduous study, could advance from humbler callings to a high degree of proficiency. James Renwick was of this latter group. He began as an engineer and was able, when only twenty-four, to win a competition for Grace Episcopal Church, Trinity's rival as spiritual home of New York's elite. The edifice, completed in 1846, established his reputation, and it surprised nobody when he was chosen to design St. Patrick's Cathedral, meant to be, as it still is, the largest Roman Catholic church in the nation.

During the Middle Ages, it often took more than a century to complete a Gothic cathedral. Notre Dame de Paris was begun in 1163, its nave was completed and roofed in thirty-three years, the towers were finished about 1245, but construction ended only after 1300. St. Patrick's, though it went up faster, still took time. The cornerstone was laid in 1858, five years after Renwick's plan was accepted. By 1879, construction was far enough advanced to warrant dedication, but it was 1887 before the Lady Chapel behind the high altar and the twin spires, well over three hundred feet high, got their final touches. Gothic on the grand scale has always been an expensive taste and one not satisfied overnight.

The city's Episcopalians, not to be outdone, secured a charter in 1873 to build their own great cathedral of Saint John the Divine. The first stone was set in place in 1893, and the nave acquired its full length in 1941, but even today the structure is incomplete and seems likely to remain so. Taste for the

110

Opposite: *Friendship quilt; ca. 1846. Each block was made by a different person.* Below: *Hair wreath; ca. 1860. Hair is from family members' heads—except the black, which is from a horse's mane.*

Gothic remains high, but it is not firm enough to outweigh the current exorbitant cost of creating it.

Renwick's interest in medieval styles was not limited to churches, and he designed buildings for other purposes, too. In fact, he became as eclectic an architect as any in the business. If what was wanted was "picturesque," he was ready to try it, for he was an admirer of A. J. Downing, who had made that term a household word. Two large buildings in Washington illustrate both Renwick's range and his boldness.

Castle on the mall

In 1852, Renwick designed a sprawling red sandstone castle for the Smithsonian Institution. It makes a few concessions to symmetry, especially along the front of the main block, where five evenly spaced bays on either side of the front entrance have single-arched windows on the first floor and foliated windows on the second. But above the porticoed main door, the central bay rises to dissimilar tow-

ers, two of the many, all different, projecting skyward. Halfway up the central bay is a wheeled window, Romanesque ancestor of the rose window in Gothic cathedrals. Wings on either side of the main block differ from each other in every detail. The whole was as if Renwick had tried deliberately to combine as many medieval elements as possible and also to demonstrate that a building so designed could be as attractive as any in the neoclassical mode.

Jefferson, as a committed classicist and as the man who had done most to commit official government structures to the Roman style, would have been startled, if not horrified, by the structure. As it was, those in charge of government buildings saw to it that the Smithsonian was located on the south rim of the Mall, not near any of the buildings that did conform to the Jeffersonian ideal. American opinion of the building then and since has never quite coalesced. Some visitors to Washington, seeing the Castle for the first time,

are delighted, while others are nonplussed. Opinion at the time was divided along different lines, for believers in continuity and convention, and virtually all academic architects, deplored it, while less tradition-bound viewers saw it as symbolic of the Romantic triumph over outmoded neoclassicism, and a portent of the future.

If the latter was Renwick's intent, rank and file citizens were in a mood to endorse it. They had discovered, in their enthusiasm for the Greek Revival, that a small elite minority was not the only group in the population with the power to determine national taste. For them, it was encouraging that at least one prominent architect recognized and shared their high regard for individualism and nonconformity.

The eclectic impulse

Most people who saw the Smithsonian Castle may not have fully realized that it was a monumental expression of eclecticism—the combining in a single building of styles from widely separated periods of history. It was not new. Jefferson surely was aware that the Roman style he favored was a composite of elements from earlier eras, including the Greek and the Tuscan. Even his idol Palladio had merged different styles in the sixteenth century. Vernacular houses all over America, moreover, mixed Elizabethan with Georgian or Federal styles, and sometimes the mixing was even built into great mansions.

Few other buildings, however, were as conspicuously eclectic as the Smithsonian. One that went even further in combining styles was Philadelphia's Masonic Temple. Dedicated in 1837, it included Ionic, Norman, Oriental, and Egyptian elements. But it was the Castle that encouraged designers and their clients to ignore tradition and do as they pleased without worrying about consistency or convention. Some tried to revive styles of particular cultures previously overlooked. For instance, Napoleon's Nile Campaign had prompted Benjamin Latrobe, as early as 1808, to propose an Egyptian exterior for the Library of Congress; but the suggestion was premature.

Not until the 1830s was taste ready to approve the Egyptian. It provided the inspiration for a prison in New York, officially named the Halls of Justice but better known, to this day, as the Tombs. In the same year, 1838, a debtor's wing added to a Philadelphia hospital was also in the Egyptian style. But the style never gained much favor, perhaps because of its association in popular thinking with ancient despotism. Another exotic style, closely related and sometimes called Near Eastern, was chosen for a few synagogues, insurance company headquarters, and such public works as the Croton Reservoir, where the New York City Public Library now stands.

Whether or not these experiments in unfamiliar styles gained general favor in American taste, they had a greater chance of being considered in the free atmosphere of Romanticism than was conceivable under neoclassical restraint. People were ready to admire one-of-a-kind exotics that represented extreme—or eccentric—forms of individual taste. For instance, Longwood in Natchez, Mississippi, added to lavish Gothic fretwork a conspicuous onion dome that gave the whole its reputation of being Oriental. The term *Persian* was applied to Iranistan, built in 1848 near Bridgeport, Connecticut, by that city's most famous mayor, P. T. Barnum. Had it not burned down, within a decade, it might serve today as the supreme

example of unrestrained taste. On a much more modest scale, several dwellings were designed to be circular, or octagonal like one in Afton, Minnesota; and at Mount Holly, New Jersey, somebody built what he called a "Chinese cottage" that was admired by A. J. Downing, the arch champion of simple, "picturesque" dwellings.

The mansard mania

Renwick reentered the arena of competing styles in 1858 when William Corcoran, a wealthy Washington banker and art collector, commissioned him to create a gallery suitable for the display of his treasures, as a gift to the nation. With his customary independence and courage, Renwick adopted for it the style of a new wing added to the Louvre the year before. Known as Second Empire, and first popular in Paris, it is an easy style to identify by its almost vertical lower roof, called a mansard roof. But instead of the gray stone used for the walls of the Louvre addition, Renwick chose red brick and sandstone, which gave the walls a very different texture. The Civil War interrupted the project. When the gallery was at last completed, in 1874, it drew strong disapproval. But like the Smithsonian, it was immune from the charge of being a misuse of public money. Such are the vagaries of taste that today, renamed the Renwick Gallery, the building is a landmark beloved by Washingtonians and visitors alike.

Taste did not wait until the next century, however, to shift from condemnation of Renwick's innovation to widespread approval. By 1876, buildings with mansard roofs were quite common, even on government buildings. One across Pennsylvania Avenue from the Renwick and a close neighbor of the White House has a mansard roof topping a mass of Greco-Ro-

man columns and porticoes; it has served as headquarters for both army and navy and the State Department, and is currently the Executive Office Building. The mansard roof proved especially popular for private town houses, and the style became known in the last years of Grant's administration as either the General Grant style or the mansard roof style, depending on the viewer's politics.

The Italianate style

Renwick's gallery built for Corcoran was an innovation in another way, the use of contrasting warm colors for exterior walls, which John Ruskin in England strongly advocated. Taste for this device developed very gradually, becoming popular only for substantial houses built in what was called the High Victorian style, which peaked in the late 1870s. Victorian taste in exteriors was more widely influenced by the firm of Town and Davis, who advertised, during the 1850s and 1860s, house styles they were prepared to supply. The list is impressive: "American Log Cabin, Farm Villa, English Cottage, Collegiate Gothic, Manor House, French Suburban, Switz Chalet, Switz Mansion, Lombard Italian, Tuscan from Pliny's Villa at Ostia, Ancient Etruscan, Suburban Greek, Oriental, Moorish, Round, Castellated." All were no doubt ordered and built, somewhere and for somebody. But all of them prove, on close examination of the sketches and floor plans, to be far less different than their names suggest. They sift down to three basic types: classical, medieval, and Italianate. It was the latter style that was ultimately the highest in popular taste.

In Europe, the Italianate style developed as a sophisticated version of the classical, inspired by Renaissance paintings of classical landscapes. But in America it grew

out of—and away from—the Gothic. Pointed arches were not abandoned, but they could be so flattened that the points were hardly perceptible. Neoclassical symmetry was avoided, as it was in almost every style after the Greek Revival. Stress was on horizontal rather than vertical lines; roofs were nearly flat and projected some distance beyond the walls. Towers were fairly common, but not in Gothic form, for their walls were pierced with numerous windows and they had the same roof overhang as the rest of the house. Oddly located porches and balconies broke the facades, and there was a variety of decoration ranging from Greek columns to scroll-saw brackets. The name "Italianate Gothic" became a misnomer as Gothic elements receded, but "Italianate" itself was misleading as the style grew more

eclectic and elaborate.

Any building, even the most eclectic, can be tasteful if its components are intelligently proportioned and harmonized; if they are not, the result may be ludicrous, whether the house is small or large. The mansion that Ruggles Sylvestre Morse built in Portland, Maine, met all the requirements of eclectic taste because funding was liberal and the builder-furnisher was highly skilled.

Morse, who had been born in a small Maine village, made a fortune in hotel operations in New Orleans. When he married in the late 1850s, he determined that his wife would have, as a summer residence, the finest house in Maine. To create it, he chose a man he could rely on, Henry Austin of New Haven. Construction took four years, from 1859 to 1863, and cost about four hundred thousand

dollars. Known today as the Morse-Libby House or the Victorian Mansion, it rivals the Longfellow house as Portland's most famous residence; it is also one of the nation's best examples of the Italianate style.

Built of brownstone, which is also used for the elaborate exterior trim, the house is asymmetrical but well balanced. Paired Ionic columns frame the massive front entrance and support a small balustraded balcony. At the left, similar columns lead up from a generous porch to another balcony, and at the right a protruding bay has three tall rectangular windows close together. A single window over the entrance has a very plain pediment, but the pediment over a three-part window on one side has ornate carving. The central bay rises to a square tower that displays a group of slender arched

Main entrance hall, Mark Twain House; Hartford, Conn.; 1874.
Redecorated in 1881 by Lewis Comfort Tiffany & Associated Artists.

windows on each face, under the broad roof overhang.

The interior stuns the senses. Once past the vestibule with its marble floor and stained-glass windows, the first eye-catcher is the unsupported stairway with 337 hand-carved mahogany balusters. Above the entrance hall is a huge lighting fixture, then called a gasolier, suspended from the third-floor ceiling and lighting all three floors; it is unmatched in this country. Each main-floor room is decorated in a style from a different period: the parlor is Louis XV, the music room Louis XVI, the library Gothic, the dining room late Renaissance. Ceilings and walls are frescoed in many colors, and there is even some painting on flat ceiling surfaces that gives a three-dimensional illusion—the trompe-l'oeil effect. The house has seven fireplaces carved in Italy, like their mantels, from Carrara marble. To find a house of equal magnificence, one would have to travel to Italy, source of the Renaissance splendor it was intended to rival.

Cast-iron fronts

The Morse house was far beyond the reach of most Americans, but it was a supreme example of what most of them considered the ultimate of domestic taste. In houses Town and Davis designed for the mass market, just a few small details combining different styles could produce the Italianate effect. Theoretically, at least, every Italianate building could have been unique, so many were the options to choose from and combine. Nor was there any reason not to choose and combine them for structures other than dwellings—schools, churches, and commercial enterprises. It was for these last that technology provided the means for adopting eclectic design, with the cast-iron front.

Alexander Davis had experi-

mented with ready-made cast-iron units in 1835 but had been more interested in other uses of iron. The effective pioneer of the cast-iron front was James Bogardus, a New York foundryman. Asked by the owner of a store on lower Broadway in New York City to help make it more attractive to customers, he suggested covering the brick facade with cast iron pieced in designs currently in vogue. It took just three days to achieve. First he cast in his foundry hundreds of large and small pieces. Then he supervised his workmen as they bolted the pieces together on the site and raised them into place.

The speed of fabrication and installation, the low cost, and the "new look" were widely reported in the press, and within a few years iron fronts were popular in all parts of the country, for new commercial buildings as well as old. Painted to resemble stone, they gave a building the visual impression of being a palazzo transported bodily from Italy, and they greatly expanded the range of operative eclectic taste. Indeed, buildings with cast-iron fronts outlived most other buildings in the eclectic mode, losing their popularity only in the twentieth century with the general shift to steel skeleton construction and with the decline of taste for elaborate decoration.

Foreign malice

The English were no less Victorian than their American cousins and only slightly less enthusiastic about change and the exercise of individual freedom. But whereas Americans visited Europe in search of culture and forms to imitate, numerous English men and women crossed the ocean with notebook in hand and, it often seemed to Americans, with malice in their hearts. The books based on

their observations and their notebook records tended to be condescending and critical, sometimes downright hostile. Those strong in tone sold well in England, where a good many people welcomed any evidence of American crudity and immaturity. The Big Three of this denigration were Frances Trollope, Harriet Martineau, and Charles Dickens.

Mrs. Trollope, whose son Anthony was to become a major novelist, went to America to recoup the family fortune, opened a "bazaar" in Cincinnati, failed to make a go of it, and blamed the debacle on the uncouthness of the local citizens and their lack of taste. Back home in 1832, she reported her impressions in *The Domestic Manners of the Americans.* It was an instant best-seller. In her unpublished notebook, she had written, "They want taste, and they want grace—the acquirement of the latter is, I believe, the natural consequence of the diffusion of the former." Her use of *want* for *lack,* it may be noted, illustrated the difference Noah Webster had pointed out between English and American usage. But of deeper concern to her was the gap separating the standards of taste in the two countries.

Two years later, Miss Martineau, already well known for solid works on political economy, visited the former colonies and reported her own adverse opinions in *Society in America* (1837) and *Retrospect of Western Travel* (1838). But least forgivable of all was criticism from Dickens. A great favorite with American readers, he was honored and lavishly entertained wherever he went in America. His *American Notes* (1842) was abrasive enough, but he compounded the felony in the next novel he wrote, *Martin Chuzzlewit.* American readers were understandably indignant. The more charitable among them attributed his caricature of this nation to his bad manners and bad taste, and Dickens later admitted they were right.

Bad habits

One of the most offensive remarks made by Dickens was that the city of Washington was "the headquarters of tobacco-tinctured saliva." He was not inventing, for chewing tobacco and spitting out the juice, into cuspidors if they were handy, onto the ground or floor if they were not, was a general male habit and not condemned, as it is in modern times, as atrocious taste. Another male habit, not quite so obnoxious, was the downing of large quantities of food at midday followed by rushing back to work. The composer Jacques Offenbach, on his visit in 1876, was one European who reported it, along with much else in America that he had difficulty understanding. Food was plentiful and cheap, as it always had been. Only the fear of missing a chance to turn a profit could explain this habit of bolting food—and so much of it—at top speed.

When men dined out of an evening, or when traveling, they may have eaten more leisurely, but they still consumed prodigious amounts of food. Scholars have suggested that this penchant was a carryover from life on farms, where men needed extra food for energy to support the long hours they spent at hard physical labor. But menus from the period suggest that women also ate heavy meals. One menu from the Gibson House in Cincinnati, for September 21, 1862, shows a table d'hôte dinner of ten courses. First was a choice between oyster soup and broiled whitefish. Then came a boiled course with five possibilities, a roast course with nine, "Large Dishes" with seven, and "Cold Dishes," also with seven choices.

Next are listed sixteen side dishes, nine relishes, fifteen vegetables, a pastry course, and desserts. Not everyone who patronized the Gibson House, presumably, tried all the courses, but the price of the meal permitted it. Some bills of fare today offer comparable variety but seldom for a standard meal. Devouring even a judicious sampling of what was offered would satisfy most of us today, but a century ago the same large meal was provided both at noon and in the evening.

The author's grandfather, as a boy of fourteen, served briefly as surgeon's steward aboard the U.S.S. *Marion* on a training cruise in the summer of 1863. Here is his diary entry, verbatim, for a typical day, September 12: "Had a bully breakfast had nice flour bread and beefsteak. I am fleshing up some. What they had in the Ward Room for dinner: First they had a course of soup, second fish, third turkey, ham, boiled mutton, roast beef, onions, green corn, squash, beets, peppers, tomatoes, fourth, lobster salad, fifth boiled fruit pudding, sixth, two kinds of pie, grapes, pears, apples, peaches, seventh, raisins, almonds, ice cream, eighth, coffee." He did not record the speed with which this amplitude was ingested.

Unheeded critics

The hostile comments of European visitors, if put into books a century earlier, would have been more deeply resented than were those published in the mid-nineteenth century. Sensitivity to criticism was giving way to its opposite, complacency and indifference to "the good opinion of mankind." Headstrong and confident, the Victorian generation was quite ready to brush criticism aside and to ignore both foreign defamers and their own best critics.

One of these, perhaps the

shrewdest of all, was Ralph Waldo Emerson. He was exasperated by what he considered the continuing deference to European culture. "We imitate," he wrote in 1841. "Our houses are built with foreign taste; our shelves are garnished with foreign ornaments; our opinions, our tastes, our faculties lean, and follow the Past and the Distant." America was finding itself, moving rapidly toward a distinctive culture, but even in the process it was still leaning on Europe past and present. Emerson spoke and wrote forcefully but in a manner that left ordinary citizens rather baffled. Satisfied as they were with their freedom to choose, and with their emancipation from elitist prescription, being reminded that their eclecticism still rested on past and distant models could hardly sit well. As a result, Emerson's great influence on the culture was indirect, through a handful of individuals who could grasp and implement his radical ideas. In his lifetime, he was generally held in great respect and even awe, but he had relatively little direct impact on taste—less than Bryant exerted, or Olmsted, or Downing, or Stephen Foster.

Beards and bustles

Emerson pleaded for nonconformity in matters of major importance but not in such things as apparel or appearance. One could easily have mistaken him for any English gentleman of the period, from his frock coat of finely textured black wool to his rather long sideburns. He was a little too old to grow a beard, as his young friend Henry Thoreau and other men born after 1815 had chosen to do by mid-century. It is a myth that beards won favor in taste during the Civil War when shaving was difficult under battlefield conditions. Shaving had been no easier during the Revolution, which produced no bearded generals or privates. The Victorian taste for hirsute splendor was a phase of the rebellion against classical restraint. Regular shaving was Roman and smacked of discipline and conformity to authoritarian standards. Ancient Greeks, the archetypical democrats, had all been well bearded.

No such consideration influenced American women in their makeup, hairstyle, or dress. As Mrs. Trollope had reported in the 1830s, they "powder themselves immoderately, face, neck, and arms, with pulverized starch; the effect is indescribably disagreeable by day-light, and not very favourable at any time." She found a partiality for false hair. "It is less trouble to append a bunch of waving curls here, there, and every where, than to keep their native tresses in perfect order." She was no less critical about clothing: "If it were not for the peculiar manner of their walking, which distinguishes all American women, Broadway might be taken for a French street. . . . The dress is entirely French; not an article (except perhaps the cotton stockings) must be English, on pain of being stigmatized as out of fashion." The money American women spent on clothing was out of proportion, Mrs. Trollope thought, to their general style of living, but was "very far (excepting in Philadelphia) from being in good taste."

The prevailing feminine mode in the decade just before the Civil War followed that of Europe— great puffed sleeves, double capes, flounces, ruchings, cravats, and large bonnets. Such things emphasized the Victorian concept of the "feminine" woman—delicate, graceful, helpless. But not all women shared this concept. One rebel, Elizabeth Miller, proposed something new and sensible— loose trousers gathered at the ankles and worn under a short skirt.

The notion appealed to Amelia Bloomer, an advocate of women's rights, who gave it favorable publicity in her reform magazine, *Lily*. The only result was derision, so general that the offbeat style was quickly named for her. Bloomers, carrying no foreign sanction, simply had no chance of being accepted by general taste, even after the gathering was raised to the knees.

The postwar decade brought further elaboration in dress. Tassels sprouted from shoulders and elbows, and bustles from every fashionable rump.

Patternmakers

The Civil War did have one important effect on clothing. The sudden urgent need for tens of thousands of military uniforms spurred industry to expand its capacity for mass production, and when peace returned, the factory owners turned to civilian production. Uniforms conformed to precise specifications, but for ordinary clothing there had to be a considerable variety. Designers were added to the factory staffs and became a new breed of tastemaker. At the same time, relatively inexpensive and efficient sewing machines simplified dressmaking at home. To aid the home seamstress, one designer, who signed herself "Mme Ellen Demorest," created a new industry by making and selling dress patterns made of tissue paper. She is said to have bought her pattern paper five thousand reams at a time and to have sold up to fifty thousand copies of some of her designs.

In almost no time at all, a tailor named Ebenezer Butterick borrowed the Demorest idea for the male of the species by offering stiff brown paper patterns for men's shirts and boys' suits. He did well enough but soon realized there was much greater profit on the distaff side. By the early 1870s, the firm of E. L. Butterick was selling to American women more than 6 million dress patterns each year.

The upshot of these innovations was that clothing, for the first time in American history, was not disproportionately more expensive than food and shelter. It was also more varied, within the range of current styles, as factory designers and patternmakers competed for patrons and profits. Much the same development affected furniture. The nation's burgeoning industry, and the trend toward mass production, were steadily undercutting the elitist control of taste formation. The process accelerated in the postwar years.

Styles unlimited

After about 1825, not even Duncan Phyfe, for all his earlier fame as America's premier furniture designer, had much success in adapting new foreign styles. His place in the sun was taken by Lambert Hitchcock, who in 1818 built a factory in Connecticut to turn out a new kind of chair that was, of course, unsanctioned by taste abroad since it was of American design. Basically a version of the American Empire style, the Hitchcock chair was distinctive for its native maple frame, concave horizontal back slats, and painted surface—usually brownish and stenciled with designs in gilt or bright colors. By the 1830s, it stood first in American popularity. Almost as high in favor was the Boston rocker, another native product, with a similar colorful surface. Both rocker and Hitchcock chair were simple in construction, as the humble Windsor chair had always been, but were fancy enough to appear in the front parlor.

The Victorian taste for multiplicity being what it was, Americans continued to look also to foreign styles in furniture, adapting those of centuries past just as readily as those of the present. England was no longer the major source of models. At any given time, several different styles from as many countries were in favor, but it is possible to project this rough sequence: Louis XV after 1825, then Renaissance, Louis XVI, and Turkish, and, after 1870, Eastlake. The variety of styles complemented the variety of available houses. No single bed or chair or table can be taken as typical of Victorian furniture. One authority, Thomas B. Ormsbee, has listed eight separate styles for the period, but even as he did so, he confessed he was oversimplifying. The old rule of one dominant style for a given period had been discarded. Victorian taste embraced as bewildering an assortment of styles, some beautiful, others merely astonishing, as ever graced rooms in American houses.

The decade of the 1840s was one of transition, marked by the appearance of such untraditional details as wavy molding and flower medallions superimposed on French Empire pieces. Next came several new forms, including the tasseled footstool or ottoman, a borrowing from Turkey; the useful lazy susan that revolved on a dining room table, for individual self-service; and the double-door wardrobe, seven to nine feet tall, one of the final such units before the long-overdue advent of closets.

Beginning about 1850, the floodgates of fanciful innovation opened wide. A designer could start with any style previously known to mankind, alter it in any way he could think of, and be confident of attracting customers. Or he could ignore all tradition entirely, devise some eye-catching novelty, and be equally certain of eager purchasers. No two Victorian rooms were exactly alike, but most were cluttered with furniture, often oddly

Opposite above left: *Lithograph of Jenny Lind in* La Somnambula; *New York; 1850.* Opposite above right: *Music corner, parlor of the Durgin House; Willowbrook at Newfield, Maine; mid-19th century.* Opposite bottom: George Washington, *by Horatio Greenough; 1841.*

mismatched, and also with objets d'art that served no purpose other than decoration.

According to one scholar, the profusion of objets d'art relates to the Victorian belief that woman's place was in the home. By his reasoning, the introduction of pressed glass about 1830 multiplied the availability of small pieces at low cost, some of them useful, most of them not. These, together with similar, supposedly artistic objects made of ceramic or china, proved irresistible to stay-at-home wives and daughters, who took delight in buying them.

Women's work

Whatever the credibility of this theory, with its overtone of male chauvinism, it is true that women of the prospering middle class had few opportunities to participate in the vibrant life that men knew. Higher education for women became available in the 1830s but caught on very slowly, whether in women's "seminaries" (in the East) or coeducational colleges (west of the Appalachians). Most girls, both urban and rural, stayed at home until they married, spending their energies learning how to manage a household and on domestic arts of all sorts—their private share in the folk-art movement. Knitting produced scarves and sweaters and afghans. Hooked rugs, rare before 1820, rapidly grew in popularity; some followed designs bought from peddlers, and others reflected individual talent, in designs that were geometric or floral or pictorial.

By the mid-1850s, even such practical things as pieced bed quilts acquired extensive design. Many patterns were given specific titles—"Wild Goose Chase," "Underground Railroad." Step or block patterns were popular, as they also were for hooked rugs. Cooperative quiltmaking turned

rural quilting bees into social occasions. On what were called "friendship" or "signature" quilts, common before the Civil War, a name was inscribed on each square block.

Along with cooking and dressmaking, these "hobbies" were ordinarily for practical purposes, but young women also painted, played the harp or piano, raised exotic plants, and spent endless hours producing such attractive oddities as hair jewelry and hair wreaths. The hair used in these pieces was from the heads of members of the family, although horsehair was sometimes used to provide additional colors. Some ambitious rural families turned these arts to profit by a form of "cottage industry." Even young children could develop skill in braiding straw or knotting fringe at the request of milliners or shawlmakers.

Two patriotic symbols, the eagle and the shield, retained their popularity as designs for many objects. A new one, the American Indian, apparently originated in England and gained favor in America late—it was used on the small penny, first minted in 1859, and more conspicuously for wooden or metal Indians placed at doorways of retail stores. It was, of course, predictable that some forms of folk art would be adopted by business to advertise their products.

Mark Twain at home

Huck Finn's description of the Grangerford "mansion" captures the essence of Victorian taste as it could have been found in the lower Mississippi valley before the Civil War: Big brass firedogs on the hearth, a mantel clock with a townscape painted on its face, a crockery cat and dog, a basket filled with brightly colored artificial fruit, an oilcloth table cover emblazoned with a red and blue spread eagle. On the walls, litho-

graphs of Washington, Lafayette, and the signing of the Declaration —no doubt taken from John Trumbull's painting. A well-thumbed copy of *Friendship's Offering*, "full of beautiful stuff and poetry." On the piano rack, the sheet music for "The Battle of Prague" and "The Last Link Is Broken."

Such was domestic taste in a new section of the country as Mark Twain recalled it in 1875. By then, he was enjoying his own version of Victorian taste and conspicuous consumption—in his Hartford house, completed in 1874, with its nineteen rooms, eighteen fireplaces, and five bathrooms. It is not as ornately impressive as the earlier Victorian mansion in Portland, nor is it Italianate, but in some ways it is comparable. No two rooms are alike, nor are they furnished in the same style. The main door, guarded by a porte cochere over the driveway, opens to an ample, elaborately decorated entrance hall of irregular shape. From it, a massive stairway ascends at an angle. The library has one of the largest and most elaborate fireplaces in existence, in no recognizable style, with a mantel brought from Scotland. Books line the walls; Twain was as great a reader as he was prolific in his writing. This room, cluttered with unmatching furniture, mementos, and pictures, gives onto a conservatory, facing the southern sun. The dining room is less crowded, and its matched table and chairs have an odd boxlike look. Over an equally solid sideboard is a colored-glass window, one of Louis Comfort Tiffany's many contributions when he redecorated the first-floor rooms in 1881. There is a main-floor guest suite of bedroom and bath that William Dean Howells called "a princely chamber." The master bedroom upstairs has a large four-poster bed. Cherubim from Venice look down with benign smiles from the wall above the pillows.

All the rooms display intentional irregularity and stylistic variety. Dominating the third floor is a huge billiard room and assorted other amenities of masculine socializing. It opens to a porch resembling the deck of a Mississippi riverboat. The asymmetrical exterior is of warm polychromatic brick, and there are balconies of various shapes at unexpected places. The house was exactly what Mark Twain wanted and, despite its individuality or perhaps because of it, it is a typical example of expensive Victorian taste.

Like the furniture they contain, however, no one Victorian house can really be called typical. Each is reflective of individual taste, in the context of Victorian freedom of choice. No single Victorian house, in any event, could exhaust the available variety of forms. Yet there was a modicum of consistency. Exterior form almost always influenced the interior—size and shape of rooms, ceiling height, the spacing of furniture, and the number of separate pieces. Looking backward, the add-on frame houses of the seventeenth century called for dark, heavy pieces and Federal mansions needed light and delicate chairs. So with the varied forms of the Victorian years: the Morse mansion in Portland could not have been furnished like Twain's Hartford home.

Knicknacks and whatnots

For Ithiel Town, who announced publicly his readiness to design modest dwellings in any desired style, furniture was a detail of architecture and ought to contribute its share to the idea suggested by the chosen exterior. At the same time, popular books of instruction for young married women advised furnishing each room to accord with its function and even advo-

cated changing the decor from time to time. Victorian diversity could accommodate such contradictory positions. Agreement was general, however, that the husband should choose the exterior form, while responsibility for the interior decoration was assigned to the wife. Without the guidance of a single standard as in earlier periods, and with the great variety of styles to choose from, taste was of necessity an individual matter.

Housewives faced with this freedom found it more and more difficult to carry out the furnishing of a house. Victorian brides, initially happy at the prospect, discovered after the honeymoon that the freedom could be a burden. The many available books of instruction helped, but the ever-increasing variety to choose from was bewildering. Each newly introduced style or object demanded consideration; and there was always a limit to the space in any house.

The final Victorian years produced their share of new forms. The étagère, a Continental piece that was quickly very popular, was equipped with shelves of different lengths and was ideal for displaying oddly shaped souvenirs. The corner "whatnot," with its tapering stack of shelves, was crowded with smaller objects: roses and portraits embedded in glass; hollow glass balls that produced miniature snowstorms when shaken; decorated spoons brought back from Florence; teacups picturing Victoria and Albert on their wedding day; miniature volumes with metal clasps, and somewhat larger albums containing daguerreotype likenesses of friends and relatives; and other such knickknacks or, rather, the "whatnots" that gave this repository of beloved junk its familiar name.

By the 1870s, stoves were increasingly the major source of heat in cold weather. Like cast-iron

building fronts, they were available in a variety of styles—square or potbellied, plain or decorated, short or tall. Freestanding and airtight, they radiated heat in all directions and lost less of it through the exhaust vent and up the chimney than the fireplaces they blocked. These often suffered the ignominy of being sealed off. But the old mantels continued to hold flower arrangements, elaborate candleholders containing seldom-lighted candles, and assorted other objects, including, more often than not, one or more Rogers pieces. For many years, these were overwhelming favorites in Victorian taste for ornamentation.

Sculpture for the many

John Rogers, born in 1829 and trained as an engineer, was forced by failing eyesight to give up that profession and work as a machinist. He turned to clay modeling as a pastime. His interest grew, and after about a year of study in Italy, where virtually every American sculptor had learned the trade, he set up a shop in New York. By 1859, the year he introduced *The Slave Auction*, showing blacks on the block and eager white bidders, he needed twenty workers in his shop. The number of workers eventually rose to sixty. During the Civil War, he specialized in turning out war-related subjects— *The Wounded Scout, Wounded to the Rear,* and the like. Each Rogers piece was cast in plaster and then painted, and was titled at the base in large letters to make sure that nobody missed the point. Demand steadily increased with returning peace, especially for depictions of familiar events and sentimental situations. One great favorite was *Going to the Parson,* a group that portrays a bashful young couple meeting a clergyman who seems quite ready to join them in eternal bliss.

Priced modestly, from six to twenty-five dollars, these pieces were within the means of many Americans, who bought them by the thousands. More than one hundred thousand of them, by one estimate, were retailed in the thirty years after 1860. Their subjects resembled those of genre paintings but were generally more sentimental. What Rogers discovered had been established earlier by Currier and Ives with their tinted lithographs—that the public would buy, in unlimited numbers, copies of art that had the right kind of appeal.

Art on a pedestal

These same Victorian Americans could hardly have been unaware that sculpture of a different kind existed, on a level beyond their ability to appreciate as they did the Rogers pieces. Painters had more or less thrown off the restricting shackles of neoclassical convention, and many of them were producing pictures that could be understood and enjoyed. But sculpture in America was too new for that. Early in the century, the government had had to turn to Europe to obtain talent adequate enough to produce the governmental statuary it desired, and the man it chose, Jean Antoine Houdon, had set the classical standard still accepted for important sculpture. In an age when Romanticism had long since succeeded neoclassicism in almost every facet of the culture, sculpture of that sort was a lonely exception. It was still art on a pedestal, out of ordinary reach and remote from the people's taste.

The man generally considered the first real American sculptor, Horatio Greenough, set out for Italy in 1826, the same year the painter Thomas Cole departed and for the same reason—access to better teachers and more advanced techniques. He settled in Florence

and lived there until 1851. With the help of Washington Allston, he was commissioned by the United States government to create a statue of George Washington suitable for placement in the Capitol rotunda. That was in 1832, but it took him eight years to finish the work. In 1841, it crossed the ocean aboard a warship, all twelve tons of it, and was at last set in place. But the lighting was inadequate, and it was too heavy for the floor, so the next year it was moved outside to the East Lawn, where it braved the weather for half a century before being put in a dim alcove at the Smithsonian. Today it is more favorably placed in the Museum of History and Technology in Washington, D.C.

The Father of His Country seated as if in the Roman Senate, wearing sandals and clad in a toga that left him bare from the waist up, roused no ecstatic praise when it was unveiled, for by 1842, public taste had cooled for evocation of Roman grandeur. Two other expatriate sculptors, Thomas Crawford and Hiram Powers, were also victims of shifting taste—or of their unawareness, living as they were so far from home, that classicism was no longer in vogue. Crawford studied in Rome under the Danish classicist Albert Thorwaldsen. He earned much of his income by furnishing parts of the Capitol—bronze doors for the Senate wing, statues for its pediment, and a nineteen-foot bronze *Armed Freedom* for the top of the great dome. At that height, some three hundred feet above ground level, its carefully detailed carving is best seen through the eyes of the Capitol pigeons, or through binoculars, and only art hunters ever bother to look.

Powers followed a different course. Like dozens of Americans with lesser talent who opted to live in Italy and drank up antiquity as copiously as the local wine, he turned out busts and torsos and full-length stone portraits of mythical and historical personages, mostly women. Bryant and Emerson and other travelers visiting old friends in Rome and Venice found their friends' studios crowded with Zenobias and Cleopatras, Eves and Venuses and Minervas. Some of the expatriates were torn between prudery and the impulse to glorify the human body, as Hawthorne noted in 1860 in his Roman novel, *The Marble Faun.* Sculptured clothing dated a work, of course, because fashion changes quickly. But nudity could hardly be carved without frequent, guilty observation of living models. The result, Hawthorne thought, was often "a cold allegorical sisterhood who have generally no merit in chastity, being really without sex."

This was certainly true of the *Greek Slave,* modeled in 1843 when sympathy for the Greeks was still strong. Powers must have read that the Turks made slaves of nubile Greek girls, for the one he carved has her wrists chained. Her left hand happens to conceal her pudendum, but bared breasts could still shock viewers and distract from the intended moral. Powers was enough of a businessman, though, to exploit the notoriety his *Greek Slave* created by exhibiting it in major cities in the United States and Europe. It invariably aroused controversy, with puritans expressing outrage and sophisticates defending it as highly moral. The result was continued interest and, for Powers, large profit from admission fees.

Enough people liked the *Greek Slave* to warrant replicas: a few in museums, the same size as the original, and thousands of miniatures, on parlor mantels, discreetly encased in glass and often competing with Rogers pieces for atten-tion. Like them, its appeal was increased because it told a story. The work also spawned imitations, the best of them Erastus Palmer's *The White Captive,* today considered its superior.

People in substantial numbers, for the first time, were viewing the work of an American sculptor, and talking about it. As sculpture, its smooth perfection maintained the neoclassical standard set by Houdon and, though the subject was not from antiquity, it evoked thoughts of the country where classicism originated. Continuing preoccupation with classical mythology, in any event, year by year made American sculpture more anachronistic as Victorian culture advanced. Rogers pieces owed much of their immense popularity to the fact that they were not classical in either subject or execution but honestly related to American actuality.

In the Civil War years, another sculptor gave the art a fresh direction. Born in England, William Rimmer spent his boyhood in Massachusetts, became a cobbler in Brockton, and turned to a career as a physician before starting to carve in stone. His expert knowledge of anatomy gave such authority to his work that French critics insisted his *Falling Gladiator* must have been cast from a living human body. But Rimmer's important contribution was as lecturer on sculpture and anatomy, for he was able to persuade young hopefuls to abandon neoclassical conventions for something closer to realism.

Heard melodies

Musical taste was also slow to develop, but not as slow as sculpture. Numerous professional musicians who came to America from Europe after the Revolutionary War earned reasonable incomes by selling instruments and musical

Opposite top: Lola Has Come, *lithograph; New York; ca. 1852. The notorious Lola Montez. Opposite bottom:* Chromolithograph of Joseph Jefferson in Rip Van Winkle; *1872. Jefferson's most famous acting role.*

scores, and by giving instruction. However, they had few opportunities to perform until—largely as a result of their own efforts—permanent orchestras were established: the Handel and Haydn Society in Boston in 1815, the Musical Fund Society in Philadelphia in 1820, the Philharmonic Society in New York in 1843. All three construed their mission to be the publishing and performing of "correct" compositions, meaning those of such European giants as Mozart, Handel, and Beethoven.

The most active promoter of music for the people was native-born Lowell Mason. He organized conventions of music teachers, conducted frequently, and composed some twelve hundred hymns, including "Nearer, My God, to Thee" and "From Greenland's Icy Mountains." The hymns won widespread recognition, being sung in most Protestant churches. But the musical taste Mason worked hard to create was quite conventional, limited to music already established as "classical."

Under the circumstances, there was little chance for native composers to get a hearing for their work, even if it imitated that of the great Europeans, as it usually did. Concert programs throughout the nineteenth century remained static, with new compositions of any sort rarely attempted. One man who tried to change the pattern was William Henry Fry. He wrote the first American opera, *Leonora,* which had its premiere in Philadelphia in 1846 and had sixteen performances, an extraordinary number for the period. As music critic for the New York *Tribune,* Fry was a gadfly, criticizing the musical "establishment" for its indifference to native compositions and the public for preferring imported stars to local talent. From 1852 to 1853, he gave a series of ten lectures, in one of which he said that "There is no taste for, or appreciation of, true Art in this country. As a nation we have totally neglected Art. We pay enormous prices to hear a single voice, or a single instrument [but] will pay nothing to hear a sublime work of Art performed, because we do not know enough to appreciate it, and consequently such a performance bores us terribly." It was high time that "we had a Declaration of Independence in Art, and laid the foundations for an American School of Painting, Sculpture, and Music." Until Americans discarded "their foreign liveries" and learned to support American artists, "Art will not become indigenous to this country, but will only exist as a feeble exotic."

If Fry had one "single voice" in mind, it was no doubt that of Jenny Lind, the "Swedish Nightingale," who had just completed the hundred and fifty engagements that P. T. Barnum had scheduled for her at a thousand dollars a concert. Such was her fame that for her debut at Castle Garden in New York, choice seats sold for as high as $250. She gave her fee to New York charities, a gesture that further endeared her to Americans, but what made her tour a spectacular success was the remarkable range and quality of her voice. She was one of the most gifted coloratura sopranos in history, and taste for such singing demonstrably existed in America. The "single instrument" that Fry spoke of may have been the violin of Ole Bull, a Norwegian who entranced audiences for many years in all parts of the country. He played mostly his own compositions and Norwegian folk songs. One evidence of his appeal to Americans is a statue of Bull, playing his violin, in a Minneapolis park. Fry was right, no question about it, but people paid for what they liked, and taste just then was for the finest individual talent in Europe.

One young pianist turned the tables by dazzling European audiences. Louis Moreau Gottschalk, son of a wealthy New Orleans couple, was a child prodigy who was sent to Paris at thirteen for better training than was available anywhere in America. His ability to play from memory any piece he heard only once was uncanny, and he won high praise from Chopin and Berlioz. Europe loved him, and so did Americans when he finally returned in 1853, just after Jenny Lind left. But he discovered that what Americans liked best in piano music were flashy works of slight merit. Asked why he composed the two best-known of his works, "The Last Hope" and "The Dying Poet," he answered, "It is only mediocrity that pays, and, as I must live, I must be willing to please others, if not myself." Eminently sensible; but what an indictment of the contemporary level of musical taste in America!

Gottschalk's best compositions were based on the folk songs of Louisiana, both black and white, that he had heard as a boy. But they lacked the appeal of songs by Stephen Foster, who learned what he knew of Afro-American music from E. P. Christy's minstrel troupe, for which he wrote some of his best-loved works. Their verbal simplicity led listeners to suppose that they were authentic folk songs; the fact that they were not made little difference to white Americans, who liked minstrel shows almost as much as warmed-over English plays and the freaks in Barnum's Museum. Tens of thousands of mid-century Americans heard Jenny Lind. More than 20 million viewed Gen. Tom Thumb and the original Siamese twins, Chang and Eng.

A major social event in 1863 was the wedding, in New York's fashionable Grace Episcopal Church, of Tom Thumb and another Barnum midget, Lavinia Warren. On their wedding trip, they were honored guests at a White House dinner given by President Lincoln. The public loved it, just as it loved all celebrities, especially visiting foreign royalty. In democratic theory, everybody was equal, but a crown prince or grand duke was something special.

Tied to the tracks

Somewhat the same kind of thinking affected the theater of the period. No matter what play was performed, or how poor the supporting cast, a famous name as lead assured enthusiastic applause. If the possessor of the famous name was foreign, and somewhat notorious, full houses were assured. Lola Montez, known as former mistress of Bavaria's King Ludwig, was a mediocre actress, but her Spider Dance, in which she plucked away parts of her costume as if they were spiders, was a finale seldom matched on stages from the East Coast to California mining camps. Other actors had to depend on their own, more conventional talent. There were plenty of would-be stars who were willing to endure one-night stands and the uncertain support of local amateurs. Taste for theatricals was strong everywhere, and it was not very sophisticated.

Until well after the Civil War, dramatic fare in the United States was limited. Very few works by native playwrights were performed. For lack of effective copyright protection, any of the best foreign plays could be staged without payment of royalties to their authors. Potential native talent was discouraged. In an 1845 review of one play written by an American, Edgar Allan Poe wrote that "compared with most American dramas it is a *very* good one

[but] estimated by the natural principles of dramatic art, it is altogether unworthy of notice."

Native dramas at the time had two main themes, glorification of nationalism and Romantic escape to the far away or the long ago. Both were also popular in fiction, poetry, and painting. Combining the two was the surest way to write a hit, but hits by native playwrights were scarce. Among the best were Elizabeth Smith's *Old New York, or Democracy in 1689; Witchcraft, or the Martyrs of Salem,* by Cornelius Mathews; and *The Lion of the West,* by James Kirke Paulding, a comedy whose character Nimrod Wildfire resembles Davy Crockett.

As schooling improved gradually and reached more of the population, taste became more sophisticated; and as the railroad network grew, traveling groups of actors performed in more and more parts of the country. Dramatic fare also changed, but it did not improve much. Flag-waving plots yielded to melodrama, and Romantic escape was only updated—to a dramatized version of *Rip Van Winkle,* a favorite for the rest of the century. *Uncle Tom's Cabin* was also recast as a play, with phenomenal success. Its rebuke to slaveholding was almost lost to its heavy sentimentality, and little Eva's ascent toward heaven on nearly invisible wires was a finale that no viewer ever forgot. But Victorian taste reserved its highest approval for the "crook" melodrama. It seldom strayed far from the tried-and-true formula well illustrated by *Under the Gaslight,* written by Augustin Daly and first performed in 1867. This masterpiece involves a kidnapped heiress, a girl whose identity is mistaken, and a one-armed newsboy who in trying to save the heroine places himself in jeopardy and is tied to the railroad tracks. Just as an ex-

press train is rounding the bend, she chops her way out of a locked room with an ax and rescues him. One wonders how Poe would have reviewed such stage heroics.

The Victorian era

Not too long ago, it was fashionable to deplore everything Victorian, from what Lewis Mumford called the visible smut of rampant early industrialism to the mass-produced tawdriness and the use of euphemisms—*limb* for *leg, white meat* for *breast, deceased* or *departed* for *dead,* among many others. According to this view, good taste should somehow have restrained the culture by providing direction and preventing the flagrant abuses of freedom. But that kind of taste, after enjoying high success for two centuries, was a vagrant in the third, disregarded and impotent. Romantic individualism and democratic equality were in the saddle, riding roughshod over every former standard and putting every new style and fashion, however extravagant, on equal footing. Popular sovereignty, having gained the ascendency in politics, had extended its baleful influence to every facet of the culture. The later stages of Victorian development comprised, in the memorable phrase of Mumford, the "Brown Decades," when almost nobody paid attention to the few concerned individuals who sought to restore order and rational progress.

More recently, reviving interest in Victorian artifacts has blunted the edge of that criticism. Whether this revival will persist or prove only a passing fad, it demonstrates the fact that discrediting an old taste cannot prevent its resurrection. But more to the point, taste as the faculty of discrimination can operate most freely when the alternatives are multiple; and multiple they were in Victorian America.

From Centennial
to World War

(1876–1914)

Preceding pages: *General view, Court of Honor, Columbian Exposition; Chicago, Ill.; 1893. The statue overlooking the lagoon is* The Republic, *by Daniel Chester French.* Above: *Mabel Lucy Peirce, age 5; Massachusetts; ca. 1882.* Above right: *Anna Held; 1900. At the time, she was one of America's most admired women.* Above far right: *Picture of graduate on graduation day, Bradford Academy; Bradford, Mass.; 1897.*

T he final quarter of the nineteenth century opened with a celebration that surpassed, in exuberance and self-congratulation, any earlier event in the nation's history. Editors and clergymen and politicans, scholars and poets and orators belabored the centennial theme in millions of words. From May to November, in Philadelphia's Fairmount Park, the evidence of progress since 1776 was proudly displayed at the Centennial Exhibition, the largest world's

fair ever mounted up to that time.

Setting the style

William Dean Howells, the most perceptive reporter of the exhibition, was perplexed by its lack of any unifying theme. Of course, had the organizers chosen, for instance, to build all the buildings in a single style, the great show would hardly have been representative of the culture or a true reflection of contemporary taste. The vast majority of visitors to the exhibition accepted the diversity, for as Victorians they were used to it.

The show featured 249 separate structures, no two of which were identical. Of the five major buildings, the two largest, Main and Machinery halls, were somewhat similar. Both were immense, and both had no counterpart anywhere in the world. If they suggested any familiar style at all, it was the commercial, with cast-iron front (without the usual imitation of ancient designs) and internal iron column supports. These buildings bore very little decoration of any sort. They did have low towers, which were purely decorative except for one near the center of Main Hall that could be ascended for a bird's-eye view of the grounds. Otherwise, they were models of functional simplicity at a time when unadorned functionalism had not yet entered the thinking of even the most progressive architects. They were liked well enough, however, to rouse hopes that they would be left standing when the exhibition closed. But they were disassembled, over the strong protests of many people.

Had they been preserved, they might have served as models for other large buildings, particularly factories. They were relatively inexpensive to build, and with their great expanses of glass in the upper walls and on the roof, they were light and airy, as most factories were not. But their structural principle, that of interchangeable modular units, was probably too revolutionary for 1876.

A third major building, Agricultural Hall, although quite adequate for its purpose of displaying farm products and implements, made less impression on the viewing public, and there was no storm of protest when it was demolished. The only major structures left standing when the exhibition was dismounted were the art gallery—Memorial Hall—and Horticultural Hall; both had significant influence on future architectural taste.

It is regrettable that Horticultural Hall, after years of inadequate maintenance, was damaged just enough by a hurricane to justify its demolition in 1954. Even though it was the smallest of the major structures, it was the largest conservatory in the world at the time it was built. Its designer, Herman Schwarzmann, a German immigrant who had first been named engineer of the grounds and then the chief architect of the buildings, had incorporated into the hall details of various large greenhouses he had studied in Europe. It was his inspired adaptation of Near Eastern features, though, especially the horseshoe arches at the entrances made of black-, red-, and cream-colored brick, that most delighted visitors and won general praise from critics. These and other Moorish or Saracen forms included in the building prompted writers to dub the style "Moresque." The interior of the building, with its fountains and pools set amid lush foliage, was equally enchanting to viewers. As a greenhouse, Horticultural Hall was a veritable pleasure dome instead of merely a place where exotic trees and plants were arranged in neat rows. Its influence on later greenhouses in city parks was great, both in design and in ambiance, but few others ever matched it for elegance.

The art gallery, also designed by Schwarzmann, had an even broader impact on taste. In 1876, museums were rare in the United States—there were only five, and two of them were unfinished. All were small. Not surprisingly, Memorial Hall's great popularity among the exhibition crowds provided a strong impetus to the construction of new art galleries in major cities. These tended, more-over, to be in the same style and of the same immense scale as Memorial Hall.

Schwarzmann had discovered the Beaux-Arts style used for Memorial Hall in Paris while touring Europe for ideas to borrow for the exhibition. Essentially neoclassical, with columns and arches and domes, this style is marked by elaborate decoration, inside and out, exceeding that of most neoclassical styles based on Renaissance adaptation. Memorial so impressed visitors that the style won instant approval and was borrowed not only for art galleries in Chicago, Milwaukee, Brooklyn, and Manhattan but also for large city libraries—New York Public, Library of Congress, Free Library of Philadelphia, and others. The public found such symmetry and classical organization a welcome relief from the Victorian irregularity of facade and, by the 1890s, had made the style the unchallenged standard for luxury hotels, fashionable clubhouses, railroad terminals, municipal buildings, and mansions of the very rich.

Of the lesser buildings at Fairmount Park, only two had a measurable effect on taste. The most exotic was Japan's, prefabricated in Japan and assembled with strange tools and methods that amused American observers but drew their admiration when the pavilion was finished. It did much to correct the widespread misconception that Japan was at best half-civilized. The fine bronzes, ceramics, screens, and lacquerware that Japan displayed in Main Hall further astonished visitors. The result was a taste for Japanese art that has endured to this day, less evident in architecture than in room decoration—screens, panels, and objets d'art.

Queen Anne revived

More influential on American

building style than the Japanese, though, was St. George's House, erected by the English government. With exposed exterior beams in the half-timbered tradition and glowing inside and out with rich colors, it offered a marked contrast to the buildings that several states erected nearby, most of them variants of the Victorian Gothic built of wood and sporting the exaggerated scrollwork ornamentation known as gingerbread. St. George's House was a fine example of what in England was called the Shavian Manorial style, after Richard Norman Shaw, whose designs for country houses stood high in favor among prosperous Englishmen. Shaw was a prominent leader of the Aesthetic Movement, which considered the dwellings built for the gentry during the reign of Queen Anne (1702–14) the most pleasing in design.

The exhibition was mounted during a financial depression that had begun in 1873. By the time the economy recovered, late in 1877, many families that had put off building new homes turned away from whatever Victorian style they might have liked earlier in the 1870s and chose the Queen Anne (or Shavian Manorial). It could be built at any price, but the best examples, closest to the Shavian Manorial idea, were necessarily quite expensive. All had a few features in common: off-centered front doors, windows of different sizes and often oddly placed, wide porches, external chimneys, and somewhere a rounded bay rising to a peaked turret.

Within a decade, the Queen Anne style had produced an offshoot, the Shingle style, easily recognized by the shingles, painted or left to weather, that completely cover the exterior. Limited to rather sizable houses, many examples of the style survive, less for

year-round living than as vacation homes at fashionable resorts up and down the Atlantic coast, especially in the Northeast. The Queen Anne was for city dwellings; the Shingle style looked most at home beside the sea. But it could also be used for other structures, like the churches and public buildings designed by the Maine architect John Calvin Stevens.

Just as rural builders had done with the Georgian style in the eighteenth century, homeowners with limited resources modified the Queen Anne to suit their pocketbooks. Thousands of small houses of the sort earlier advertised by Ithiel Town and A. J. Davis were altered to make them resemble the Queen Anne style. Taste could be satisfied with just a few Queen Anne elements, such as a small tower, a porch at one side, or an enlarged window.

Houses for Hansels and Gretels

Before the Civil War, Town and Davis had pretty much monopolized the business of producing small houses. By the 1870s, numerous firms were competing for

the trade, advertising widely in magazines and newspapers. Like Town and Davis, moreover, they were ready to provide whatever style a potential customer might want. One firm in New Jersey offered a patented construction method based on room-size prefabricated modules that could be joined together and even, if desired, separated and rejoined later in some other pattern. Mass production was not to be denied.

Well into the 1880s and 1890s, styles familiar before the Centennial held their popularity alongside the newer Queen Anne. Taste for the carpenter Gothic had never died. Now, carried to extremes, it produced the so-called Gingerbread style, which must have seemed to the Hansels and Gretels of the time, whatever their economic status, the ultimate in good taste. Housebuilding firms could supply the desired scrollwork appendages, but most of the gingerbread woodwork was the work of individual carpenters who began a folk art of porch decoration.

A community that reached its peak during the gingerbread craze

Opposite: *Shingle-style Baptist Church, designed by John Calvin Stevens; South Waterboro, Maine; 1890, destroyed by fire in 1911.*
Left: *Crocker mansions; San Francisco. At left is William Crocker's Queen Anne mansion; 1887. At right is Charles Crocker's neoclassical mansion; 1876.*
Below: *Shingle-style resort home; Kennebunkport, Maine; ca. 1900.*

Above: *Hotel del Coronado, designed by James and Merritt Reid; San Diego, Calif.; opened 1888, completed 1890.*
Above right: *Wainright Building, designed by Louis Sullivan and Dankmar Adler; St. Louis, Mo.; 1891. A milestone in modern architecture.*
Right: *Ponce de Leon Hotel, designed by John Carrère and Thomas Hastings; St. Augustine, Fla.; 1889. Built for railroad magnate Henry Flager.*
Below right: *Romanesque Revival railway station of Boston & Albany Railroad; designed by H.H. Richardson; Framingham, Mass.; 1883.*

and then stabilized is Sea Cliff, a village on the north shore of Long Island that became a favorite summer resort in the 1880s. Visitors can wallow in nostalgia as they stroll past its elegant Victorian structures, including such well-preserved examples as the cream-colored Woodshed, the nearby privy converted into a picturesque toolhouse, a conspicuous red house with stained-glass windows, and other relics in yellow and pink and blue, all delightfully reminiscent of the period taste for bold colors and uninhibited decoration. But gingerbread decoration could be found almost everywhere in the country. In San Francisco, there are rows of houses boasting scroll-saw ornamentation that differ in detail from door to door.

At the same time, there was a trend in the opposite direction, toward minimal decoration. Probably in reaction to the current excesses, the element of the population concerned about its dignity preferred soundly built homes in the Victorian tradition but without what they considered faddish ornament. Whether plain or ornamented, these houses usually have a gable end facing the street.

Fancy hotels

Returning prosperity after the centennial revived interest in large resort hotels. Saratoga Springs regained its former popularity as a spa and center of horse racing. Its famous old hostelries, including the Congress and the United States, were enlarged, and their interiors were redecorated in bright new colors and attractive fabrics. New resorts much more remote from the population centers were also attracting vacationists—and attention. One on the Pacific coast was the Hotel del Coronado, on a peninsula across the bay from San Diego. Opened in 1888, it had 390 rooms, each with a fireplace

and a wall safe for personal valuables. The dining room could seat a thousand people. Soon dubbed "the Del" by patrons with a taste for luxury amid lavish surroundings, it had all the latest conveniences: running water, gas heating, electric lighting, telephone and telegraph service. Built of wood like most other resort hotels of the time, it was like no other in style; it has, however, been called "ornate Victorian," a vague catch-all term for any unique design in the spirit of total originality.

The next year produced the Ponce de Leon in St. Augustine, built by the railroad magnate Henry Flagler, who did much to promote and develop Florida. To design it, he engaged two young architects, John Carrère and Thomas Hastings, sent them abroad for two years to collect data, and gave them considerable freedom when they returned. The result of their collaboration was breathtaking. The hotel and its grounds take up an entire city block—six acres—and the hotel is built of coquina mixed with cement, forming walls of great strength. The general style is early Spanish Renaissance, although the main gateway and a few other details are Italian. No longer a hotel, its landscaped grounds are still enclosed by a stout fence of spiked iron balls instead of links. Like the del Coronado on the opposite shore of the continent, it was the only one of its kind. Victorian taste was broad and accepted such singularity of design if it was interesting enough, especially if it was magnificent, as these two were.

"A vicious love of fashion"

The eclecticism of the High Victorian Age knew no bounds and was certainly not without its critics. During 1876, the Big Three of the magazine world carried articles decrying both the Victorian styles in

fashion and the general disregard of what a home ought to be. H. Holley Hudson, writing in *Harper's Monthly Magazine*, insisted that continued imitation of foreign models was utter folly. "Until, however, we come to possess a vernacular style, we must content ourselves with copying." In the *Atlantic*, Wilson Flagg was even more caustic. Counterfeit villas and ornate houses, he wrote, revealed "a vicious love of fashion and display" that architects did nothing to discourage. John Burroughs, in a *Scribner's* essay titled "House Building," also faulted the supine behavior of the nation's architects. "A house is for shelter, comfort, health, hospitality—to eat and sleep in, to be born and die in." Added decoration was a bid for attention and had nothing to do with living. He particularly disliked the mansard roof. It might be acceptable in cities, he thought, but it gave a rural house a dapper, unnatural appearance. He blamed all the cheap gingerbread ornamentation on the invention of the scroll saw. Only the very poor lived in truly picturesque dwellings. Such simplicity inevitably ended with greater income and yielded to pride and ostentation.

Burroughs was a disciple of Emerson, who had offered his own comment in 1870 on the taste for showy houses: "A man builds a fine house; and now he has a master, and a task for life; he is to furnish, watch, show it, and keep it in repair the rest of his days." The house in Concord that Emerson bought in 1835, where he lived out his days, was ample but simple, a vernacular adaptation of the Federal style. Two of his Concord neighbors, however, had been unable to resist the influence of shifting taste. Hawthorne, returning from Italy in 1860, added a tower in the then-current trend toward the Italianate, and Bronson Alcott had earlier dressed up his simple vernacular house with a Greek Revival portico and pediment. It took Thoreau's kind of radicalism to demonstrate how life could be fully satisfying in a hut. But as a lifetime bachelor, Henry could indulge his nonconformist taste.

Mavericks and innovators

In an age of rapid technological progress, architects as a group were singularly uninterested in adopting new methods and materials that could have helped create an indigenous style. The cast-iron front, for instance, was a product of industry, not of architecture. And it was carpenters, not architects, who somewhat earlier in the century had introduced—first in Chicago—the "balloon" type of construction with wood. Instead of relying on heavy timber framing joined with wooden pegs for the main support, balloon construction called for wooden studs, usually two inches thick and four wide, fastened together with machine-made nails. The result was a frame as strong as that made with the heaviest posts and beams but one that was much lighter. Balloon construction greatly reduced both the physical labor and the cost involved in a building, but the more important result for prospective occupants was greater interior space. Architects, however, accepted the innovation reluctantly.

There were mavericks, however, in the ranks of professional architects, who were dissatisfied with merely adapting traditional styles and who dared to innovate. One was Henry Hobson Richardson who, early in his career, began a revival that had no counterpart in Europe—the Romanesque. His Trinity Church on Boston's Copley Square, completed in 1877, is the most famous Romanesque Revival building in America. Taste for it developed quickly, especially in New England, where numerous buildings with a wide variety of purposes—schools, libraries, railroad stations, commercial structures, and a few dwellings—followed the Richardsonian style. They are easy to recognize by the liberal use of massive rounded arches over entrances and windows, square towers with pyramided roofs, stone and brick exteriors. Richardson's major triumphs outside New England were the Marshall Field wholesale store in Chicago, completed in 1887, after Richardson's death, with seven stories of rough-cut gray stone, and the State Senate Building in Albany, with its striking mixture of pink-gray marble, golden Mexican onyx, yellow Siena marble, and polished red granite.

Although it caught on quickly, the Romanesque Revival was short-lived. Richardson himself did not stay with it long. In 1874, even before Trinity Church was completed, he joined forces with Stanford White in designing an elaborate neo-Gothic mansion in Newport. He shared White's fascination with the union of all the plastic arts—sculpture, painting, and architecture—to a degree that overshadowed his interest in Romanesque or any other particular style. What counted most for him was the total effect of a building.

Effect, indeed, was what a great many Americans seemed to want, whether in a sumptuous mansion or in a ready-made house with one or two features that could justify its claim to "picturesqueness." In Chicago, however, a group of serious young architects experimenting in the 1880s with new forms and methods were challenging the picturesque and stressing utility instead. The leader of these radicals was Louis Sullivan, remembered today for his maxim "form follows function." Decide first what purpose a building is to serve, Sullivan insisted, and develop the building's form around that purpose.

The idea was revolutionary, so contrary to every concept accepted by current taste that it was dismissed contemptuously and even openly derided by most architects before 1900. Writers of magazine articles had called for greater functionalism, as Emerson had before them, but writers were neither architects nor builders. The radicals —or progressives, as they preferred to be called—were, however, undeterred. Sullivan and his partner Dankmar Adler found enough clients in Chicago and St. Louis to keep them in business, and they went on to pioneer the "organic principle" in large business structures that today are virtual classics.

Progressive architecture as Sullivan and his friends in Chicago were developing it had only a limited endorsement in other parts of the country, and in the large eastern cities had virtually none at all. In contrast, the Gingerbread style of the same era had a strong appeal to popular taste, although it led nowhere and left no progeny. But gingerbread decoration was mostly applied to dwellings, which were closer to the lives of people than the structures the progressives were most concerned with. Taste has commonly been divided along this line—perhaps because a house is a man's own castle, as no other structure ever can be.

The prince of architects

By the time Richardson died—in 1886, when he was only forty-eight years old—a star of greater magnitude was already dazzling the inconstant public, and just behind him was a whole constellation of talent that was to dominate architectural taste for the next thirty years.

Far left: *Tribune Building, designed by Richard Morris Hunt; New York, N.Y.; 1875. From a picture in* Leslie's Illustrated Newspaper. Left: *Flatiron Building, designed by Daniel Burnham; New York, N.Y.; 1902. With 20 stories, the city's first modern skyscraper.* Below: *Singer Building, designed by Ernest Flagg; New York, N.Y.; 1906.*

The new brilliance was shed by Richard Hunt. After studying at L'Ecole des Beaux-Arts in Paris—the first American to enroll there—he returned to the United States before the Civil War and gained experience by designing in various styles. One of his first major buildings was the Lenox Library, in 1873, on the present site of the Frick Museum on Fifth Avenue in New York City. He next proceeded to build one of the city's first skyscrapers, the Tribune Building. When the great English biologist T. H. Huxley approached New York in the summer of 1876 on his only visit to the United States, he was told that the tallest buildings on the skyline were those of the Tribune and the Western Union Telegraph Company. "Ah," he said, "that is interesting: that is American. In the Old World the first things you see as you approach a great city are steeples. Here you see, first, centres of intel-

ligence." Whatever the pious may have thought of this comment, it reflects an American habit that has grown stronger ever since—of building business structures that dwarf even the tallest church spires.

If, as some experts insist, a skyscraper is any tall building with passenger elevators, the nation's first was the Equitable Life Assurance Building, completed in 1870. Elisha Otis had developed a safe elevator in 1852, but the public was suspicious, and most elevators were used only for hoisting freight. The Equitable, by installing passenger elevators, was a pacesetter, but with only six stories—130 feet—it did not rise much higher than most other New York buildings. The Western Union and Tribune buildings, both completed five years later, were considerably taller, with ten full stories, and had to have elevators. Both had towers with clocks and

the neo-Gothic decoration that current taste demanded. But for the Tribune Tower, Hunt rejected most of the decorative motifs then familiar and substituted original forms of his own devising, among others very flat arches over the windows on the ground and fourth floors and, above the windows projecting from the mansard roof, pediments resembling nothing in antiquity.

By 1876, however, Hunt had, like his contemporary Richardson, turned to the accurate reproduction of specific models. When Commodore Vanderbilt died in 1877, the family asked Hunt to design a suitable mausoleum. He recalled a Romanesque chapel he had seen at Arles in southern France and adapted it so skillfully that the younger Vanderbilts made him virtually their private architect. For one of the grandsons, William K. Vanderbilt, he designed a chateau in the flamboyant French

Top: *Biltmore, designed in the French chateau style by Richard Morris Hunt; near Asheville, N.C.; 1895.* Above: *Great hall of the Breakers, designed in Italian palazzo style by Hunt; Newport, R.I.; 1895. The largest of the Newport "cottages" built by millionaires.*

style of the Loire valley. At its completion in 1879, it won the instant admiration of New Yorkers, and for years afterward it was imitated by the socially ambitious and the newly rich who had previously been satisfied with Italianate row houses or brownstone boxes. One chateau after another rose along Fifth Avenue as it was built up steadily toward the north.

Few of the French chateaux built in New York in the 1880s and 1890s survive. Most have been victims of the irresistible force of metropolitan growth. In the wisdom of hindsight, it is clear that a busy city street was never a proper place for a chateau, which ought to have ample grounds and broad vistas. For a glimpse of Hunt's talent, and of a chateau in its most appropriate setting, one would be well advised to journey to Asheville, North Carolina, ask the way to Biltmore, now open to the public, and feast on its glories.

A most palatial estate

George Washington Vanderbilt, another grandson of the Commodore, must be considered one of the poorest of all that famous tribe. He was willed a mere pittance, 10 million dollars, whereas his brothers, Cornelius II and William, received 67 million and 65 million respectively. But money went far in those days before the federal income tax, and George, a philanthropist at heart and interested in forestry, managed to create a most palatial estate and still have several million dollars left.

Only the very best talent would do. To manage the adjacent forest of 130,000-acres, he hired Gifford Pinchot, later governor of Pennsylvania, and gave him a budget larger than Congress then allotted to the Department of Agriculture. To lay out the formal grounds immediately surrounding the mansion, he called on Frederick Law

Olmsted. Hunt did not disappoint him in designing the house itself. First he toured the chateau region of France, settling on Blois for his model, and then he drew up the plans with great care. Construction took five years, from 1890 to 1895.

It is hard to exaggerate the splendidness of Biltmore. The banqueting hall is seventy-five feet high and its walls are hung with Gobelin tapestries. The library, with a ceiling painted by the Venetian artist Tiepolo in the eighteenth century, shelves twenty thousand volumes, all richly bound. George Vanderbilt loved to read. He also loved company: there are forty master bedrooms. The roof was the largest in the nation up to that time, for any building private or public. What the crusty old Commodore would have thought of Biltmore, or of the other magnificent piles erected by his heirs, we are not privileged to know. But his son had more than doubled his fortune, in astute railroad management, and the third generation saw no better way to use it than to build palaces.

Before he died in 1895, Hunt gained all the laurels any architect could hope for. He could name his own fees and he never had to worry about cost overruns. The Breakers at Newport, Rhode Island, which he built for Cornelius Vanderbilt, is probably the nation's most conspicuous evocation of Italian Renaissance splendor. Other wealthy families considered themselves lucky if they could lure him away, however briefly, from the Vanderbilts to design for them town houses or Newport "cottages," with rooms in various styles—Jacobean, Moorish, Byzantine, Italian Renaissance—but always lavish and elegant. Workmen loved him for his genial good nature and for giving them assignments that called for exquisite

craftsmanship. The public loved him, too, for providing palaces they could gaze upon with awe and dream of owning. Yale, Princeton, and Harvard all gave Hunt honorary degrees, and foreign academies elected him to membership. The Royal Academy of British Architects awarded him its gold medal, the first it ever gave to an American.

And just what was Hunt's influence on American taste? In a nutshell, his major contribution was to delay the acceptance of modern architecture in America. To those who deplore the modern with its repudiation of tradition and decoration, this makes him rather a hero.

White city beside Lake Michigan

The Centennial Exhibition in Philadelphia had mirrored the multiplicity of styles set forth by the diverse taste of 1876. Seventeen years later, the Columbian Exposition in Chicago, commemorating the four-hundredth anniversary of the discovery of America, just as faithfully signaled the restoration of classicism to its old place at the summit of taste. It was not any earlier version of neoclassicism, however, but rather the new Beaux-Arts interpretation of classical design that gave the fair of 1893 its particular character.

Admirers of the Beaux-Arts style welcomed its revival of classical forms as an American Renaissance. Hunt had prepared the way with his adaptations of French styles to suit the desires of millionaires. But Hunt was not narrowly committed to any one style at that time; his was an eclectic enthusiasm, and the Beaux-Arts was just another style that he could accept and devote his great energy to promoting. When he finally accepted it, about 1890, he was a major force in bringing the style to the forefront of general taste.

The most important figures in the American Renaissance were, however, the members of a New York firm of architects, McKim, Mead, and White. William Rutherford Mead was the businessman, giving the firm its sound financial base but not interfering with his gifted partners, both of whom had trained in the office of Henry Hobson Richardson. Charles Follen McKim had dabbled briefly in the Shavian Manorial and other late Victorian styles but soon turned to classical forms. Stanford White had also worked in other styles, but his real genius was for sumptuous interiors, for which he loved everything old—woodwork, furniture, period motifs. Hearty and genial, he could talk a client into paying the extra thousands of dollars that meant the difference between an adequate building and one of rare distinction. One of the firm's early efforts was the Newport Casino, a classic of the Shingle style, but it soon turned to the classical and its Renaissance derivatives, with the Boston Public Library and New York's Madison Square Garden. Leading artists and sculptors were asked to share in the projects —two frequently called on and firmly established in general taste were Augustus Saint-Gaudens and John La Farge.

When the city of Chicago first decided to mount the exposition, the most eminent architects in the country were summoned as consultants. When they assembled, all deferred politely to Hunt, who wanted to center the exposition around what he called a Court of Honor lined with Beaux-Arts buildings. In the months following, the huge buildings went up, one varying only slightly from the next and each with the same columns and arches and domes no matter what it was intended to be used for. So strong was the desire for consistency that even the Agri-cultural Building, designed by Mc-Kim and White, displayed its farm machinery, animals, and produce beneath a Roman dome and behind a portico with four Corinthian columns supporting a huge pediment. No visitor could have guessed the contents of any of the Court of Honor buildings by looking at its facade. The gleaming white classical uniformity had only one counterpart in the nation, the group of federal buildings in Washington that conformed to Jefferson's dream; but those were austere, with almost none of the extensive ornamentation that the Beaux-Arts style demanded.

Gondolas and golden doors

Unlike the federal buildings, the Greco-Roman temples in Chicago that awed millions of visitors in 1893 were not intended to be permanent; they were made of staff, a mixture of cement, fibers, and plaster that could not have survived a severe Chicago winter. One critic at the time dismissed the great show as so much "whipped cream baroque"; it was hardly more durable than whipped cream. Lewis Mumford in *Sticks and Stones* (1924) used a different kind of imagery: the joe-pye weed and the swamp maple, he suggested, had been rooted out and replaced by elegant but sickly shrubs that could not thrive in American soil. But as long as the Court of Honor held together—less than a year— its sheer magnitude did much to confirm the taste for neoclassicism as superior to every other style.

Outside the Court of Honor, other styles were permitted. One quite unlike the neoclassical enjoyed remarkable longevity—Louis Sullivan's Transportation Building, with its great golden doors and unclassical cupola. There was also a Fisheries Building, Roman-esque in style and decorated with crustacean motifs that the ancients had somehow overlooked. Both buildings had to be at some distance from the Court of Honor in order not to strike a jarring note. Sullivan's building had its admirers at the time, but not for many more years did it gain the general respect of critics and architects that it deserved, as a monument of nonclassical individualism.

One of the great attractions of the exposition was the lagoon that stretched the length of the Court of Honor. To provide an Italian atmosphere, Venetian gondolas and gondoliers had been imported. Gliding in a real gondola and listening to Italian love songs while surrounded by architecture suggestive of Venice must have been the climax of any visit to the fair. If the ride were at night, as Winslow Homer showed it in one of his paintings, it would have had to be doubly unforgettable.

Rising out of the lagoon near the open end of the Court of Honor and facing Hunt's Administration Building was *The Republic,* an immense gilded statue by Daniel Chester French, who had been rising in fame since 1875 when he won the competition for the minuteman statue at Concord's North Bridge. Sixty-five feet tall, on a solid square base, *The Republic* represented the nation as a woman in Roman garb, crowned with laurel and holding in each hand symbols of Roman imperialism. It was the largest of the many pieces of sculpture at the show, most of which were by established sculptors. None of them were at all shocking except, perhaps, the nude *Diana,* which had been borrowed from its perch atop Madison Square Garden. *Diana* was the work of Saint-Gaudens, who, in a moment of euphoria at Chicago, exclaimed to a friend, "Look here, old fellow, do you realize that this is the greatest meeting of artists since the fifteenth century?"

"Fashionable Calling Toilettes"; from The Delineator; *1899.*

Opposite: *Chromolithograph*
Christmas card and valentine; late
19th century. Above: A Storm in
the Rocky Mountains—Mt. Rosalie, *by*
Albert Bierstadt; 1866. Left:
Memorial Hall, Centennial Exhibition;
Philadelphia, Pa.; 1876.

139

Distractions in the windy city

Replicas of the *Niña, Pinta,* and *Santa Maria* riding at anchor just off shore from the exposition were its closest tie to Columbus and the founding of America. Of greater interest to the throngs that flocked to the show was a midway called "Streets of Cairo," now a quiet lawn on the University of Chicago campus. There people in 1893 could enjoy, or pretend to, rides on donkeys and camels or rise two hundred feet in the air on a huge Ferris wheel. None of the animals that performed at the Hagenback wild animal show displayed the verve of a dark-complexioned girl billed as "Little Egypt." Adding to the atmosphere were alleged Laplanders, African tribesmen, and South Sea islanders, all moving about in supposedly authentic native habitats. Numerous beer gardens and restaurants were enlivened by Viennese waltzes. These had more appeal to the fair-goers' taste than did the music of Wagner played by bands scattered about the exposition grounds and supervised by the nation's premier conductor, aging Theodore Thomas.

Of all the main buildings, the most popular displayed the latest applications of electric power—lamps, stoves, fans, and primitive dishwashers. Electric lighting was a curiosity to most rural visitors, who at home knew only kerosene lamps. Equally unfamiliar was the telephone. Both were in common use in Chicago, as in other major cities, but gas was still used for lighting in many other urban areas. Daniel Peirce, who lived in the village of Hyde Park close to the exposition grounds, had displayed a certain urban smugness in an 1880 letter he wrote to his little sister back home in rural Maine: "Last evening Lizzie and I went up to the city to attend the Vermont Dinner. It took place at the Grand Pacific Hotel and was a

brilliant affair. The hall was lighted with the *Electric* light. Over 350 sat down to the tables with a colored waiter for every two persons.... It is seven miles to the city but it does not seem very far away when we want to talk with many of those we do business with for we have a Telephone by which we talk back and forth as easily as if we were in the same room."

Unless they had relatives in Chicago or its near suburbs, visitors to the fair were unlikely to get a glimpse of how the residents of the area lived day to day. If they strolled about Hyde Park, they might have seen the Daniel Peirce residence and many others like it, all with the mansard roof in the current style, and if they ventured as far as the city itself, they could have seen the great stone water tower or the elaborate castle that Potter Palmer called home, both in the same battlemented medieval style. They would have had to wait until 1896, however, to see the mansion of Francis J. Dewes, a beer baron inspired by the exposition to build in the best style of Rhenish Prussia, where he was born. Few houses anywhere in America could match it for ornate German baroque splendor. As a style, it was rather limited—it may best be called a substyle.

Some visitors to the city may have been awed by Sullivan's most elaborate building, the newly completed Chicago Stock Exchange. It had four hundred skylights framed in cast iron and a ceiling with so intricate a design that it required fifty-five different colors of paint. Its interior was as sumptuous as any of those by Hunt, or McKim and White, but it differed in that it borrowed nothing from classical times or the Renaissance.

The exposition, in any event, gave the firm of McKim, Mead, and White so towering a reputation that they were kept busy

working in classical modes. Their designs for New York's University Club (1896) and the Morgan Library (1906) were in the Italian Renaissance style; Rosecliff (1902), one of the most attractive of the Newport "cottages," closely followed the Trianon at Versailles. The Pennsylvania Station (1906–10), now unfortunately demolished, was modeled on the Baths of Caracalla in Rome.

Talbot Hamlin, an art critic writing in the 1940s and an admirer of revived classicism, said of the Columbian Exposition, "In the choice of the classical style the consulting architects only symbolized popular taste." In 1951, the historian Henry Steele Commager wrote that the exposition "condemned American architecture to the imitative and the derivative for another generation." Both men were right, despite their antithetical attitudes. And both these attitudes persist to this day. Most modern critics agree with Commager, yet who among us, aware of the progression of styles in American history, and of the frequency of revivals, would be brash enough to dismiss the possibility of a restored Classical America?

The Eastlake boom

Was the choice of the classical style for the exposition symbolic of popular taste, as Talbot Hamlin thought, or were the consulting architects tastemakers? From the evidence, the latter seems more probable, in this particular case. But the architects were strongly influenced by the nation's wealthiest families, who should share the credit—or the blame. One thing seems certain: the chief casualty was vernacular style, not only in architecture but in furniture as well. As Lewis Mumford pointed out by way of example, the Windsor chair, so long accepted for practical use if never quite ap-

Water Figure, by Jackson Pollock; 1945.

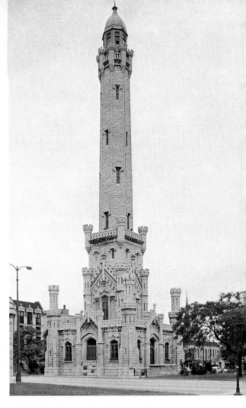

proved by cultivated taste, lost favor and by 1900 had retreated to the attic to gather dust.

During the latter part of the nineteenth century, homes became more and more cluttered with heavy furniture. The revived taste for classicism applied to large public buildings and grandiose houses but offered nothing for less affluent householders. Certainly furnishings appropriate for mansions like those of the Vanderbilts would have been absurd in most Queen Anne or post-Victorian dwellings, or even in large Shingle-style vacation homes beside the sea.

An English writer, Charles Eastlake, tried to be helpful in 1868 with his *Hints on Household Taste.* In it, he not only specified the proper furnishings for Victorian houses but pointed out what to avoid. His stated purpose was to modify "extraordinary ebullitions of uneducated taste generally." With the first American edition in 1872, the book had an immediate impact on the nation's taste.

Eastlake shared the ideas of John Ruskin, firmest advocate of a return to honest craftsmanship, and the English poet William Morris, founder of the Arts and Crafts

Movement and producer of wholly handcrafted furniture, stained glass, and textiles. *Hints on Household Taste* offered specific advice on the designing, constructing, and decorating of a wide variety of household articles—furniture, wallpaper, carpeting, draperies, clothing, metalware, jewelry—all of which, he believed, should be as close as possible to the art of the Middle Ages. The keys to beauty, he thought, were simplicity and solidity. His sketches of desirable furniture illustrate his dislike of curvilinear forms and machine-carved ornaments applied to pieces of furniture in the last stage of manufacture.

By 1876, furniture in the Eastlake style was being made on a large scale, not by hand but by machinery. American ingenuity had devised special machines to produce its component parts and to attach ornaments at the final stages, which Eastlake deprecated. Pieces displayed at the Centennial Exhibition further popularized the style. At first the factory methods did not cheapen the product, for in small factories—in such cities as Williamsport, Pennsylvania; Jamestown, New York; and Mus-

catine, Iowa—the American Eastlake was made by well-trained, conscientious workmen. Quality continued to be high in a few factories, but increasingly it fell off as rival firms departed even further from the basic principles of design. One device for lowering production cost was to finish pieces with varnish instead of by hand. By 1890, the poorest examples were alienating taste for the style, and its boom collapsed.

Bedroom furniture, for reasons not known, remained closest to the Eastlake ideal. Parlor furniture, in contrast, acquired new decoration, much of it inspired by the Japanese art shown at the exhibition: inlaid marquetry or tiles showing butterflies, cranes, cherry blossoms, fans, chrysanthemums all became popular. Despite Eastlake's strictures against curves, many of the American pieces had circles and arches, some very small, others forming the basic shape of the piece. More were rectilinear, however, with blocks piled upon each other and squares protruding from corners. As a style, Eastlake owed nothing to any past culture and, for that reason, could be almost infinitely varied in the hands of

Opposite left: *Potter Palmer's "medieval castle"; Chicago, Ill.; ca. 1885.* Opposite right: *Rough-hewn limestone water tower; Chicago, Ill.; 1869. A prominent Chicago landmark, 186 feet high.* Far left: *Main stairway, baroque mansion; Chicago, Ill.; 1896. Built for beer baron Francis Dewes.* Left: *Daniel Peirce House; Chicago, Ill.; 1878. Mansard roof, widely popular for large urban residences.*

American furnituremakers. Some of it departed so far from Eastlake's own designs that it became virtually a distinct new American style, one still considered tasteful at a time when the ornate Beaux-Arts architecure was nearing its zenith in taste. The country was growing, of course, and was large enough to accommodate trends in opposite directions.

Homes without style

Criticism of Victorian styles was revived in the mid-1890s by Edward Bok, editor of the popular *Ladies' Home Journal,* who launched a campaign to reduce the clutter in houses and to change the designs of the houses themselves. By then the Eastlake style was just one more of the many styles of furniture available to buyers, and there was also a new contender for favor —carved oak furniture with little pretense to beauty. Rooms became miniature museums of contrasting styles as freedom to choose, still operative, produced the tyranny of too many things chosen.

In his *Journal,* Bok offered plans and elevations of houses that he said could be built for as little as $1,500. Construction costs could

be reduced, he insisted, by eliminating the traditional parlor and its equally traditional fireplace, which most people no longer used since heat from stoves and the even newer furnaces was cleaner and more efficient. Bok assumed, however, that even families with restricted income would have servants, for he made a great point of the need for cross ventilation in servants' bedrooms, presumably for health reasons. But the main thrust of his campaign was to dispense with whatever was not essential to family living.

Bok's houses were built in sufficient numbers to make professional builders take notice. They had no recognizable style except the absence of any, which set them apart from virtually all other houses in the nation. In the long run, however, they had no detectable influence on domestic architecture. For an upwardly mobile population, a dwelling without a trace of style was a confession of failure to grasp America's vaunted opportunity and to rise in life. It was also taken as evidence of total deficiency in taste, which has always meant choosing from among available styles.

A. J. Downing and the firm of Town and Davis had been aware of this hunger for style when they proposed houses less well planned than Bok's but with details that would put them in one or another category of recognized style. At the turn of the century, large-circulation magazines competing with the *Ladies' Home Journal* displayed a comparable awareness of this hunger. During 1903, *Delineator* printed a series of articles, generally titled "Homes of the Past and Present," that described different styles of houses, each of which in both exterior and interior design evoked memories of the historic. All were larger than Bok's minimal house, which, by implication, was merely the zero milestone from which to measure family advance toward affluence and the reputation of being tasteful.

Mission furniture and bungalows

Bok was not alone in advocating simple dwellings. Nor was he the pioneer. In the 1880s, Gustav Stickley and Henry Wilson, working independently of each other, set in motion a somewhat complex development that in time yielded the bungalow, among the most

Top: *Rosecliff, designed
by McKim, Mead and White; Newport,
R.I.; 1902. Built for Hermann
Oelrichs; modeled after the
Grand Trianon at Versailles.
Above: Morgan Library,
designed by Charles Follen McKim;
New York, N.Y.; 1906. Inspired
by Palladio's Villa Medici. Right:
Getty family mausoleum, designed
by Louis Sullivan; Graceland
Cemetery, Chicago, Ill.; 1890.*

popular of all American building styles.

Both men were among the American disciples of William Morris. Stickley, as editor of the *Craftsman,* urged readers to learn the simple skills of home repair and maintenance and offered ideas for the heavy, rather boxlike furniture he made in one shop after another in eastern communities. His greatest following was not in the East but in California, where people of modest means gladly adopted his suggestions and provided names for his styles—Craftsman House for dwellings, Mission style for furniture (because of its supposed similarity to pieces previously made for the old Spanish missions). The best monument to the Craftsman aesthetic is the David Gamble House in Pasadena; its interior woodwork, rugs, and lighting fixtures have an unusual integrated effect that was achieved by the not-inconsiderable talents of Charles and Henry Greene. Completed in 1909, the Gamble House climaxed the Craftsman Movement, which thereafter evolved to the simpler design of the American bungalow.

Wilson, independently of Stickley, designed the first real bungalow. The term was derived from a Bengali word denoting a low thatched dwelling common to India. Wilson's original design also owed a little to the Swiss chalet. The first bungalows were square, with one story, no entrance hall, and a verandah (another term borrowed from India) running the width of the house under the shallow overhanging roof. It was not long, however, before low-ceilinged rooms lighted by small dormer windows were added under the roof. Stickley spoke of the wholesomeness of such a design, and Wilson, of its coziness. Both descriptions were no doubt appropriate, although "cozy" can be a euphemism for "cramped."

Small, cheap to build, and with no wasted space, the bungalow caught on fast, especially in California. Unlike the houses advertised earlier in the century, bungalows were built with no effort to make them look like houses of particular foreign countries. They may be called, accordingly, a vernacular development. And owing nothing to established styles, they could easily be modified to suit the climatic conditions of different parts of the country. By 1910, their fame reached the Middle West, where they were sometimes called Spanish Mission style, and by the eve of the war in Europe, they were everywhere, one of the commonest of all American domestic forms.

Meanwhile there were other men who tried to put Americans in houses they could afford. In 1880, George Pullman, founder of the Pullman Palace Car Company, created a town near Chicago for his employees, an early example of a planned community. It was considerably better than most "company" towns, but it was managed as paternalistically as any other. Rent was taken out of wages, and a family could be evicted on ten days' notice for letting the premises deteriorate in any way. Even by the time of the Columbian Exposition, Pullman, Illinois, was still a showplace that drew the attention of businessmen attending the fair. But by 1894, it had gained notoriety with one of the bloodiest of all American strikes.

Garden City, New York, had quite a different history. It was founded in 1869, on a seven-thousand-acre tract on the Hempstead Plains of Long Island, by Alexander T. Stewart, who conceived it as a community for families with modest incomes. The streets were unusually wide, and the house lots large enough for ample vegetable gardens to aid slim budgets. The very expansiveness, however, attracted people with higher incomes, and by the 1880s, the village had a growing social set. In the 1890s, after McKim, Mead, and White had remodeled the Garden City Hotel in their inimitable style, "Stewart's Folly" became fully established as one of New York's wealthiest suburbs.

A taste for fine art

After Stewart died in 1876, his extensive collection of paintings and objets d'art was sold at auction. The most spirited bidding was for paintings that were neither by old masters nor by recent artists of any solid stature. Jay Gould stopped bidding for a cattle scene by Troyon but took home, for $21,300, one of Ludwig Knaus's moralistic genre pieces, *Children's Party.* The sculpture was generally better than the paintings but went for much lower prices, which suggests that sculpture lagged behind painting in cultivated taste.

It was a little too early in history, no doubt, for rich connoisseurs of art to have developed highly sophisticated tastes of their own. To compensate, Stewart, like other wealthy collectors, hired an art advisor to roam Europe and buy whatever he thought was worth the asking price. If he were uncertain about a piece, he would telegraph Stewart, who more often than not would telegraph back authorizing the purchase. One work titled *1807* was bought in this way for $66,000; at the auction, it sold for the same amount. This practice of sending agents abroad grew more common as the century neared its close, for men who ruled the national economy had neither the time nor the knowledge for conducting such raids on Europe's art. What they did have was the money and a growing sense that art had intrinsic and increasing value, both aesthetic value and monetary value.

As art collecting by people of means became more fashionable, and as donors supplied cash for galleries to display their recent acquisitions, opportunities for viewing paintings multiplied. By 1900, most cities from coast to coast had art museums, supported by both public funds and private philanthropic donations.

The chromo culture

The most immediate result of the well-publicized collecting, however, was a widespread demand for copies of familiar masterpieces. Lithographs, especially those of Currier and Ives with added tinting, had been popular since the 1860s. The advanced technique of chromolithography was costlier but could produce better copies with true color. For middle-class families with social aspirations, it was essential to display on the parlor wall a Mona Lisa, a Titian Madonna, a Blue Boy, or some other equally famous work.

Some less formal room in the house, the family dining room, perhaps, or the den, was likely to be graced by a "Gibson Girl," the first great American glamor girl. Aloof, assured, capable, versatile, and completely feminine, she was thought somewhat daring for her time but in a ladylike way. Tall and graceful, with her starched shirtwaist and her boater hat perched atop her pompadour, she not only set the style for but was the envy of every young woman for more than twenty years. An ardent outdoor girl, she made tennis popular among women. What was more, she was real, for Charles Dana Gibson's model was his wife, a Langhorne of Virginia and sister of Lady Astor, the first woman member of the House of Commons.

With the improved methods of

Top: *Library in the home of T. B. Winchester; Beacon St., Boston, Mass.; photographed during the 1890s.* Above: *Library in the home of John Fiske; Cambridge, Mass.; 1877–78. Fiske was a philosopher and historian.*

pictorial reproduction and the mass production of a great variety of household decoration, folk art declined in popularity. Why spend long hours making valentines when better ones, in good color, could be bought for a few pennies at the nearest stationer's? Chromolithographs, soon shortened to "chromos" in the popular vocabulary, so flooded the country in the late nineteenth century that Lawrence Godkin's use of the derisive description "chromo civilization" in *The Nation* seems entirely justified. Fine copies of good paintings were numerous and had a genuine value for art appreciation, but relatively few chromos were copies of great art. Instead, most were gaudy, trivial, and so ephemeral that very few of them have survived.

Louis Prang, a refugee from the German revolution of 1848 who began selling chromos at his shop in Boston after the Civil War, greatly expanded his business when he offered the first Christmas cards in the 1870s. These and valentines pioneered the greeting-card trade. Other cards in great demand by collectors today carried portraits of sports heroes—pugilists, baseball players, track and field champions. Many others were handouts to advertise industrial products. Thread sold faster if the card naming its maker showed children at play. Larger advertisements pictured fire engines racing to flaming buildings, sturdy tugboats at work in choppy harbors, race horses, or sylvan nooks. The inside covers of cigar boxes became elaborate and colorful. So did cigar bands. What collectors today call "paper ephemera" had existed for many years, but with advertising a growing industry, they multiplied in striking designs and bright colors. Some frankly commercial chromos, including pictorial calendars, were appealing enough to

housewives' taste to be put up on kitchen walls, a practice still widely popular.

The paper patterns sold by the tens of thousands to home dressmakers suggested to one shrewd businessman the paper doll, with assorted wardrobes. Trunks and suitcases, for the fashionable trade, were given bright linings. Straw hats acquired brightly colored paper bands above their rims, and readers marked their place in books with paper bookmarks. For students of the period, all this chromo paper, even though little of it survives, yields a vivid record of "the smiling aspects of life."

The popularity of chromos continued for at least half a century, declining after the First World War with the advent of plastics and other sophisticated materials and with the development of colored comic books, moving pictures, and television as popular distractions.

Storytelling art

The phenomenal popularity of chromos did not preclude taste for art at a higher level. With the steady growth of magazines, in both numbers and circulation, editors welcomed good illustrations and could pay enough to attract talented artists. The same talent was exploited by book publishers, especially for novels. All parties, including the nation's readers, benefited from this situation, which produced what has since been recognized as the Golden Age of Illustration.

Winslow Homer began his long career in art just before the Civil War, which he reported in numerous on-the-spot drawings for *Harper's Weekly*. Whereas John Rogers had emphasized the heroics of that war in his popular plaster pieces, Homer stressed its drabness and discomforts, and its occasional humor. His switch to watercolors, and to his famous paintings

of the sea, came in 1883.

Homer was not long without rivals in the field of illustrations. In 1871, Edwin Abbey joined the Harper firm in New York and began with pen-and-ink sketches to accompany poems of English authorship. A more lucrative field, however, was the illustration of children's literature. For decades, youngsters grew up firmly convinced that Robin Hood and his merry band, and the Knights of the Round Table, looked exactly as Howard Pyle had depicted them. A. B. Frost worked the same magic for Joel Chandler Harris's Uncle Remus characters. But adults also liked their fiction illustrated. The more than 2,700 paintings and drawings of the Far West by Frederic Remington, reproduced in such popular magazines as *Harper's Monthly, Collier's,* and the *Century,* created an intense interest in Indians, cowboys, and their horses and prepared the nation to accept the myth of the West.

The summit of taste

There was less popular awareness of the most gifted artists of the period. John Singer Sargent and James McNeill Whistler, by settling permanently in England, in effect eliminated themselves from the sweepstakes of American taste. Whistler compounded his alienation by adopting the styles of his friends Manet, Degas, and Toulouse-Lautrec and could not hope for enthusiastic acceptance in his native land until they too won American approval. A dandy and a wit, often embroiled in controversy, Whistler cared not at all whether Americans liked his work. Some of them did, especially his *Arrangement in Gray and Black,* which they insisted on calling *Whistler's Mother.*

Sargent was a generation younger, living until 1925. He was the first American honored by election

other thirty years.

Eakins's use of a nude male model drew censure, and, under pressure, he eventually resigned from the Pennsylvania Academy of the Fine Arts, where he had taught for twenty-five years. His influence, however, was still felt years later when three of his pupils, Robert Henri, William Glackens, and John Sloan, became members of the Ashcan School of painting, a school committed to Eakins's uncompromising brand of realism.

Art Nouveau, a substyle

Louis Comfort Tiffany had no such handicaps to overcome. He had studied with Inness in Paris but owed more of his style to the brilliant primary colors that he saw in Africa during a visit to Morocco and to the Art Nouveau style he became acquainted with in the France of the 1880s. Back home, he turned from painting to the decorative arts and was quickly hailed as a master. So great was the demand for his work that he organized an interior decorating firm in New York. It specialized in *favrile* glass, characterized by iridescent colors and natural designs and used for vases, lamp shades, and stained-glass windows. Tiffany himself redecorated the downstairs rooms of Mark Twain's Hartford home and, in 1882, refurbished the White House interior for President Chester Arthur.

Art Nouveau bore some relation to the Aesthetic Movement that had influenced the Shavian Manorial and Queen Anne styles; it could also be linked, with a little effort, to both the earlier Pre-Raphaelite painting and poetry and to the highly stylized work of Oscar Wilde and Aubrey Beardsley in the 1890s. Its main development, however, was in France, where a Czech named Alphonse Mucha became its most celebrated exponent, beginning with his posters advertis-

to the French Academy of the Fine Arts. One critic compared his portraits of socialites to the fictional characters of Henry James, also an expatriate and with the same restricted standing in taste.

Two other painters of real talent were Mary Cassatt and Childe Hassam, both of whom were strongly influenced by the French impressionists. One Cassatt work, *Modern Women,* was painted on a wall at the exposition in 1893—in the Women's Building—but she spent much of her life in France and was not widely appreciated in the United States until after her death, in 1926. Childe Hassam's sprightly landscapes, urban scenes, and interiors show the in-

fluence of his exposure to impressionism during the few years he spent in Paris as a student.

More significant than any of the expatriates was Thomas Eakins, the great realistic painter of the nineteenth century. His insistence that painters should copy life directly made him a radical in the eyes of most critics. *The Surgical Clinic of Professor Gross,* a huge canvas showing medical students watching a master surgeon performing an actual operation, was refused a place in Memorial Hall at the Centennial Exhibition and was hung in the medical exhibit instead. Realism was generally accepted by 1876 for fiction but not for painting; that would take aning Sarah Bernhardt, the actress known to her admirers on both sides of the Atlantic as "the divine Sarah." Mucha crossed the ocean several times, to paint portraits and murals, and was so well known that the New York *Daily News,* on April 3, 1904, issued a special supplement containing reproductions of some of his works. The American industrialist Charles R. Crane subsidized a series of twenty large paintings, *The Slav Epopée,* that Mucha finished in 1930, but Americans now must travel to Prague to see it. Showings of the first completed parts, in 1921, at the Brooklyn Museum and in Chicago are said to have attracted more than half a million viewers.

Art Nouveau represented a break from academic tradition, for it was an effort to create a distinct new style that had no historical precedents. In America, despite the artistic and commercial success of Louis Tiffany and the attention paid to Mucha, it never quite caught on. The timing was wrong, and it can only be called a substyle with no long hold on taste.

The Ashcan eight

In 1907, the three young painters who had studied under Eakins and five others who understood his plea for realism organized as "the Eight" to educate American taste for the modern. One member of the group, Robert Henri, stated its creed very clearly: an artist must be a social force, an individual who "creates a stir in the world." But not even the startling exposure of life's sordid actualities by the journalistic muckrakers in that decade nor the naturalistic determinism of the literary realists could prompt the public to accept the Eight's portrayal of life's drab commonplaces. Instead, they were dubbed the "Ashcan School" in response to their preoccupation with such

urban phenomena as Bowery derelicts, burlesque-show queens, elevated trains spewing smoke and grime, dismal winter streets, and wretched slum alleys.

Three of the Eight—George Luks, John Sloan, and William Glackens—submitted paintings for a 1907 exhibit of the National Academy of Design, only to have them rejected. The next year all eight were represented in a show of independent artists held in a small Manhattan gallery, but neither there nor in the other cities the show toured was much interest shown in their work.

The Eight held together for some years, grimly confident that such painting as theirs would someday win the approval of taste. A late recruit, George Bellows, delighted in prize fights and religious revivals. His brutally realistic lithograph of Firpo knocking Dempsey out of the ring in 1924 did create a stir in the world, but by then the Ashcan label was no longer a handicap to acceptance.

From 1900 until the First World War, most Americans considered art to be remote from ordinary life. Copies of works by old masters were hung on parlor walls to give tone to dwellings, but few people took painting seriously, and fewer yet thought it should create a stir anywhere.

The energy of Alfred Stieglitz

Photography, meanwhile, was still not accepted as an art form. The "sun pictures" that could be made after 1837 by Daguerre's complicated process excited Americans, and in time, as methods became simpler, photography largely replaced portrait painting as a means of immortalizing family members. Brady's Civil War photographs were well received, as a form of reporting, and the camera became an essential tool of scientific research. But readers were cool to

Opposite top: *Victorian bedroom, George Finch home; St. Paul, Minn.; mid 1880s.* Opposite bottom: *Mahogany Guest Room, Mark Twain House; Hartford, Conn.; ca. 1873. Bed and dresser are in the "pure Eastlake style" popular during the 1870s.* Top: The Sweetest Story Ever Told, *by Charles Dana Gibson; cover of* Collier's Weekly; *1910. A typical Gibson girl.* Above: *Advertising color lithograph for Cincinnati, Hamilton & Dayton R.R.; 1894.*

photographs in magazines and had no use at all for them as illustrations for books. The same was true in fashion periodicals, long after 1900.

By that year commercial photographers could fare reasonably well by recording the happy faces of young graduates, brides and grooms, and small infants. Artistic camera work, though, was an unrewarding sideline, hardly more than a hobby. Its most tenacious champion was Alfred Stieglitz, whose views of New York streets and buildings are now highly prized. He edited camera magazines and maintained a private gallery called "291," but he and his few disciples were disparaged as "the Mop and Pail Brigade," a clue to their affinity to the Ashcan School of painters.

One now-famous Stieglitz photograph, *Steerage,* shows a mass of immigrants ready to set foot on the Promised Land in 1907. America in theory welcomed "the huddled masses yearning to be free, the wretched refuse" of Europe, as Emma Lazarus had written in the sonnet at the base of the Statue of Liberty, erected in 1883. But the first decade of the twentieth century set an all-time record for immigrants, nearly 9 million, and comfortable descendants of former "refuse" were uneasy about it. Pictures of penniless peasants about to disembark were rather distasteful to them, whether painted or photographed. So were books about the miserable slum life of the very poor, like Jacob Riis's *How the Other Half Lives* and Stephen Crane's *Maggie: A Girl of the Streets.*

At "291," in addition to artistic photographs, Stieglitz showed paintings by avant-garde artists, both French and American. In time, the idea emerged to mount a larger exhibit, in some ample hall, carefully chosen and arranged, and well publicized, to educate the public. Stieglitz became its prime mover and, in so doing, effectively broke the bonds of a restrictive taste that had prevailed much too long.

Tempest in an armory

The 69th Regiment Armory in New York was a happy choice for the exhibition. It was large enough to hold a sizable crowd and to allow for generous spacing of displays. Publicity was effective, attracting some four thousand people to the opening, on the evening of February 17, 1913. The ensuing criticism in newspapers and magazines roused curiosity, and attendance during the next four weeks rose steadily to a total of at least one hundred thousand, a large figure though not the quarter-million the sponsors claimed. Reporters had a field day: their prime target for ridicule was Marcel Duchamp's *Nude Descending a Staircase,* which was to remain the major symbol of the Armory Show.

No such paintings, in unfamiliar forms and techniques, had been seen in Memorial Hall at the Centennial Exhibition in 1876 or at the Columbian Exposition in 1893. Nor were they being bought by private collectors, or by the directors of art galleries, who were still loyal to Peale's dictum, a century before, about hanging only works by established artists. The Armory Show did not redirect taste at once, but it did prompt young collectors and open-minded critics to rethink their values. About a third of the displayed paintings were by French post-impressionists and cubists. Being exposed to them suddenly without preparation was a jolt—which was just what Stieglitz and his colleagues intended. They were delighted with the results.

Most of the published opinions of the show were hostile, for the simple reason that most important critics were committed to archaic conventions. One distinguished authority on art reviewed the show as he might have an earthquake or a fire that destroyed half a city. Another remarked that Seurat's pointillism, Van Gogh's wavy lines and strong primary colors, and Gauguin's shapely Samoan women violated every accepted rule and were an affront to good taste. A third counseled patience; the whole thing, he suspected, was a clever hoax and posed no threat to true art. The author of a review titled "Ellis Island Art" warned that modern art by foreigners and recent immigrants was a menace that had to be taken seriously. He called Cézanne an ignoramus, Van Gogh an incompetent, and Picasso a showman in a class with Barnum. One of the few temperate comments was that of Theodore Roosevelt. A Navajo rug he owned was better art, he asserted, than most of the cubism on display, but he was pleased by one Cézanne and summed up by saying that he had found nothing commonplace at the Armory and much of real merit.

Despite the generally adverse opinions, between two and three hundred of the paintings were sold off the walls. Somebody liked them—or rather, quite a few somebodies. The Metropolitan Museum of Art paid the highest price for any picture on exhibit, $6,700—for a Cézanne, the first to enter an American museum. No less important, the show inspired Abby Aldrich Rockefeller (Mrs. John D., Jr.) to start adding modern art to her collection and later to help found the Museum of Modern Art.

After New York, the show was taken to Chicago, where more people saw it and where condemnation was more vehement. The president of the Law and Order League ful-

minated against the French nudes and said that if a saloon had hung such pictures, it would have violated local ordinances. Other Chicagoans were content to call them obscenities. The final showing, in Boston, under the auspices of the Copley Society, was an anticlimax. Copley Hall was too small to display any but the foreign paintings, and nobody saw fit to question their decency.

One historian of the Armory Show, writing in 1963 on its fiftieth anniversary, questioned whether it would find a more receptive audience in that year than it had in 1913. But even if only a relatively small fraction of the American public has any genuine interest in modern painting, or in any great art, the Armory Show unquestionably broadened the taste of those that do. Pre-1913 taste, in any event, was doomed.

Established tastes, however, do not quickly abandon their hold. The Beaux-Arts style of architecture still appealed to millionaires well into the twentieth century, and the Panama-Pacific Exposition in San Francisco's Golden Gate Park, celebrating the completion of the Panama Canal in 1915, was as elegantly neoclassical as the Court of Honor in the 1893 exposition. It hardly needs saying that the paintings displayed there included nothing that had been in the Armory Show. The Palace of Fine Arts in San Francisco, however, was a last gasp of the spirit of ornate overdecoration. Since the First World War, World's Fairs have all been modernistic or futuristic in their architecture.

The magazine age

In literature there was less cause for cultural shock than in the fine arts. Readers had been exposed to new trends in style and content for half a century, time enough to develop a degree of sophistication.

Americans had always been avid readers, and with steadily increasing leisure time and none of today's mass entertainment—moving pictures, radio, television—the demand for magazines multiplied both their numbers and their circulation. By the time of the outbreak of the Civil War, about two hundred were being published, but at century's end, there were more than a thousand. *Harper's* had more subscribers than the *Atlantic,* among the quality monthlies, but fewer than the *Century,* which went out to more than two hundred thousand addresses. Even more

people—about 270,000—took the *Ladies' Home Journal,* but the *Youth's Companion* set the pace with 385,000. Editing and proofreading were consistently excellent —they had to be or the magazine risked falling behind in the heady competition for readers. As for the contents, "safe" and "solid" are the most suitable adjectives, for all popular magazines were intended for family consumption.

During the final quarter of the nineteenth century, the literary magazines changed little in what they offered to readers. A volume of *Harper's,* then titled *Harper's*

New Monthly Magazine, for the half-year from June through November, 1876, had 952 pages, each with two columns of text and no advertisements. Opening at random to the September issue, one would find an article on Long Beach, the New Jersey beach resort where Grant maintained his summer White House, and a second long article on "The Mikado's Empire"; shorter pieces on the Baltimore oriole, Eton College, carnivorous plants in Florida, and Mason and Dixon's Line; five short stories, one of them translated from the German; installments of four serialized novels; five poems; twenty pages of editorial departments; and finally a humor miscellany titled "Editor's Drawer."

Other magazines did carry advertisements, mostly for patent medicines and such feminine essentials as corsets. An ad in 1878 for Allan's Anti-Fat, with before and after pictures, assured potential customers that this great remedy for corpulence was purely vegetable and perfectly harmless. Considering how much food most Americans ate every day, it is hardly surprising that many such concoctions were available, and that corsetry was so much in demand. Cooley's corset that had "Cork in lieu of Bone" was unbreakable, porous, light blue, and launderable, its maker announced, and the Kabo corset with no brass eyelets, advertised in *Delineator* in 1878, was being bought by "3,600,000 satisfied women" every year. Men, meanwhile, were advised when looking for ready-made essentials to ask for True-Fit shirts, sized for every build.

Delineator was primarily a fashion magazine, one of several that kept women informed, mostly by pictures, of styles that would assure their wearers of public approval. The steady changes in fashion, and the multiplicity of particular styles, suggests the expediency of resorting here to the same device the literary magazine editors used—of letting pictures tell the story, and of letting readers form their own judgments. Women in "the Gilded Age" had every encouragement to dress well and to overdress. The same went for children. As for men, it may be reported that they commonly wore long-john underwear all year round and ignored every suggestion that their trousers should be pressed. Otherwise they dressed much like men today but always with vests, and their hats were brown derbies.

Fauntleroy and Finn

Magazine serialization of novels had little adverse effect on their sales in bound copies. If anything, they helped these sales, for readers impatient to learn "how it all came out" could buy the book at a low price, commonly a dollar. Besides, a serial could create a desire to buy other books by the same author.

Fiction that sold the most copies between 1876 and 1900 showed the same wide range of type as Victorian houses and furnishings. The variety was so great, in fact, that setting up categories would be difficult. Yet in general the most popular novels fell into relatively few groups.

Hawthorne's "d—d mob of scribbling women" still appealed to reader taste, but less for sentimental fiction of the sort he detested than for memorable books for children. Among the top bestsellers of the period were *Little Lord Fauntleroy,* by Frances Hodgson Burnett (1886); Kate Douglas Wiggin's *Rebecca of Sunnybrook Farm* (1903); and Eleanor Porter's *Pollyanna* (1913). Taste for escape fiction in its purest form was gratified by Rider Haggard's *She* (1887) and *King Solomon's Mines* (1886); Anthony Hope's *The Prisoner of Zenda* (1894) and *Rupert of Hentzau* (1898), both set in the imaginary country of Ruritania; and Charles Major's *When Knighthood Was in Flower* (1898). Charles M. Sheldon's *In His Steps* (1896), Lew Wallace's *Ben-Hur* (1880), and H. Sienkiewicz's *Quo Vadis?* (1895) appealed to one kind of religious taste, William Thomas Stead's *If Christ Came to Chicago* (1895), questioning the reception Christ would have if he were to appear in modern America, to quite another.

The American Winston Churchill advanced the taste for fictionalized history—*Richard Carvel* and *The Crossing* for the Revolution, *The Crisis* for the Civil War. His *Coniston,* a remarkable dissection of New Hampshire politics, attracted fewer readers. F. Hopkinson Smith's *Colonel Carter of Cartersville* created sympathy for the Old South and its impoverished aristocracy. A new and equally durable myth was born in 1902 with the publication of Owen Wister's *The Virginian,* prototype of all the "Westerns" in moving pictures and television.

Tom Sawyer offended taste in the "best circles" but was a bestseller in 1876, as was *Huckleberry Finn* in 1884 despite its "bad English" that fastidious elders found distasteful. But the great writer for boys was Horatio Alger, Jr. A Harvard graduate who rebelled against his strict Puritan heritage, he tried the bohemian life of Paris and returned to become a Unitarian preacher, only to give that up for the more lucrative career of writing juvenile fiction. Between 1867 and his death in 1899, he turned out some 130 action-filled books, all based on the principle that with pluck and luck, any boy could rise above poverty and temptation to wealth, power, and happiness. His books reconfirmed the

Three views of the David B. Gamble residence, designed by Charles Greene and Henry Greene; Pasadena, Calif.; 1908. Top: *Exterior.* Center: *Entry with Tiffany glass, main stairway, and living room to the left.* Above: *The library table, chairs, and carpet.*

Puritan ethic his father had tried to drill into him—that hard work and moral living are crowned by material success. Alger did not believe it, but most of his generation did, and his books sold by the tens of thousands.

In somewhat the same vein, but on a more adult level, was *Acres of Diamonds* (1888) by Russell Conwell, a Baptist clergyman who founded Temple University and was its first president. He gave *Acres* thousands of times as a lecture, and as a book it was equally popular. Like the Alger stories, it stressed individual initiative, but it also tried to reconcile orthodox Christianity with laissez-faire capitalism. Since most defenders of free enterprise unfettered by social controls were orthodox Christians, the book was firmly approved by dominant taste. A liberal Christian, Edward Bellamy, in the same year took an opposite stance in *Looking Backward: 2000–1887*, also a best-seller. Uncontrolled capitalism, he suggested, was destined to be replaced by A.D. 2000 with a completely socialized economy. That two books so opposed to each other in message were both bought and eagerly read by a vast number of people, at the same time, is evidence of a deeply divided taste.

The big change in literature

In the last few years of the century, a group of conservative editors and scholars tried to control reader taste, or, more specifically, to preserve their own standards of idealism, tradition, and gentility from destruction by literary radicals. George Santayana later coined a name for the group—the "Genteel Tradition." Others have called them "Defenders of Ideality," which they would have liked better. Since the Civil War, they had been opposing the stronger forms of realism, especially the

in *A Modern Instance* (1882). He somewhat redeemed himself in 1891 with his *Criticism and Fiction,* wherein he argued that fiction should be pure because in America, the Young Girl was among its most devoted readers—as she no doubt was. Many novel readers agreed. But Howells soon proved that he could not be relied upon to support the standards of taste that Aldrich and his fellow conservatives endorsed. He wrote favorable reviews of realistic novels, including Crane's *Maggie: A Girl of the Streets,* and he was a close friend of such literary "wild men" as Mark Twain and Hamlin Garland. In 1894, he was highly critical of contemporary capitalism in *A Traveler from Altruria,* a utopian novel in reverse. His most radical action, though, was his strong defense of Governor Altgeld of Illinois for pardoning some of the men convicted in the Haymarket Riot of 1886. Before 1900, there was little sympathy for labor, and industrial violence—if engaged in by workers —was condemned.

In the 1890s, the most talented offenders against the Genteel Tradition's notion of good taste were Stephen Crane and Frank Norris. Crane's *Maggie* was a stark picture of slum life and a virtual object lesson in the power of environment to destroy an innocent individual. A Horatio Alger here might have found a way to overcome such handicaps, but Maggie could not. Almost nobody read the book, even after Howells praised it in print. But Crane's next book, *The Red Badge of Courage* (1895), appealed to thousands of readers. Worlds removed from the usual Civil War novel replete with heroics and romantic episodes, it revealed the irony in human existence, which could turn an arrant coward into a regimental hero by no action of his own. Continuing the same theme, Norris ex-

kind of fiction that exposed sham and corruption, and the drift away from formal diction toward the colloquial, as in *Huckleberry Finn.* The infusion of naturalism, or deterministic philosophy, into fiction about 1890 roused them to action; in their fight, they had the strong support of many Americans who did not like to be told that each individual is not the captain of his soul and the master of his fate.

If one of this small but influential group was typical, it was Thomas Bailey Aldrich. Born in Portsmouth, New Hampshire, the setting of his delectable semiautobiographical *Story of a Bad Boy,*

he was repelled by New York's strident commercialism and retreated to Boston, glad to escape, as he put it, with his English still correct. As editor of the *Atlantic* from 1881 to 1890, he did all in his power to keep its pages undefiled. Nobody could fault his own writing, whether in travel accounts or in the amusing tour de force "Marjorie Daw." But it was not in his nature to be critical of American life or to be enthusiastic about writing that was.

Aldrich's predecessor at the *Atlantic,* William Dean Howells, had violated the taboo against mention of marital disharmony and divorce

Top: *Uplands II, Charles Templeton Crocker Estate; Hillsborough, near San Mateo, Calif.; 1913.* Above: *Palace of Fine Arts at the Panama-Pacific International Exposition; San Francisco, Calif.; 1915.*

plicitly detailed, in *McTeague* (1899), the inevitable destruction of a man too weak to overcome his own inherited flaws; in *The Octopus* (1901), he described the equally inevitable defeat of innocent people by a ruthless corporation with profit its only motive.

Muckraking

That *Red Badge of Courage* stood high enough in reader taste to become a best-seller, while Norris's long novels were almost as widely approved, suggests that the Genteel Tradition was losing its battle to preserve its lofty standards. It did have a success in 1900, when Theodore Dreiser's first novel, *Sister Carrie*, was withheld from circulation because the publisher's wife considered it immoral. Carrie, as Dreiser traced her career, gained fame and fortune not by virtuous deeds or even intelligence but as a result of events beyond her control. By 1913, however, when *Sister Carrie* was released for sale, it caused no outcry of offended taste. In the years intervening, realistic writing in its strongest form, naturalistic determinism, had received a powerful assist from journalism, in the writing of the muckrakers.

They were given that name by Theodore Roosevelt, who based it on a character in *Pilgrim's Progress* so intent on raking muck that he could not see the celestial crown he might have worn. The modern rakers of muck were investigative reporters employed by S. S. McClure and rival magazine editors locked in a fierce battle for subscribers. What the raking exposed was horrendous corruption in the nation's business and politics. Based on intensive research and skillfully written, the articles profoundly affected public opinion, for they provided documented evidence that giants of industry and governmental officials were as crooked as

cynics had suspected. Mark Twain had fictionalized such chicanery in *The Gilded Age* (1873), but with copious humor. There was nothing to laugh at in what the muckrakers wrote. Admiration or amiable tolerance of the rich and powerful turned to rage and a grim hope of reducing their invidious control of economic and political life.

The best of the muckraking writers were Ida M. Tarbell and Lincoln Steffens. Miss Tarbell's articles in *McClure's* were the basis of her two-volume *History of the Standard Oil Company* (1904), which led to the breakup of that greatest of all American monopolies. Steffens, managing editor of *McClure's*, aimed his deadly pen at the graft in local politics, not only in such major cities as Philadelphia and St. Louis but even in as small a community as Greenwich, Connecticut. The resulting book, *The Shame of the Cities* (1904), is the classic of its kind and is still fascinating reading.

The Armory Show shocked many viewers because they were in the habit of allowing conservative art experts to guide whatever awareness they had of fine painting and sculpture. The muckraking movement shocked on a much larger scale. It jolted hundreds of thousands of magazine readers into the painful awareness of being gulled and exploited by unscrupulous financiers and politicians. No longer could anybody ignore the gap in privilege between rulers and ruled, or the fact that if not controlled, the gap would continue to widen.

The desire for a greater voice in national affairs had been largely responsible for the election of Andrew Jackson in 1828; now it resurfaced in the form of pressuring Congress to enact reform legislation. Congress responded. It investigated the insurance companies in 1905. The next year it

passed the Meat Inspection Act, prompted by *The Jungle,* a novel by Upton Sinclair that turned readers' stomachs with its nauseating account of stockyard methods. Congress also dissolved the tobacco and Standard Oil trusts. In 1913, year of the Armory Show, the Sixteenth and Seventeenth amendments were adopted, authorizing a federal income tax and the election of senators by popular vote.

Whether or not the muckrakers expected such results, the hard facts they reported in forceful language convinced the majority of the population that Howells had been wrong, and that the smiling aspects of life were not, after all, the more American. What the literary realists had been suggesting for thirty years was vindicated, and the campaign of the Genteel Tradition to suppress it was thoroughly discredited. Without intending to, the muckrakers had redirected taste to approval of the realism that has marked American writing ever since.

On the concert stage

Cultural evolution, however, is uneven; it may spurt ahead in one area of the culture and lag behind in others. Musical taste, for a conspicuous example, was still dominated in the first decades of the twentieth century by an almost total deference to foreign composers, conductors, and performers.

In 1908, to coincide with the twenty-fifth season of the Metropolitan Opera Company, Edward Krehbiel, music critic of the New York *Tribune,* published his *Chapters on Opera.* He devoted most of its 435 pages to the many famous foreign operas, artists, and directors in the Met's history, although he did find space to list American singers who had made their mark. At one point he mentioned New York's Academy of Music, chartered in 1862. Ole Bull, the Norwegian violinist, serving as the academy's manager for the final weeks of its first season, offered a prize of $1,000 for the best original opera by an American composer "on a strictly American subject." The offer lapsed when Bull left, but Krehbiel made the comment that "It is doubtful if the competition would have produced anything more than a curiosity." He may have been right, but his phrasing reflects the tendency within the music establishment to dismiss American musicians and their music.

Krehbiel, who was not foreign-born but a native of Ann Arbor, Michigan, championed the music of Wagner, Brahms, and Tchaikovsky when they were little known in America. Like almost everyone else in his profession, he had a high regard for the traditional standards taught at the music centers in Germany. The few conservatories in America—the first at Oberlin College in 1865, and others founded soon afterward in Cincinnati, Chicago, Nashville, and Boston—also trained young aspirants according to those standards and helped maintain the taste for European music, German in particular. The Romantic German music of the nineteenth century was, admittedly, the best in the world in its time, but narrow preoccupation with that best made it very difficult, if possible at all, for taste to develop for music by Americans and with American themes. Not until the present "Big Three"—Eastman, Juilliard, and Curtis—opened their doors, after the First World War, did American schools of music begin to challenge the German centers and train musicians who subsequently gained favor and the approval of taste.

One of the very few American composers who was successful abroad before 1900 and whose

works are still played was Edward MacDowell. He studied in France and Germany in the 1870s and 1880s, and in 1889 was enthusiastically applauded for a piano recital he gave at the Paris Exhibition. In 1896, he became Columbia University's first professor of music. As a Romantic composer who managed to avoid cliches and to develop an individual sense of harmony and melody, MacDowell earned an enviable reputation, first abroad and then in his own country, before death cut short his career in 1908, when he was forty-seven.

Study abroad and good press notices for European concertizing were the next best thing to being born abroad and bearing a foreign name. Some American performers actually changed their given names: Lillian Norton, born on a remote farm in Maine, became the famous soprano Mme Lillian Nordica. Late nineteenth-century composers—John Knowles Paine, Dudley Buck, and George Chadwick among them—were only slightly less gifted than MacDowell but, despite study and successful concerts in Europe, met a barrier of indifference at home. They comprised the second school of American composers—the first were William Billings and his fellow tunesmiths a century earlier—but American taste never gave them its full and fair endorsement. In contrast, concert audiences in America immediately accepted *From the New World,* a symphony composed in 1893 by a Czech, Anton Dvorak, who had spent some time in the United States. Its major theme, as he pointed out, was based on "a plantation song." Perhaps the native-born composers should have drawn more from Afro-American music, but that was still well below the threshold of American taste, being generally associated with black-face minstrel shows and whorehouse jazz.

One gifted American composer of the period, Charles Ives, who wrote music as an avocation during a successful business career, was too far ahead of his time to be appreciated. Fascinated by harmonious and dissonant combinations, he created discordant quarter-tone pieces by disfiguring or distorting popular tunes and hymns. Not until 1939 was there any public acceptance of his music, which was authentically indigenous and which anticipated, by decades, the modern idiom. In 1947, he received a Pulitzer Prize for his Third Symphony, written many years earlier. Taste had finally caught up with Charles Ives.

Behind the footlights

Comparable conditioning worked to the disadvantage of native playwrights bold enough to try new kinds of drama. The boldest of all was James A. Herne, who tried to do on the stage what dozens of realistic writers were doing with success in novels and short stories. His *Hearts of Oak,* first staged in 1879, had to wait twenty years for approval, winning it only then because he rewrote it and gave it a new and less formidable title, *Sag Harbor.* The plot concerns a girl who marries one man, realizes too late that she really loves his brother, and is consoled by a story in a similar vein told her by a wise old sea captain. Much stronger is *Margaret Fleming* (1890), a play about marital infidelity that offended contemporary taste when, just before the final curtain, Margaret opens her blouse to nurse her infant child. Herne pleased audiences more, in 1892, with *Shore Acres,* which features a homespun philosopher but incorporates a liberal dose of melodrama.

Theatergoers were simply not ready for honest realism on the stage, and Herne never won the esteem heaped upon his one-time collaborator David Belasco, who could fill theaters with a wide variety of genres: domestic problems, crook melodramas, farces, Civil War and frontier plots. Almost everything Belasco wrote was a box-office success; he had a keen sense of what the public wanted. Two of his plays so appealed to Puccini that he adapted them to Italian operas—*The Girl of the Golden West* and *Madame Butterfly*.

Belasco succeeded because his plays were romantic, set in a never-never land that served as a welcome escape from humdrum daily life. As literature, they were low in quality by modern standards; but so was most of the theatrical fare beloved just then by Americans. Producers took their cue from England rather than from the Continental playwrights—Ibsen, Chekhov, Strindberg, Maeterlinck—whose characters talk like real people and express genuine emotions. The two English playwrights who did anticipate modern dramatic standards, Oscar Wilde and Bernard Shaw, were too intellectual to appeal to American taste of that period.

The plays Americans liked most were those of Shakespeare, heroic tragedies, plays with country bumpkins, and adaptations of sentimental novels. Among the top favorites in the late nineteenth and early twentieth centuries were Clyde Fitch's *Barbara Frietchie* (later set to music as *My Maryland*), William Gillette in *Sherlock Holmes*, Gillette's own play *Secret Service*, and the perennial *Rip Van Winkle* and *Uncle Tom's Cabin*. It would take the major upheaval of a world war and the emergence of an exceptionally gifted playwright, Eugene O'Neill, to elevate America's taste in drama.

Despite the social anxieties of the middle class, and even despite the wretchedness of the poor, life in America toward the end of the

Left: Dempsey Through the Ropes, *lithograph by George Wesley Bellows; 1924. Based on first-round incident of Dempsey-Firpo match at Polo Grounds in 1923.* Below: Buffalo Bill's Wild West, *lithograph; 1899.*

Gilded Age was generally enjoyable. The "Gay Nineties" were not misnamed. The Edwardian period, between Victoria's death in 1901 and the outbreak of war in 1914, was even more exuberant—on the surface. Anna Held personified the decade and its spirit, as a chanteuse, a star in show business, and as a fashion plate. Her hourglass figure was the envy of her sex and the cynosure of male interest.

The general hedonism and avoidance of serious matters, and the endless quest for novelty, no doubt concealed a basic unease, a discontent with life as it was organized. This discontent was strong enough, with prodding from the muckrakers, to force those major amendments in 1913 and the passage of regulatory laws. The taste for high living, however, might have been even stronger if Americans had had any inkling of what lay just ahead.

157

VI

Twentieth Century Limited

(1915–1945)

Preceding pages: Field Workers, *by Thomas Hart Benton; 1945.* Above: Girl in Orange Gown, *by George Luks; late 1920s. Ashcan School.*

On June 28, 1914, a Serbian terrorist shot and killed the heir to the Austrian throne, setting in motion a chain of events that led to general war in Europe. The causes —territorial, imperialistic, economic—were of minimal concern to the United States, but warhawks demanded intervention. Isolationist sentiment was stronger, however, and in 1916, Woodrow Wilson was reelected president on the slogan "He kept us out of the war." But when Germany stepped up its submarine warfare and some American lives were lost at sea, public opinion forced Wilson to ask for a declaration of war; Congress promptly acceded, in April, 1917. A new slogan became popular: this was to be a crusade "to keep the world safe for democracy." Soon after the armistice in November, 1918, however, it became clear that the world was no safer for democracy than it had been in 1914, and the crusading enthusiasm that had carried the nation through the war was replaced by disillusion.

Reading about war

The war "to end war" and the dubious peace had a significant effect on the behavior and enthusiasms of the following decade. Previously, Americans had viewed war as ennobling and romantic, despite General Sherman's declaration that war is hell. Although some antiwar literature and drama had been written, it had never won much favor. John William De Forest's novel *Miss Ravenel's Conversion from Secession to Loyalty* had exposed the horrors of war in 1867, but the book was never fully appreciated until its reissue in 1939.

The brief war with Spain in 1898 was widely opposed by intellectuals, but neither William Dean Howells's powerful short story "Editha" nor such astringent poems as "On a Soldier Fallen in the Philippines," by William Vaughn Moody, had any perceptible effect on popular sentiment. In contrast, the First World War, more objectively reported in the press, could not be glossed over, especially the factual descriptions of trench warfare and mustard gas. By 1921, less than three years after the armistice, the novel *Three Soldiers,* by John Dos Passos, had won broad popular approval. One of its three protagonists is a mindless conformist eager only for promotion, but the other two desert, and at the close of the book one of them is facing execution by a firing squad with calm defiance. Deserters as fictional heroes? This would have been unthinkable before 1917.

In 1922, readers were excited over E. E. Cummings's account of his confinement in a French concentration camp, *The Enormous Room.* War could be hell, the book made clear, even for noncombatant volunteer ambulance drivers. The classic of this antiwar genre, however, is *A Farewell to Arms,* by Ernest Hemingway. To write the novel, Hemingway drew upon his own war experience, especially the disastrous Italian retreat from Caporetto. The desertion of the fictional Lt. Frederic Henry, like that of the two Dos Passos doughboys, did not offend reader taste in 1929.

Revolution in poetry

Realistic fiction had already won its long battle with idealized romanticism before the war began. An independent but comparable break with the literary past occurred in poetry, chiefly through the efforts of a determined Chicagoan, Harriet Monroe. In 1912, she founded *Poetry: A Magazine of Verse,* welcoming to its pages fresh talent and rejecting anything smacking of the tired old conventions characteristic of the verse used by editors to fill out short pages to give "tone" to their periodicals. Such verse remained in favor among the undereducated element satisfied with superficial sentimentality, but *Poetry* redirected more discriminating taste to what was quickly called the New Poetry. It still goes by that name, justifiably, because its revolutionary character profoundly altered the nature of serious poetry as it is still being written.

Abetted by Ezra Pound, an expatriate living in England, Harriet Monroe opened *Poetry* to translations from foreign languages and also to position papers with strongly opposing views. Controversy attracted new subscribers and stimulated interest among people who had never given poetry more than a passing nod. Older poets committed to traditional forms and themes defended them vigorously, but their effort was a "last ditch" campaign of the Genteel Tradition. Good poetry in conventional forms continued to be written, but not with the subject matter that had appealed to earlier generations. Taste declined for smoothly textured lines that skirted the hard facts of life and increasingly favored rugged themes that were relevant to the immediate facts of existence. Whitman had pioneered the break with the past, but he had been born too soon, and had been repudiated at every level of taste. Now his star, so long occluded, emerged in all its brightness as biographies, critical studies, and new editions of *Leaves of Grass* were in sudden favor.

Like Whitman, the New Poets rejected the honored old conventions of English poetry as too restrictive and invented new forms of their own as vehicles for their ideas. The two with the greatest initial following, Vachel Lindsay and Edgar Lee Masters, ignored formal convention the most markedly and chose subject matter that was highly original. Their enthusiastic acceptance by the public suggests how greatly taste had changed, and how rapidly, in the second decade of this century.

Lindsay, torn in youth by conflicting ambitions, settled on a quest for beauty. For an extended period, he roamed the country, trading poems for bread, sleeping in hay barns or under the sky, and learning what ordinary Americans were like—and what they liked. Most of them, he discovered, shared his wistful dream of a life that held more than plodding existence from cradle to grave—a life touched with the beauty that eluded their grasp. During the winters, when vagabondage was difficult, Lindsay survived by lecturing on "The Gospel of Beauty," and in 1912 he began to write longer poems—"The Santa Fe Trail," "General William Booth Enters into Heaven," "The Congo."

This last, when printed, contained his marginal stage directions: "Heavy accents, very heavy," "With pomposity," "Like the wind in the chimney," "Sung to the tune of 'Hark ten thousand harps and voices'." His public reading of such poems comprised a successful one-man show, packing auditoriums with people who sat spellbound as he half-recited, half-sang his magical word pictures. His closest rival for magnetic appeal was the evangelist Billy Sunday, whose eloquence prompted people in droves to walk the sawdust trail and repent their sins in public. The salvation Lindsay offered was a glimpse of transcendent beauty. Sunday left nothing as appealing to subsequent taste as "The Chinese Nightingale," Lindsay's masterpiece for sheer beauty.

Edgar Lee Masters, a successful Chicago lawyer, won his own high place in current taste with a single volume published in 1915, *Spoon River Anthology*. A series of interrelated epitaphs in free verse, each written as the deceased might have worded it, the book tells of pathetic unfulfillment and failed human relationships. Spoon River, with its limited access to success and happiness, was anybody's small town in the mythology of the period. The *Anthology* soon had its counterparts in other genres—Sherwood Anderson's *Winesburg, Ohio* in the short story, Sinclair Lewis's *Main Street* in the novel, and, somewhat later, Thornton Wilder's *Our Town* in drama.

Two of the most intellectual and influential of the New Poets, Ezra Pound and T. S. Eliot, were held in awe but never had broad appeal except in academic circles. One reason for this may have been that both spent most of their lives abroad, Pound in Italy, Eliot in England, becoming an English subject in 1927, twenty-one years before winning a Nobel Prize. Perhaps the best American poet in the first half of the twentieth century was never considered a New Poet

—Edwin Arlington Robinson, some of whose finest poems were written in the 1890s. He was America's first professional poet, living as he did for poetry alone and waiting with stoical patience for taste to catch up with him, as it did about the same time it caught up with Charles Ives in music. The delay in recognition contributed much to Robinson's deep pessimism, which was out of joint with late Victorian confidence and faith in boundless progress.

One welcome phenomenon of the years between the two world wars was the emergence of women poets of a high order of genius. Most earlier "poetesses," as they were often called when women were commonly assumed to be inferior to men in intellectual capacity, had prospered with frothy sentimentality—"newspaper verse" of the sort Mark Twain had burlesqued in *Huckleberry Finn*. The new breed could hold their own with male poets, and readers grew accustomed to judging them not on their sex but on the quality of their work. Edna St. Vincent Millay gained acceptance as a Vassar undergraduate with *Renascence* (1912), which exhibited technical virtuosity and startling freshness. Amy Lowell was the leader of the Imagist Movement; her "Patterns" (1916), strongly antiwar, is among the finest poems ever written that uses clear, hard images. Marianne Moore appealed to readers with her disciplined but unconventional metrics and her witty, ironic tone. These three and others gained such a respectable place in reader taste that the difference between men and women poets was minimized.

Sandburg and Frost

By mid-century, the New Poets most highly regarded were Carl Sandburg and Robert Frost. Frost revived the glory of rural self-suffi-

ciency as Americans had lived it a century earlier and fostered the notion that such an existence was still possible in remote parts of New England. He reminded his readers, most of them city-dwellers, of the rugged individualism of their forebears, which they missed—or thought they did—in modern civilization. With superb craftsmanship and strongly accented conversational diction, he played upon this sentiment until his admirers were ready to name him poet laureate and applauded when John F. Kennedy invited him to read one of his poems at the 1960 presidential inauguration. When an official biographer revealed Frost's deliberate life-long creation of an illusion he knew was an illusion, it caused a storm of protest. But taste can be nurtured by illusion.

Whereas Frost blandly ignored the hard facts of American life, Carl Sandburg was of, by, and for the common wage-earner, sincerely and undeviatingly. More versatile than Frost, he wrote one of the great biographies of Lincoln, numerous short stories for children, a vibrant novel (*Remembrance Rock*), a memoir of the photographer Edward Steichen, his brother-in-law, and other prose. His poetry ranges from exquisite impressionistic pieces—"Cool Tombs," "Grass," "Nocturne on a Deserted Brickyard"—to brutally realistic verse—"To a Contemporary Bunk Shooter," "I Am the People, the Mob."

Both poets drew large audiences to their numerous stage appearances and strengthened the taste for readings that had broadened Lindsay's fame. Frost, who was given to commenting on critics of his poetry, was listened to almost with reverence. Sandburg, more of an entertainer, sang some of his poems to his own guitar accompaniment, to the delight of audiences. Both these poets, in their quite different ways, broadened and strengthened the taste for not just the New Poetry but for poetry itself, as something to be taken seriously.

Revolution in drama

If poetry made giant steps up the ladder of taste after 1912, drama was close on its heels, in the person of Eugene O'Neill. He "arrived" in 1920 with the production of his first full-length play, *Beyond the Horizon,* and for the next fourteen years, other plays of his were constantly being performed in New York and other major cities. The secret of his success as a playwright was twofold: he restored to drama the principles of the ancient Greek tragedies; he also borrowed the newer techniques of Ibsen and Strindberg. Once O'Neill had proved that breaking with the old theatrical conventions was commercially feasible, audiences were no longer satisfied with the star system and the plays they had long been familiar with.

O'Neill was not, however, the only playwright with talent, for the taste he redirected was served during the 1920s by several other serious playwrights—Elmer Rice (*The Adding Machine*), Maxwell Anderson (*What Price Glory?*), and Sidney Howard (*They Knew What They Wanted*). The 1930s saw the rise to fame of William Saroyan, Lillian Hellman, Robert Sherwood, and Clifford Odets. American drama would never again be the same.

Taste for self-satire

Besides introducing the antiwar novels cited earlier, new talent affected taste in fiction in other ways after 1920. That year saw the publication of *Main Street* by Lewis and the equally sensational *This Side of Paradise* by his fellow Minnesotan, Scott Fitzgerald. The banner year of the decade, though,

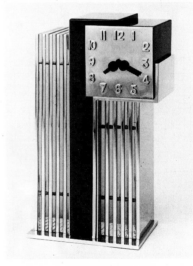

Top: *Art Deco furniture from the Grand Lounge of Radio City Music Hall; New York, N.Y.* Left: *Art Nouveau sculpture of a woman.* Above: *Art Deco clock.*

163

was probably 1925, when Lewis published his most serious novel, *Arrowsmith,* and Fitzgerald *The Great Gatsby,* a classic of the Jazz Age—a term he invented. Also in 1925 were *Manhattan Transfer* by John Dos Passos, Dreiser's masterpiece *An American Tragedy,* Ellen Glasgow's *Barren Ground,* and, on the lighter side, *Gentlemen Prefer Blondes,* by Anita Loos, and *The Private Life of Helen of Troy,* a spoof of the Homeric saga, by Professor John Erskine of Columbia. Fresh talent seemed unlimited, responding to an almost insatiable hunger for good books in the modern mode.

In 1930, Sinclair Lewis won the Nobel Prize for Literature, the first American to be so honored. Though some critics charged Lewis with superficial writing and narrow reliance on caricature, most readers applauded, partly because the Nobel selection committee had at last recognized an American but also because Lewis so effectively pictured the foibles of Americans in that period. The most compelling of Lewis's books was *Babbitt,* which in 1922 appealed to the postwar generation, disillusioned, sophisticated, and ready for his merciless exposure of urban emptiness. Zenith as he described it became the imaginary prototype of brash midwestern cities on the make, and "Babbitt" instantly entered the national vocabulary as a synonym for any narrow-minded, pompously self-satisfied, upwardly mobile, morally ambiguous American plagued by no sense that his material possessions are not the ultimate of civilization. The 1920s were among the most interesting of decades. The superficiality of its Babbitts was one of its conspicuous elements; another was the taste for self-satire.

Magazines of the twenties

That same taste accounts for the

popularity of H. L. Mencken, iconoclastic Baltimore editor whose green-bound *American Mercury* was "must" reading every month, from 1924 until 1933, for supersophisticated American readers. Mencken's series of *Prejudices* challenged traditional complacency and sanctimoniousness, and stimulated the growth of modern secularism. But *The American Mercury,* influential as it was, fell far short of the established weeklies in circulation, especially *Collier's,* the *Saturday Evening Post* (allegedly founded by Ben Franklin), and *Literary Digest.* All three were challenged in the 1920s, however, by new weeklies that in time superseded them and are still high in popular taste. *Time,* launched in 1923, caught on quickly with its comprehensive survey of current events edited with a flippancy that was often outrageous. The *New Yorker,* first issued in 1925, was "not for the old lady in Dubuque," as its founder, Harold Ross, liked to remark. Yet it steadily gained readers everywhere, even in Dubuque, with its crisp, whimsical style, its "The Talk of the Town" written chiefly by E. B. White, and its stories and articles by such writers as Alexander Woollcott, James Thurber, and Clifton Fadiman, not to mention the glory of its cartoons by Peter Arno and Charles Addams. Two humor magazines, *Life* and *Judge,* folded in the late 1930s, unable to meet the new standards set by the *New Yorker.*

Harper's Weekly died in 1916 after six influential decades and was absorbed by the *Independent,* but that honored old weekly, even after merging with the *Outlook,* survived only until 1935. *Youth's Companion,* which for some years had had the largest circulation of any magazine, gave up in 1929. Taste had simply changed. *The Nation,* founded in 1865 and now the oldest weekly in the country, survived with vigorous editing and good writing, even after the birth in 1914 of the *New Republic,* a strong competitor in the political arena. As for monthlies, the *Century* expired in 1930; the *North American Review* in 1939, after 124 years; and *Scribner's* also in 1939, leaving only *Harper's Monthly* and the *Atlantic* to carry on the old literary tradition. Readers with a taste for solid literary matter had presumably declined in number.

Taste for good reviewing, perhaps complementing the taste for new kinds of literature after the world war, encouraged the founding in 1924 of the *Saturday Review of Literature,* for long the most respected of all reviewing media. Urban newspapers also instituted book review sections. Publishing itself profited by the better reviewing and by the expansion of reading taste that it encouraged, enough so to prompt the organizing of two book clubs that have flourished ever since—the Book-of-the-Month Club in 1926 and the Literary Guild in 1927.

Great audiences

In the first issue of *Poetry Magazine,* in 1912, Harriet Monroe quoted a line from Walt Whitman, "To have great poets there must be great audiences too." With her magazine, Miss Monroe probably did more than anyone else to create a great audience for modern poetry. But not every art form had the benefit of a Harriet Monroe to work hard and long to promote a taste for its newer forms. The talent had to exist first, of course, before the taste in a particular art form could develop, although in some cases, as in drama, that taste could be formed, or redirected, by some single exceptionally gifted artist. But there were numerous other factors influencing the course the various art forms took—the disillusionment after a war that had settled nothing, a population increasingly more complex in ethnic background, boredom with conventions too long established, or simply an advance in sophistication or tolerance.

Consider music and its new form, jazz. Developing out of spontaneous work songs, dance tunes, and spirituals of black slaves and their free descendants, this genuinely indigenous music was unrelated to the traditional music of Europe in its harmony, rhythm, and melodic structure. Because most white musicians considered it too primitive to merit serious attention, jazz was left to develop on its own until, by the 1890s, it could produce its own classics—the ragtime piano works of Scott Joplin, for example. Joplin, a black pianist, had mastered the keyboard while playing in St. Louis saloons and bordellos, virtually the only institutions that would welcome such unorthodox music and would pay for it. Word got around, however, that it had qualities for entertainment that no ordinary music could offer, and white or mixed bands, mostly in New Orleans and later in Chicago, began competing for the favor of local pleasure-seekers. An audience for jazz existed, and grew.

Despite Joplin's personal reputation as composer and performer, prejudice against black musicians and ragtime itself persisted among the genteel. Not until January 16, 1938, when Benny Goodman led a racially mixed orchestra in a jazz concert at Carnegie Hall, did a cultivated audience accept jazz on its own merits. Goodman, known as the King of Swing, was one of the major figures of the Big Band era, which was at its apogee in popular taste just then. It faded during the new war and was replaced by bebop, played by smaller bands to

Opposite top: *The Grand Foyer of Radio City Music Hall; New York, N.Y.; 1932. Over the Grand Stairway is Ezra Winter's mural,* Author of Life. Opposite bottom: *Auditorium, Radio City Music Hall. In the pit is the Radio City Music Hall Symphony Orchestra.*

til 1903, and thereafter was on the road almost continuously until 1909. It shared the immense popularity of the always-successful crook melodrama. Late in the nineteenth century, the Kiralfy Brothers presented one dance production after another, some classical, others with original plots and scores. Their *Nero, or the Fall of Rome* had a cast of over two thousand that danced on a Staten Island stage three hundred feet wide and eighty feet deep.

Such theatrical spectacles were sometimes billed as ballets, but they had little of the refined body movements associated with classical ballet. That dance form had had a long history in Europe, especially in Czarist Russia and France, and became familiar to American audiences in the 1920s when Russian ballet troupes, refugees from the Russian Revolution, toured the United States regularly. The high-water mark was set in 1933 when the Ballet Russe de Monte Carlo gave an extended series of performances in New York. Earlier, however, individual Russian ballerinas had displayed their art on American stages; in 1910, the immortal Pavlova danced at the Metropolitan Opera House.

Once introduced, classical ballet became a fixture in the United States as one of the most exacting of all art forms, and taste for it has steadily grown. But dance took on a new dimension in the 1930s with the emergence of a distinctly American ballet. Purists often disparage the use of the word *ballet* to describe such productions, as though the word were synonymous with the *danse d'école*—dance according to particular rules that may not be broken—but the word is simply derived from the Latin for "dance." In America, much as classical ballet came to be admired, there was rebellion against what the theater executive

much smaller audiences.

Let there be dance

As early as 1922, a ballet with a jazz base was successfully produced in New York. It was titled *Krazy Kat,* from a popular comic strip, and, to avoid any possible misunderstanding, was subtitled "A Jazz Pantomime."

There had been an audience for dance for a long time—since 1767, in fact, when, on command of the royal governor, John Street Theatre in New York presented

Harlequin's Varieties to entertain visiting Indians from South Carolina. At frequent intervals thereafter, dance routines enlivened plays and concerts, and celebrated foreign dancers starred in full-length classical ballets or gave solo performances—some of them risqué like the notorious Spider Dance of Lola Montez in the 1850s. One notable dance production, *The Black Crook,* opened at Niblo's Gardens in New York on September 12, 1866, ran for 475 nights, had numerous revivals un-

Top: The Seiners, *by Rockwell Kent; 1910–13.* Above left: Host, *by Elie Nadelman; ca. 1917.* Above right: The Last Waltz, *by Jack Levine; 1962.*

Lincoln Kirstein called the "spectral blackmail" of a worn repertory formula and also against the often-unnatural steps and gestures of classical ballet convention.

The rebellion was limited but evident before 1930, as gifted choreographers developed original routines and as no less gifted dancers learned to express emotions through body movements unauthorized by *danse d'école*. In 1937, the Ballet Theatre was founded, and from the time of its first production the next year, it was the acknowledged leader in developing a native ballet. It presented established foreign ballets like *Les Sylphides* but also such original works as *The Great American Goof*, for which William Saroyan wrote the story. Others with familiar American themes included *Billy the Kid, Filling Station,* and *Frankie and Johnny*. One new element hardly known to classical ballet was humor, especially as developed by Agnes de Mille, one of the greatest native choreographers.

With Aaron Copland's *Rodeo*, in 1942, American ballet became firmly established as an art form, indigenous and fully approved as tasteful. Its audience multiplied, however, when its routines were adapted for musicals, including *Oklahoma*, in 1943. Since that time, no musical has much chance of success if it does not include elements of modern ballet, whether or not the enthusiastic audiences ever realize its lineage from Russian tradition. Parent and rebellious offspring are both high in contemporary taste and likely to remain so. Classical ballet appeals to tens of thousands; modern ballet to millions.

Revolution in music

The decision to finance radio by advertising rather than from public funds or user fees as in other countries made broadcasting a powerful force in directing and shaping taste. For years the Ford Motor Company paid for Sunday afternoon live broadcasts of symphony orchestras, greatly expanding the audience for classical music. For even more years, Saturdays brought operas into living rooms direct from the stage of the Metropolitan Opera House, sponsored by Texaco and making Milton Cross a household name for his lucid and enthusiastic plot summaries. Here was culture for the millions, and the effect on taste was immeasurable.

Recordings steadily improved in quality, along with turntables, amplifiers, and speakers, as demand increased. In the 1950s, sales shot upward with the introduction of long-playing records, unbreakable and weighing less than the "78s." Another recent advance is the stereophonic sound track, replacing the older monaural reproduction of sound.

No classical recording ever approached the tremendous sale of the latest hit by a popular singer, but over a span of years, the best-loved classical music sold steadily, immune from the rapid rise and fall of quondam mass appeal. By 1940, recorded music was big business, serving a vast home audience. Unlike some other areas in the culture, choice was multiplied, from the most banal and ephemeral of popular tunes to the most exalted and durable of the classics.

Most conductors and performers of symphonic music and opera were still foreign by birth or training or both. For the foreign-born, the lure was the same as it had been for most immigrants from the very beginning—the promise of unlimited opportunity and wealth. But during the fifteen years before the Second World War, a new motive became dominant—escape from the worsening political conditions in Europe. The consequent exodus of more than twenty thousand of Europe's best scientists and artists in every field enriched the American population and helped make this nation preeminent in technology and the arts.

Jacques Barzun, who was born in France, singled out migrating musicians in his *Music in American Life* (1956) and argued convincingly that the infusion of so much talent in the area of music produced a veritable revolution in culture. It was a happy coincidence that radio broadcasting developed in the same period, providing a wide dispersion of music that would have been impossible earlier.

The most famous conductor of this time was Arturo Toscanini. From 1908 to 1914, he commuted regularly from Italy to conduct at the Metropolitan Opera House, and from 1926 to 1936, he led the New York Philharmonic Orchestra. His physical vigor, his shouting at rehearsals and his broken batons, and his capacity for magnetizing audiences made him a legendary figure. After he settled permanently in America to conduct the newly formed NBC orchestra, a post he held from 1937 to 1954, he became so popular that his open defiance of Mussolini and Hitler influenced American opinion against those dictators. His first appearance on television in March, 1948, marked the apogee of that unprecedented popularity.

Other conductors who became citizens and subsequently helped expand the taste for classical music included Serge Koussevitsky in Boston, Pierre Monteux in San Francisco, George Szell in Cleveland, Dimitri Mitropoulos in Minneapolis, and Eugene Ormandy in Philadelphia. As these names suggest, they were from numerous countries in Europe. Perhaps of greater significance was the migration of some of Europe's best

composers. In the past, a few composers had visited the United States, Dvorak and Delius among them, and had written music with American themes. But now for the first time they came to stay—Igor Stravinsky, Arnold Schoenberg, Paul Hindemith. Also for the first time, native-born conductors, artists, and composers were given a fair chance to compete with imported talent and to receive the applause they deserved. Rosa Ponselle, Lawrence Tibbett, John Charles Thomas, Yehudi Menuhin, Albert Spalding, Charles Ives, Vergil Thomson, Aaron Copland, and others like them profited, along with the general public, by the growing taste for good music. Conservatories and music departments on campuses everywhere grew in size and reputation, identifying and training fresh talent, and further increasing the audience for serious music.

Cultural lag in music

Acceptance of the unfamiliar, however, was still rather limited. Dimitri Mitropoulos, in his dozen years with the Minneapolis Symphony, almost invariably included on the Friday night programs

works never heard before, many of them by American composers. The season-ticket holders grew accustomed to the practice and applauded with varying degrees of enthusiasm; but many of these "world premieres" were also final performances. The introduction of lesser-known works by foreign composers who were already established met with greater success, and the symphonic repertory grew and changed. Hackneyed old compositions were dropped, to be replaced by works of "moderns," meaning composers of the late nineteenth century—Mahler, Moussorgsky, Borodin, Debussy —and even a few who were still living—Ravel, Richard Strauss, Elgar, Sibelius, Franck. The old distaste for Wagner resurfaced during the First World War but gradually declined, even though people knew that Hitler was using Wagnerian music to glorify his Master Race. Romanticism in music still dominated American taste. Dissonance was resisted, as were the strange harmonics and experimental accents of Stravinsky and Schoenberg.

American acceptance of the music of Sibelius is another example

of how taste can be directed by an influential supporter of that taste. As early as 1897, the Finnish government had awarded Sibelius a life-time subsidy, and by 1924, he had completed his seven symphonies and most of his tone poems and other works. The few Americans who knew of him regarded him patronizingly as a composer of what they considered potboilers, *Valse Triste* and *Finlandia.* Then Olin Downes, music critic for the New York *Times,* mounted his long and eventually successful campaign to establish the Finnish master in American taste, and concert programs began to include his Second Symphony and such shorter works as *The Swan of Tuonela.* Sibelius may not have been, as Downes insisted he was, "the greatest symphonist of the first half of the twentieth century," but by 1957, when he died at the age of ninety-two, he was as highly regarded in America as any other recent composer.

Music by American composers, though improving in excellence, was still generally neglected. Native composers of opera were particularly at a disadvantage. One native opera successfully produced

Building styles in New York City. Opposite: *Neo-Gothic.* Left: *An example of Art Deco.*

prior to the Second World War was George Gershwin's *Porgy and Bess,* but despite its Broadway run in 1935, it failed to become part of the standard operatic repertory. Two reasons may be offered: it is a story of Negro life in a slum area of Charleston—a plot that did not appeal to a generation looking for escape—and its music is closer to the jazz idiom than to the kind of music that had established the operas of Puccini, Verdi, and company in the favor of opera-lovers.

Gershwin was far more successful with musicals, including *Lady Be Good!* in 1924 and *Of Thee I Sing* in 1931, and with such showpiece compositions as *Rhapsody in Blue* and *An American in Paris,* with its taxi horns and other reminders of the French capital. Musicals, for better or worse, appealed to a much broader taste than grand opera. They were easy to understand, they included songs in the familiar idiom, and they could readily be staged by amateur groups in small towns across the nation, as grand opera could not. Combining the best features of the older revues and operettas, the musical has had, since the First World War, as high a place in gen-

eral taste as any other art form.

Calm after the storm

The tempest of protest at the 69th Regiment Armory in 1913 cleared the air for painters of the generation following the Ashcan School. That group's interest in social realism was continued by younger artists, including Ben Shahn, Jack Levine, and George Grosz. Shahn, a native of Lithuania, created a stir with a series of twenty-three paintings about the Sacco-Vanzetti trial and execution in 1927—a *cause célèbre* that prompted numerous poems, plays, short stories, and novels. Grosz was famous for his vitriolic cartoons about corruption in his native Germany. After he moved to New York as an art teacher, in 1933, he turned to milder subjects until the Second World War, when he felt impelled to paint a series symbolic of war-ravaged figures. Levine, born in Boston in 1915, also attacked corruption with a bitter, satirical style. *Gangster Funeral* is typical: the individuals portrayed are withered and distorted yet glittering.

Social realism, abhorrent to cultivated taste before the First World War, became an especially accept-

able subject during the depression years. Another accepted subject was regionalism, a descendant of nineteenth-century genre painting but with more social significance in the hands of Grant Wood, Thomas Hart Benton, and Charles Burchfield. Folk art had its most famous practitioner in Grandma Moses, whose primitive scenes delighted many citizens. There were also artists who studied in France and brought home cubism and surrealism. These styles were later fused into the "new abstraction" by Jackson Pollock who, from 1947 to 1949, adopted the drip technique —dropping fluid paint onto a canvas to produce unusual effects.

New styles and techniques no longer caused verbal tempests. By the 1930s, gallery visitors admired what appealed to their individual tastes and glanced tolerantly at what did not. Most were willing to be shown why they should appreciate paintings they could not understand and learned that nonrepresentational art was in good repute among the initiated. Archibald MacLeish had announced in 1924, in his "Ars Poetica,"

A poem should not mean
But be.

This attitude had always been accepted for most music, despite many efforts to explain particular works, and now it was being applied to paintings that satisfied a deeply felt aesthetic need but could not be explained in words.

Some of the new sculpture was equally resistant to verbal interpretation yet had a strong appeal to taste. Much of it, however, had a meaning, easy to understand, like the immense relief portraits of four presidents that Gutzon Borglum carved out of the solid rock of Mt. Rushmore in 1927. Other sculptors introduced untraditional materials for this three-dimensional art, notably different kinds of metal.

Art Deco

In architecture, furniture design, and the decorative arts, taste followed a curious detour into what came to be known as Art Deco. Its nineteenth-century progenitor was Art Nouveau, which won few American converts other than

Louis Tiffany, because taste still favored styles with historical precedents. Like Art Nouveau, the newer Art Deco repudiated historicism and was therefore eagerly welcomed by Americans in their postwar mood of rejecting the past.

Art Deco got its name belatedly, from the 1925 Exposition Internationale des Arts Décoratifs in Paris. But its typical forms were already very much part of the American scene by 1920. Faddish at first, they held on well into the 1930s, long enough to constitute a distinct period in taste.

Louis Sullivan had drawn on Art Nouveau in developing his philosophy for the decoration of office buildings he designed during the 1880s and 1890s. By the early 1920s, younger members of the "Progressive School" of architects were following his lead in surface decoration and, because by then they were nearing their victory over the Beaux-Arts tradition, most new skyscrapers and other large buildings were given the new

decorative treatment. It differed in the basic motifs that were used. Instead of floral patterns or classical details, the age of industry and electricity provided the themes. Each architect was free to choose his own motifs, and no two are exactly alike. Some designers carried their individualism to extremes: the handsome American Radiator Building on 40th Street, near the New York Public Library, has black brick and gold terra-cotta ornamentation suggesting a steam-heat radiator. A better example of Art Deco is the Barclay-Vesey Building of the New York Telephone Company, completed in 1926. Increasingly, motifs taken from nature lost ground to angular lines and curves imitative of machine-age artifacts or to primitive shapes that were borrowed from such remote civilizations as Incan, African, and Polynesian. The greatest concentration of Art Deco architecture is along Central Park West in Manhattan, which was built up in the 1920s, but the most conspicuous single monument to

the style is the Chrysler Building, completed in 1930 and briefly the world's tallest. Before the label "Art Deco" was available, all such architecture was called "modernistic," "modernist," or just plain "modern."

The lingering notion that skyscrapers should resemble Gothic cathedrals produced some oddities. Most conspicuous were the towers. The frankly Gothic topping of the 1913 Woolworth Building yielded to machine-inspired designs, often quite elaborate and sometimes almost a parody of historical Gothic. The top of the RCA Victor (now General Electric) Building in New York, viewed from blocks away, might be taken to be pure Gothic, but the finials and tracery prove on closer inspegion to be the intricate products of engineering drawing. The Chrysler Building has actual gargoyles, but instead of imitating mythological creatures, they are of metal and resemble heads of monstrous birdlike creatures from science fiction. Street entrances also evoked memories of cathedrals—massive, arched, inspiring awe, but with ornament derived from geometry, or aboriginal cultures, or pure fantasy. Buttresses can be found on some buildings of the 1930s and 1940s, including the Chanin and National Title Guarantee; but they are decorative only, and do not function as supports.

New York has so many Art Deco buildings, and so many of them that are famous—the Empire State Building, the Waldorf-Astoria, the Barbizon-Plaza, Radio City Music Hall, the Horn & Hardart automated restaurants—that it would be easy to think of Art Deco as the essential New York style. Other cities, of course, have their own examples, but nowhere else are they so concentrated, perhaps because business expanded in New York rapidly after 1920,

needed more space, and adopted Art Deco as the style just then considered most suitable and elegant. In the process, the city lost large numbers of older buildings whose sites were too valuable to warrant their preservation. Fifth Avenue above 34th Street, famous at the turn of the century for its mansions, was by 1940 almost solidly converted into a commercial street, left with only a few private homes and such other relics as the Public Library, St. Thomas and Fifth Avenue Presbyterian churches, the University Club, and the Plaza Hotel.

Countering the main current

Strong as the taste for Art Deco was, it did not preempt every other style. Gothic continued to be favored for new churches everywhere. New York's Riverside Church, built in the 1930s with modern engineering methods, is only the most famous example. Gothic was also preferred for many new college buildings. Yale and Princeton universities acquired libraries resembling old colleges at Oxford and Cambridge, and George F. Baker donated a medieval law quadrangle to the University of Michigan—only to be criticized for not giving it to one of the Ivy League institutions. James Buchanan Duke built an entire Gothic campus for Trinity College in Durham, North Carolina, which the grateful trustees renamed Duke University.

Ecclesiastic and academic taste for Gothic was a conspicuous eddy, countering the main current of Art Deco. As might have been expected, any style that so strongly repudiated historic antecedents called for interiors equally untraditional. Paul Frankel and other gifted designers set to work creating furniture with a vertical emphasis. Angular and often boxlike, it gave the impression, no

doubt intentional, that an office was no place for employees or visitors to relax. The 1920s were a decade of almost frenetic business activity, well reported by John Dos Passos in *Manhattan Transfer;* the point was underscored by no less a pundit than Calvin Coolidge in one of his most memorable statements: "The business of America is business." Underfurnished offices, housing men and women with no thought but to keep the economic wheels of the nation turning faster and faster, were symbolic of the decade and would be until the bubble burst in 1929 and the Great Depression forced everyone to slow down—and perhaps even to relax in more comfortable chairs!

Minimal furniture and furnishings were advocated by Frank Lloyd Wright, for quite different reasons, for the many homes with minimal space. It was one thing for a company president to sit in the firm's largest office and confer with a client sitting in the only other chair and something quite different for a family to enjoy the illusion of spaciousness in a small house. To help achieve this effect, Wright eliminated the wall between living and dining areas and located pieces of furniture along the walls where they would not impede movement. Like the Art Deco designers, he used as sources the Inca and other Indian civilizations from south of the Mexican border, but he used them to enhance interior warmth and the horizontal effect.

Wright designed modern factories for American industry, an earthquake-proof hotel for Japan, and the Guggenheim Museum for New York's Fifth Avenue, but his more enduring interest was in livable modern dwellings, less for wealthy clients than for families with modest incomes. In 1932, that interest was evident in an exhibition mounted at the Museum of

Living room, Pope-Leighey House, designed by Frank Lloyd Wright; originally in Falls Church, Va., now at Woodlawn plantation, Mount Vernon, Va.; 1939–40.

Modern Art to popularize modern architecture. Response was limited, for most of the house plans and elevations displayed were closer to the "International Style" currently popular in Europe than to the colonial adaptations favored for American homes, and the museum was accused of trying to foist foreign architecture on the United States. What the museum directors had hoped was that the exhibit would help Americans realize that other countries, despite the worldwide depression, were moving ahead to new concepts while American architecture was standing still or was actually in a state of relapse. But taste for the familiar was too strong. Neither the museum nor Wright had much effect on the thinking of homebuilders.

A follow-up Museum of Modern Art exhibition a few years later showed little more progress. Taste seemed to be paralyzed not only in the housing field but for every kind of building, and especially for new forms needed for the changing culture. Despite increasing air travel, the airport in Washington, D.C., was the only one designed with serious attention to the handling of passengers and freight, the parking of travelers' cars, or even the planes themselves. Nor were there effective designs for high-rise hotels and apartment houses, or for filling stations. It was almost as if Art Deco, as applied to architecture, so preempted other building styles that it exhausted the national will to replace it with something better suited to emerging needs.

Modern palaces

The very rich, meanwhile, had their own ideas and the money to implement them. But the mansions they erected between the world wars inspired far less emulation at lower economic levels than did the

French chateaux and baroque palaces built a generation earlier by the Vanderbilts and their rivals for social eminence. In 1919, on an isolated knoll overlooking the Pacific, William Randolph Hearst began construction of a vast Hispano-Moresque complex, La Casa Grande, dominated by twin towers 137 feet tall. To make sure it would last, he used concrete throughout. Instead of providing numerous bedrooms in the main house, he built three relatively small guesthouses descending the hillside, with a total of forty-six rooms. Two large swimming pools, one in the open and the other enclosed, depend on water piped from springs on higher land five miles away.

Hearst spent unrecorded millions on La Casa Grande, furnishing it with art treasures carefully selected in Europe and shipped thousands of sea miles for unloading at the small port of San Simeon at the foot of the estate. He never called his mansion a castle, but the public did, and so does the State of California, which gained it by donation in 1958 and opens it to several thousand awed visitors each week, who may choose any one of four different guided tours. The awe begins as the buses start up the winding four-mile drive and becomes vocal at glimpses of elephants and zebras and assorted other species from far countries that roam the 240,000-acre grounds. Members of the Hearst family sometimes stay at out-of-the-way rooms in La Casa Grande, just as Vanderbilts sometimes occupy remote suites at the Breakers in Newport.

What the paying guests see, whichever tour they select, is the modern epitome of the old Spanish style that missionaries introduced in the early eighteenth century and that is still very much in evidence in California and neighboring states. To a lesser extent, the same taste for Spanish baroque has survived also in Florida, where its greatest development, like that of the state itself, has been in the twentieth century. There, however, other styles have been followed by builders from the North and East, and for the most part the Spanish is recent. Yet much of it has already been demolished, so rapid has growth been and so great the need, in the tourist belt, for huge hotels and condominiums.

In Sarasota, a city laid out with ample dimensions, buildings have had a better chance to celebrate their fiftieth birthdays than along the crowded Gold Coast from Fort Lauderdale to Miami, and the Ringling Estate, conveniently close to the circus winter quarters, is an impressive showplace. It has no such spacious acreage as the Hearst Castle and is smaller in scale, but its treasures, climaxed by a replica of Michelangelo's *David* at the far end of the garden, reflect the same impulse to ransack Europe.

In Palm Beach, prime winter playground of the very rich, the Spanish style is so far quite safe from the ambitious plans of developers. Flagler's Poinciana Hotel still opens its massive Spanish doors to wayfarers with money enough to stay there, and casual tourists can, if they are lucky, catch brief glimpses of private mansions bearing Spanish names if not consistently Spanish decor. Joshua Cosden's Playa Riente sports a ballroom cantilevered over the water, and the Stotesbury Estate, El Mirasol, includes a private zoo. The most awesome palace in Palm Beach is Mar-a-Lago, built between 1923 and 1927. It has its own private golf course and a million-dollar inlaid marble dining table.

Population growth, obviously, increases the value of land, for ev-

Opposite top: *Mar-a-Lago, Palm Beach, Fla.; 1923–27. Spanish Colonial Revival.* Opposite bottom: *Corner of living room, Mar-a-Lago.* Top *and* above: *Fashion sketches from* The Delineator; *1920. These pictures appeared under the title "Fashion Divides Her Attention Between Side Attractions and New Tunics."*

ery added home reduces the nation's undeveloped acreage. When the rich build mansions, most of them like to surround them with private domains, whether or not they ever make use of them. This desire is a simple carry-over from Europe, where the deer parks and vast hunting preserves of the landed aristocracy are perquisites of their status. But some Americans, as they garnered dollars enough to erect palaces, developed their grounds for the general benefit. William R. Coe, an insurance magnate, erected a huge Tudor mansion on Long Island and created, on its 409-acre grounds, what he dubbed a Planting Fields Arboretum designed to educate the public in the planting of trees and shrubs. He had learned how, himself, as a boy in his native England. Mansion and arboretum were donated to the State of New York in 1949 and today comprise one of the great public showplaces near New York City.

The invisible rich

One major difference between the late nineteenth century and recent decades is that the architectural taste of the wealthy no longer rubs off on the less affluent. In the last century, the popular Fifth Avenue version of a Loire chateau was highly visible and could hardly fail to inspire imitation, just as its owner's wardrobe and behavior were emulated by the public. But the love of outward show gave way in a generation to a desire for anonymity, and the rich increasingly opted to live in apartments while in town and to spend the rest of the time in "second" homes well hidden from public view. The Rockefeller summer houses at Seal Harbor on Maine's Mt. Desert Island are, like many others, so skillfully located that only by trespassing could they be seen by ordinary citizens. Elsie De Wolfe,

America's first professional interior decorator, insisted that taste filters down from the wealthiest to people at lower economic levels, but by the 1920s, the less affluent didn't always know what the wealthy were up to.

Of course, multimillionaires after 1920 might still have preferred their urban mansions had real estate taxes remained steady, maintenance costs not climbed at an accelerating rate, and the supply of cheap domestic help not dwindled. Increasingly, these mansions were sold to schools and other institutions exempt from taxation, or were torn down and replaced by stores and office buildings. Mansions in less crowded cities, or in the open country, suffered these indignities at a slower rate. Those that survived intact and are now open to public inspection are highly instructive as monuments to past taste—an instruction not available to middle-class builders of the time when they were new.

Fresh influences

Partly because they were denied the guidance of the rich, Americans were influenced in other ways. In the 1870s and 1880s, there had been some interest in Heinrich Schliemann's archeological discoveries in Greece and Turkey—at ancient Troy and Mycenae in particular. But that interest could not compare with the excitement caused in October, 1922, by the opening of King Tutankhamen's tomb in the Nile valley, with its treasures intact. The beauty of the objects photographed for newspapers prompted an instant enthusiasm for jewelry and furnishings in ancient Egyptian style: bracelets in the shape of coiled adders; ashtrays resembling miniature chariots; gleaming porcelain goddesses holding large black candlesticks, usually wired for small electric bulbs. If cost was

no consideration, a fireplace could be remade to look like the entrance to the Temple of Luxor.

Fascination with "King Tut" treasures has never died, as the throngs viewing them on tours in the 1970s emphatically indicate. In the 1920s, Egyptian influence on style was great but not of long duration; for it was the nature of taste just then to approve fresh enthusiasms. One popular musical, *Kismet,* encouraged the hanging of room draperies in Middle East styles. The Fu Manchu stories by Sax Rohmer revived interest in Chinese forms, including red-lacquered coffee tables and chests of drawers set on silver feet. Even more influential was *The Sheik,* a 1921 silent film starring Rudolph Valentino, first of the screen's "great lovers." Bedrooms decorated to resemble desert tents were among its benefactions.

No single concept

In the 1920s, anything unusual and unrelated to historical styles was acceptable in current taste and was related to, if not part of, the Art Deco Movement, which was too broad to be confined to any single concept. In this respect, it can be compared to the Victorian era, which also accommodated great diversity. The two differed chiefly in the source of inspiration. Victorians looked for guidance to authors of books, whether English —William Morris, Charles Eastlake—or American—A. J. Downing, A. J. Davis. Furthermore, most Victorian styles echoed the European past, while Americans in the 1920s looked for inspiration to exotic countries and to technology.

Many of the effects of Art Deco could be achieved in the home without tools but with the liberal use of glue and thumbtacks. Le Page's Craft League in Gloucester, Massachusetts, advertised in 1925 a *Craft Book,* for ten cents, illustrated in color and with "complete directions, simple and easy to follow," for making more than a hundred articles that were "unique, dainty, practical and useful." It was folk art revived, with emphasis on glue.

Magazines offering decorating advice to homemakers changed their approach or lost subscribers. As late as 1915, rooms were still being pictured in historic styles, but after 1920, the stress was on the "modern." Instead of naming the owners of the houses, moreover, these articles named their decorators. Many Americans, whatever the direction of their individual taste, seemed to feel the need of expert advice. Elsie De Wolfe was no longer alone; interior decorating had become an established profession.

For people unable to pay the going fees for professional advice, magazines such as *House and Garden* were indispensable. In its pages could be found inspiration for rooms done in single colors—black and silver were favorites—furnished with just the right combination of details to create a novel effect. Better electrical wiring, with numerous wall and floor outlets, made floor lamps practical and popular. In keeping with Art Deco's emphasis on geometric shapes, their shades were as likely to be square or rectangular as round. Dining-room tables underwent the same change, and so did much tableware. Plates and cups acquired flat sides and square corners, in solid colors or with angular decoration.

Taste for Art Deco extended to virtually every object in everyday use, and to other objects with no discernible use whatsoever. It was particularly adaptable to new elements in the culture, such as automobiles and radios and moving pictures, which had no historical precedents to fall back on. The au-

tomobiles most admired—Packard, Pierce-Arrow, Cadillac—all had conspicuous nonfunctional decorations on hoods and hubcaps, and on dashboards. Ocean liners sporting Art Deco lounges and dining salons were favored for the crossing to Europe. Jewelry, whatever its cost, was strong on Art Deco, especially pieces devised by Louis Cartier—segmented brooches and necklaces giving the illusion of movement, and two timepieces he invented, the wristwatch and the "mystery clock," with its hands apparently unconnected to any mechanism. Another innovation, the cigarette lighter, was a natural for Art Deco. Even umbrellas and footwear took on angular shapes. So ubiquitous was Art Deco that it might be regarded not merely as a form of taste but as a way of life, roughly spanning the years from 1920 to 1935.

Death by plastic

Art Deco is today remote enough in time to warrant a revival. It is already popular with collectors, and it has been featured at museum exhibitions. One major display at the Minneapolis Institute of Art in 1971 demonstrated forcibly the extent of its influence on American life in its heyday. The categories listed in the official catalog suggest that not much in American life was untouched by Art Deco:

> Furniture
> Silver
> Stone/wood/metal/enamels
>   (clocks, lamps, boxes,
>   cigarette lighters,
>   compacts, medallions)
> Paintings and drawings
> Books and bindings
> Posters
> Costumes
> Textiles (especially carpets
>   and rugs)
> Architecture and interior design
> Plastics

That last word is one clue to the decline of Art Deco and its eventual death. Plastics, a product of chemistry, date from the discovery of celluloid in 1869, but only after 1909, when Bakelite was developed, did synthetic materials begin to attract much attention. By the late 1920s, firms in the plastic business were mass-producing inexpensive copies of Art Deco objects, as they still do on a large scale for the souvenir trade. Genuine Art Deco varied in costliness but was never as cheap as the plastic copies. It also always showed a degree of individual craftsmanship, if not always great artistry. Even the homely objects put together with glue showed loving care. Factory mass-production was its antithesis, and there was no defense against multiple identical reproduction. The end result was the triumph of kitsch, which by definition is the total negation of taste.

The Great Depression also contributed to the decline of Art Deco. Within weeks after the stock exchange panic of October 24, 1929, 30 billion dollars of paper wealth evaporated as investors sold shares or were unable to cover their purchases made on margin. The massive postwar prosperity ended abruptly, and consumer buying, formerly a flood, became a mere trickle. Recovery, moreover, was slower than it had been for any previous economic slump. Breadlines grew steadily longer, and Hoovervilles sprang up on wasteland near every major city as the number of unemployed workers climbed to 16 million.

Hardest hit of all were the people in the arts and the craftsmen, whose works almost nobody could now afford. Their one salvation was the Works Projects Administration, which supported artists, actors, and writers over the protests of hidebound conservatives, who condemned all art as a luxury and suspected the WPA of subverting national ideals. It was quite all right, however, to buy an expensive automobile. One famous advertisement told readers that buying a Packard would keep a man employed for a year. No such logic was applied to anything as useless as painting. The depression was a time of distorted values, but severe as it was, it could not halt the progression of taste.

Streamlining

The period that followed Art Deco might have been predicted—the Streamlined Decade. Beginning shortly after the stock market collapse of 1929, it overlapped Art Deco, as successive periods often do. The depression actually stimulated its advance, for by streamlining trains, ships, automobiles, and airplanes—thereby cutting down on air friction—the costs of operation were reduced at a time when money was scarce. Unlike Art Deco, streamlined shapes were based on sound engineering principles, a significant and welcome advance from the use of engineering design for ornamentation only.

Streamlining, based on both scientific theory and empirical data, served the taste for speed and efficient operation far better than did the angular shapes of Art Deco or, for that matter, than most other forms favored by earlier taste. In the preceding century, there had been only one conspicuous exception—the clipper ship, which was the end-product of decades of observation and testing. As Emerson had pointed out at the time, Yankee shipwrights had obeyed "the law of fluids that prescribes the shape of the boat—keel, rudder, and bows—and, in the finer fluid above, the form and tackle of the sails." Science had made great advances in the century since Emerson's remark, and by the 1930s, its

findings could confidently be applied to more objects than ships. Doing so created new shapes for taste to consider for approval. Americans were ready to grant approval and, with their growing sense of functional beauty, to accept one more Emerson aphorism: "The most perfect form to answer an end, is so far beautiful."

Ships, however, were the first to show the effects. Le Corbusier, the French architect whom progressive American designers were beginning to heed, urged study of ocean liners to learn how to escape the grip of Beaux-Arts historicism. He particularly liked the sharp graceful lines of the *Aquitania,* built in 1914. He did not mention the ornamentation of its interior—a Palladian lounge, a smoking room from the period of Charles II, and suites named for great painters containing reproductions of their most famous works. He may have been amused by the story, no doubt true, that H. E. Huntington, given the Gainsborough suite on one crossing, liked the copy of *The Blue Boy* so much that he bought the original for his art collection in San Marino, California.

Liners built later showed a steady advance in applied laws of fluids, and, with more efficient engines, were able to whittle down the time required for the Atlantic crossing. The *Queen Mary,* launched in 1934, was recognizably streamlined, although one wall of the dance salon displayed a centaur pursuing a naked nymph—typically Art Deco—and the forward cocktail lounge glittered with chrome and had cylindrical bar stools. By 1937, the even more streamlined *Normandie* crossed the ocean in less than four days. The most advanced marine designs, however, were for the Pennsylvania Railroad ferries on Chesapeake Bay and the island-hopping steamers on Puget Sound.

The industrial designers

Until late in the 1930s, art in industry was largely confined, as it had been for centuries, to the so-called minor arts—silverware and table china, textiles, expensive objets d'art. The depression expanded its range. Pressured by manufacturers worried by dwindling sales, designers turned to many other objects, making them more attractive to buyers, and a new profession was the result—industrial designing. Its members most in demand were individuals with broad interests, the kind who would know and appreciate avantgarde work by artists. One artist who exerted a strong influence was Rumanian-born Constantin Brancusi, who modeled his sculptures on fish and birds and seals, all naturally equipped to move easily through air or water. His 1924 marble egg, *The Beginning of the World,* and his *Bird in Space,* in the shape of a single curving wing, awed museum visitors, or mystified them, but for the industrial designers, working with hydrodynamics and aerodynamics—the laws of fluids—they were highly instructive. But Brancusi's one-man show in New York, in 1926, got him into trouble with customs officials, who insisted he should pay duty on *Bird in Space* as raw metal.

Trains changed radically in form—and in speed and cost efficiency. Designed by Raymond Loewy after Brancusi's sculptures, their new streamlined shapes with blunt rounded fronts and tapering rears met with much less air resistance; they were also outfitted with modern interiors that riders were quick to appreciate. There was less interest in streamlining automobiles, perhaps because fuel costs meant more to railroad executives than to private car owners. The 1934 Burlington *Zephyr* was very economical, costing only 31 cents a mile for

its run from Denver to Chicago at a speed of 77.5 miles per hour. Other lines quickly followed the Burlington lead, and travelers welcomed the Union Pacific's *City of Salina* (1934), the Santa Fe's *Super Chief* (1936), the Milwaukee Line's *Hiawatha* (1937), and the *Twentieth Century Limited,* added in 1938, one of the few east of Chicago. But despite the aesthetic appeal of such trains, the timing was wrong, for travel by intercity buses, partially streamlined at best, was already cutting into railroad passenger service, and what has been called "the great American love affair with the automobile" was more fervent than ever. The new streamlined trains were admired, but the desire to be at the wheel of one's own car was even closer to America's heart.

Taste for speed, however, was best served by air travel. Efficient, safe air transport was particularly dependent on aerodynamic principles, and the first crude planes evolved rapidly into machines of streamlined beauty.

Industrial design affected the forms of many other objects in contemporary life. Buckminster Fuller's Dymaxion House, and other innovative forms for dwellings designed to withstand climatic changes and permit new lifestyles, had minimal appeal; taste in domestic architecture was altogether too conservative. But smaller artifacts with no dependence on the laws of fluids ac-

Top left: *Exterior of Robie House, designed by Frank Lloyd Wright; Chicago, Ill.; 1908–10. In Wright's early Prairie style.* Center left: *House on Highland Ave.; Hollywood, Calif.; photograph taken in 1917.* Left: *The Gropius House, designed as his residence by Walter Gropius; Lincoln, Mass.; 1937. Gropius was founder of The Bauhaus in his native Germany.*

quired new beauty and efficiency as the streamlining principle was applied to them: cameras designed by Walter Dorwin Teague, the stoves of Norman Bel Geddes, Loewy's refrigerators, the cradle telephone of Henry Dreyfuss. Outdoor machinery, too—farm implements, power lawn-mowers, outboard motorboats. Streamlining also gave fresh new lines to things as diverse as aquariums, great dams, lamp posts, soft-drink bottles and the bottling plants themselves, vacuum cleaners, cocktail shakers, lunch wagons, fountain pens. The culmination of the Streamlined era was the New York World's Fair of 1939–40. It was, for the industrial designers, their model city.

The best streamlined forms were both exciting and, for people in general, deserving of full approval. But what happened to Art Deco was repeated in streamlining. The style was applied to more and more objects with less and less practical purpose, mass-produced for sale at low prices. What was worse was that the designs were cheapened.

Tubular chairs and shapeless overstuffed sofas labeled "modernistic" were symbolic of depression taste, but at least they served a practical purpose. But the consistent use of bloated, tear-shaped forms for trivia had alienated the taste for all streamlining by the time the Second World War broke out. The war itself had an impact. The sudden need for large numbers of reliable vehicles to transport military personnel gave us the jeep, one of the most useful machines ever invented and virtually indestructible, but totally devoid of streamlined beauty. Nor were the laws of fluids applied to machine guns and other lethal instruments; good industrial design was applied only where it was essential—to fighter aircraft and submarines.

As a result, taste retreated.

The planners

When streamlining was most popular and at its peak in taste, it was seriously proposed that the technology producing it, if applied to all facets of the culture, could create a planned civilization vastly superior to any in history. The term suggested for this new civilization was *technocracy,* meaning rule by technocrats, individuals presumably superior in wisdom and scientific knowledge who could be depended on to determine the most effective life patterns and procedures. But when taste for streamlining declined, so did public faith in technocratic planning.

The attack on Pearl Harbor further reduced such confidence in planning. If America's defense was so vulnerable, despite the millions of dollars spent on the military, how much real hope could there be that planning in other areas would be successful? In time, government planning came to be regarded as a threat to individual freedom, smacking of the "five-year plans" of totalitarian countries that reportedly never worked. Although the erstwhile technocrats were disappointed in government spending, when the war was over they found a ready market for their skills in private industry, where they could continue their efforts to reshape the economy and the American way of life. In one area particularly—the creation of new communities—their skills were in immediate demand.

With the rapid increase in the nation's population, from 100 million in 1920 to 150 million in 1950, the phenomenon of urban sprawl was impossible to check. Very few of the new residential developments displayed any kind of planning except the kind that would reap the quick profits most developers wanted. One exception was

Radburn, in the Borough of Fair Lawn in northern New Jersey. From the start, its designers, Clarence Stein and Henry Wright, admitted that the community was an experiment but confidently predicted that with its completion, in 1931, it would be "a complete town"; it was and still is for about 2,500 residents. Not only housing units but stores, schools, and business firms were carefully located, along with a network of pedestrian and bicycle paths separated from the streets by underpasses and bridges, and generous public space with fields and woods. Unlike George Pullman's employee town in Illinois, it was democratically organized, and unlike A. T. Stewart's Garden City on Long Island, it has resisted takeover by affluent families.

Under the New Deal of Franklin D. Roosevelt's administration, similar planned communities were created with federal money. Greenbelt, in Maryland, not far from the District of Columbia, is the best known. But instead of gaining wide support, the concept never caught on, perhaps because of people's general wariness toward any kind of planning and their preference for the individual initiative. If so, they have paid for their folly, for while subdivision developers gladly adopted some of the basic ideas of the "garden cities," especially the curving streets and odd shapes of lots, they provided few of the other advantages. Their colorful brochures and inflated promises gulled prospective buyers, but the projected parks and playgrounds, tennis courts and community swimming pools, civic centers and pedestrian paths through "forever wild" groves, had a way of being deferred year after year.

Commuter suburbs

The "garden city" concept, in a

word, faded into the single-family-house instant suburb having none of the grace of the older suburbs, which kept growing more expensive and more exclusive. All that sustained the growth of the suburbs was the urge to replace urban living with something that was a bit closer to nature. That urge was great, however. Every year more white-collar workers adjusted to the new life-style that incorporated a daily trip to work in the central city and the same long trip back home in the late afternoon.

As the suburban population grew, a distinct culture developed. The sheer distance from "downtown" deterred most suburbanites from sharing its amenities. The humblest apartment-dweller in Manhattan, for whom country living was an impossible dream, could much more easily attend plays and concerts, or visit museums, than his more successful former neighbor for whom that dream had come true. The result of the mass outward migration was the rise of a dual life-style, urban versus suburban. In the city, the superblock housing developments, some for public housing and some privately sponsored, were the response to the needs of an increased population there. A third way of life persisted in small villages and the truly rural parts of the nation, but with about 90 percent of the total population classified as urban by the time of the Second World War, and with "urban" including both the cities and their dormitory appendages, the contrast between center-city and suburban cultures is more relevant.

Tastes, or rather the range of choices, certainly differed between any Manhattan residential block and Levittown on Long Island or Hartsdale in Westchester County or Upper Montclair in New Jersey. In those and other commuter towns across the nation, living could not but be different, in obvious ways, from life in the crowded city heart. No urbanite in whatever central city could invite friends over for an outdoor steak fry in good weather, or slave over a vegetable garden behind the house, or within minutes drive through open country. Beaches and golf courses were within much easier reach for suburbanites, as was open land for counting species during the annual bird migration. In theory at least, suburban life was a welcome substitute for what had been left behind when the family moved out of the city. The numerical choices were probably about the same, urban and suburban, but they were undeniably different. A demographer, surrounded by charts and statistics, might well have been able to predict a time, not far in the future, when the suburban life-style would be the national norm and suburban standards the basis of national taste.

The radio

Wherever Americans lived, and whatever the differences in their life-styles, technological advances and advertising increasingly set nationwide standards of taste. Whether in the hearts of cities or in the most open country, homes were easier to manage with the new labor-saving appliances. The forms that these appliances took meant less to housewives than their efficiency. Even the most aesthetically attractive stove or toaster or vacuum cleaner lost its sales appeal if it needed frequent repair or gave poor service. On the other hand, if two makes were equally durable and efficient, design could determine which was more often purchased.

In any event, for the first time in the country's history, housewives were free much of the day from the endless drudgery their mothers and grandmothers accepted as unavoidable. How they spent this free time was a matter of individual choice. Many gathered at each others' homes to play bridge or, for several exciting years during the 1920s, Mah-Jongg, a game borrowed from China. The more athletic took up golf, a pastime formerly reserved mostly for men. Women's clubs flourished as emancipated housewives sought to involve themselves in worthwhile projects while they socialized. But the majority spent afternoon hours listening to radio soap operas, so called because their sponsors were often manufacturers of soap and related products that every household needed.

Radio, which began with crystal sets, developed rapidly in the 1920s to vacuum-tube instruments with ample volume and good reception. Local announcers were chosen for their ability to amuse and interest their listeners, and to persuade them to buy particular products. The best talent could hope to be chosen for national hookups, where there were more listeners to amuse and interest, and to influence what they bought. Independent local stations could survive, but there were advantages in being affiliated with others in a major chain, which reached millions instead of a few thousand. Individual performers, thanks to radio, became celebrities and virtual idols.

In 1927, two new singers—Rudy Vallee from Maine and Bing Crosby from Tacoma, Washington—won enthusiastic admirers and, in the process, created a taste for crooning. That was the year Charles Lindbergh crossed the Atlantic and became a national hero, but Rudy and Bing, simply because of their regular radio programs, were much more in evidence than was "Lucky Lindy." Another pair of rivals, Jack Benny

Left: *Spanish-style dwellings on hillside street; San Francisco, Calif.* Below: *Interior window detail, Robie House, designed by Frank Lloyd Wright.*

and Fred Allen, competed for the large radio audience that liked situational comedy. These two, and many others, were graduates of burlesque, that seedbed of American humor.

Radio also made it possible for entertainers of other sorts, all but forgotten today, to win popular favor—Lamont Cranston's mystery-solving "The Shadow"; "Uncle Don"; "The Whistler"; "Fibber McGee and Mollie"; "The Lone Ranger," with the *William Tell* Overture for his theme song; and "Easy Aces." Taste for radio entertainment grew steadily as the talent multiplied, and programs that drew the most listeners sold the most products, in a fortunate partnership of interests that fostered taste for consumer goods as well as for gifted performers.

Radio versus the movies

Being unseen, the radio stars fell short of the fame enjoyed by men and women—and children—famous for roles in the movies: Mary Pickford ("America's Sweetheart"), Douglas Fairbanks, the Marx Brothers, Greta Garbo, Jean Harlow, Errol Flynn, Harold Lloyd, and the youngsters in "Our Gang" comedies.

Not every film was tasteful by anybody's standards, but taste for motion-picture entertainment was tremendous, greater by far than it would be when television preempted much of its audience, after 1950. The most popular single genre was the Western, which had been entrenched in reader taste since publication of Owen Wister's *The Virginian* in 1902. On the screen, the good guys were easy to recognize by the white horses they rode, and the Indians were divided, as in Cooper's novels, into the noble and the treacherous. Again and again, the West was won as cavalry galloped out to rescue forlorn civilians from assorted danger and deviltry.

Serials were almost as popular, especially *The Perils of Pauline,* which prompted a popular song describing the endless hair-raising predicaments she found herself in: "Poor Pauline! I pity poor Pauline!" But she was not alone in getting into trouble: many a film star, or look-alike stunt man, dangled from cliffs at climactic moments, thus giving birth to the term *cliff-hanger.*

Radio had the advantage of sound, but lost it in 1927 when *The Jazz Singer,* starring Al Jolson, introduced the "talkies," as moving pictures with sound tracks were first called. One result of this breakthrough was an almost instant readjustment of reputations. Actors of the silent era whose vocal cords did not vibrate effectively were dropped from the stardusted pantheon. Only a supreme pantomimist like Charlie Chaplin or a deadpan comedian like Buster Keaton could survive. More important, the advent of sound expanded the range of possibilities in the art of picturemaking and, reasonably enough, increased the audience.

Land of wish fulfillment

There wasn't much in all this for high-brow taste, although Walt Disney's *Fantasia* (1940) very successfully combined classical music with appropriate screen effects in a style that would later be known as "multimedia." Novels adapted to films were seldom very effective with the exception of *Gone with the Wind,* the phenomenal bestseller of the late 1930s that broke all attendance records as a film and is still packing theaters in revival. Its enduring fame rests on its sympathetic treatment of the Confederacy in the last great "romantic" war. Like other popular films,

Gone with the Wind affected taste by prompting imitation of the hairstyles, makeup, and dresses of the Civil War period. Films generally have less influence on male clothing, but when Clark Gable, in *It Happened One Night,* revealed that he was wearing no undershirt, it caused a serious disruption in the male underwear industry.

So many people attended the movies regularly that it was profitable to build elaborate theaters to seat them all. Some of the largest, mostly in New York, might give the impression that architecture from 1920 to 1940 was totally untouched by progressive ideas. Foyers were grandiose in the baroque splendor of the 1890s, and the vast auditoriums, which could seat thousands, were decorated in spectacular Byzantine, Romanesque, Italian baroque, or Spanish Renaissance style.

The Beacon Theatre at Broadway and 74th Street in Manhattan paid conspicuous tribute to ancient Egypt and Persia, but it also posed American Indian maidens twelve feet tall with breasts four feet in diameter.

The Walker Theatre in Brooklyn, named for New York's ebullient mayor Jimmie Walker, was done in turquoise, red, gold, and beige and had twisted columns; it also displayed a pipe organ of gold and white in the center of the orchestra pit. At one time there were said to be no fewer than fifteen hundred movie theaters in New York's five boroughs that had organs, for the ultimate in moviegoer taste was a brief concert, given by a resplendently clad wizard of the keyboard seated under a spotlight in a darkened hall to set the mood for the newsreel, the animated cartoon, and the feature film that was to follow. So that everyone could see the organist, the pedestals of these organs were equipped to elevate the organ onto the stage for

the playing and then to retract out of sight. As more and more films were given sound tracks, though, the organs gradually disappeared.

Although most of the great movie palaces have been demolished, enough survive to rouse nostalgia for their decors, which tended to intermix forms of ancient cultures. Art Deco and streamlining carried taste away from historicism; the great movie houses between the wars revived it, albeit in questionable ways. No Richard Morris Hunt or Stanford White was around to insist on faithful reproduction of these styles, and young cynics who took their cue from Mencken's *American Mercury* bandied about such terms as "Bronx Renaissance," but they did not let the garishness deter their moviegoing.

More serious students of art history were less amused. But for the vast public, taste was satisfied. Hollywood symbolized wish fulfillment, a never-never land of romance that was all the more credible, however briefly, when projected in pavilions of dreamlike splendor. As if to add their personal endorsement to the illusion, the famous stars lived above the arroyos of Beverly Hills, just north of the actual Hollywood, in palaces as exotic as the theaters where their talents were admired.

The art of advertising

After the organ concert, the newsreel, and the comedy short and before the feature film began to unwind, footage from the next week's film was projected in the movie houses of the day. It was part of the ballyhoo, and it was unique in that the product itself was the medium for its own advertising, to a captive audience that took delight in being captive. The feature film itself advertised in more subtle ways. The clothing that beloved stars wore, the chairs they sat in, the way the walls were decorated and the windows curtained—all made their variable impressions on the minds of the viewers. If a superstar appeared with her hair done up in an unusual manner, the style was imitated within weeks in every part of the country. People who paid to see a film were, in effect, paying for the privilege of being influenced in their tastes.

Movie stars were among the individuals most sought after for testimonials, a valuable form of advertising. The basic principle was the creation of illusion. This soap or shampoo would turn plain girls into vibrant beauties pursued by ardent males. This after-shave lotion would enhance any man's attractiveness to those alluring beauties. This expensive convertible marked its owner as a person of distinction and excellent taste. Skillfully handled, such appeals to universal dreams of success and prestige could banish any lingering doubts about the product's intrinsic quality. Advertisers who could manipulate the public successfully became the nation's most influential tastemakers.

Studies found that food, drugs, cosmetics, automobiles, tobacco, and appliances, more or less in that order, were the most amenable to advertising. The first dry breakfast cereal, shredded wheat, was introduced at the Chicago fair in 1893; between the world wars, many other such cereals, packaged alluringly, appeared, changing the breakfast habits of millions. Bread, previously sold by local bakers, was merchandised by nationwide firms skilled in persuading customers that white bread was best and light weight a virtue. Most store-bought loaves were so light, so lacking in texture, that toasting was needed to give it body enough to hold butter (or margarine, another triumph of advertising) and whatever jam or jelly or

marmalade the family liked and could buy in shapely jars.

For three centuries, breakfast had been a hearty meal, farmer style, with eggs and meat and potatoes, grits in the South, and in New England, even pie. In the 1920s, thanks to the genius of advertisers and the perfection of electric toasters and coffeepots, it underwent a revolutionary change, differing, from season to season, only in the juice or fruit that was currently available. Citrus fruit became available year-round as industry adopted refrigerated freight cars and rapid rail transport from Florida and Texas and California. Not overnight, but in a very short time, the breakfast menu had become standardized nationwide.

To make a house a home

Appliances emancipated housewives, but their houses showed no great changes. Who wanted to live in a box, however well planned for maximum efficiency, that had no character, no personal touches? People *said* they wanted homes with the greatest possible comfort and convenience, but when offered models, as they were at the Museum of Modern Art exhibition in 1932, most were apathetic or indignant. What they really wanted, near or below the level of consciousness, was something quaint, something to remind them of the past, or what they thought existed long ago in the prescientific age. Something, in short, that would give the illusion of escape from a world increasingly mechanized. As Edgar Guest, poet laureate of the unsophisticated, once put it, "It takes a heap o' livin' in a house t' make it a home," and home was the one place, other than the favorite moving-picture theater, where the illusion of romantic love and fairy-book existence could still be preserved.

Frank Lloyd Wright and his

handful of disciples had provided an original style suited to America —the Prairie House—and Wright himself had designed some of the most interesting individual houses, repudiating all traditional forms, for clients with limited means and perhaps an understanding of architectural principles. For some reason, knowledge of architecture had never been considered essential to public school education, and taste in housing remained a conspicuous laggard in a rapidly changing culture.

What dominated taste after 1930 was the period house, whether built cheaply in mass developments or at considerable expense by people of affluence. The period house, in such forms as the Greek Revival and the Victorian eclectic, had had a long history in the United States, but by the late 1930s, more attention was being paid to specific period forms and, if there was money enough, better site orientation; also more care was being taken in providing better scale and proportion. Finally, there was a demand for larger grounds, which had a direct bearing on the expansion of city boundaries and the growth of suburbs.

Period styles most in favor between the wars were the English cottage, the Spanish hacienda, and the old New England farmhouse with pitched roof and an ell at one end that contained a garage where the stable or barn once had been. Since all these styles had a long frontage, they needed wide lots; even with these, homes often needed dense shrubbery to conceal their proximity to neighbors. Ample setbacks from the street added to the illusion of dignity. Patios, groomed flower and vegetable plots, and perhaps a small area left "wild" extended the family's privacy in the rear. Well built and with open interiors, the best of these period houses had something of the flow and informality of the Prairie style, with the same large living room that centered family life around a fireplace and the same large windows that opened onto attractive vistas. Period houses less carefully planned were apt to have numerous small rooms, all with doors, as was the common practice during the colonial era when there was no such thing as central heating. Viewed from the street, both the good examples and the less successful were easy to recognize for the historic styles they were intended to follow.

Functionalism and stark simplicity, devoid of anything without utility, has never appealed to the taste of most Americans for their dwellings. The taste for exteriors suggesting former periods produced a new wave of eclecticism. This was evident along the River Road in the Minneapolis of the 1930s: the sequence was a gleaming white Spanish hacienda; an older gray house with late Victorian scrollwork decoration; an Italianate box with an almost flat roof and broad eaves; an oversized two-story colonial farmhouse; a half-timbered Elizabethan structure; an austere Georgian in red brick; and nearby a Prairie House designed by Wright. Over the next few years, a great many such houses were built, in cities large and small, and the resulting mixture of styles within a particular neighborhood, perhaps amusing to some historians of culture, did not offend general taste. This kind of eclecticism is a distinctive phenomenon of the period and a durable reminder of the choices freely exercised in the mid-twentieth century.

Taste for quaintness

When viewed from the outside, most of these period houses reasonably duplicated domestic styles of earlier times. Within their walls,

however, there was evidence of a broad range of personal taste. Some owners chose to furnish their rooms with replicas of furniture approximating the exterior styles, but the governing impulse was to introduce objects that gave the impression of quaintness: factory-made spinning wheels that nobody could operate, if they were operable at all; wooden or plastic wagon wheels suspended over dining-room tables and wired for small electric bulbs; old cobblers' benches refurbished or copied, to be used for cocktail tables; machine-made rugs that looked as though they had been hand-braided or hooked; windowpanes that were made with deliberate imperfections.

Genuine antiques were also high in taste, as they still are. But a bedstead more than a century old was likely to have had its cording

replaced by box springs, while big copper kettles usually became receptacles for magazines or for neat fireplace logs never intended to be burned. Currier and Ives prints, or modern copies, were proudly framed in old (or old-looking) wood and hung in the living room. If a family had kept its Windsor chair or its George and Mary Washington portraits in their dark oval frames for several generations, those too were dusted off and proudly displayed. Ship models were another favorite for the mantel of the seldom-used fireplace, and making them became a profitable new industry—the trick was to make them look old. Antiquing grew as a hobby, along with other manual exercises performed at workbenches in basements or garages, equipped with power tools. Odd pieces of furniture, or entire rooms, could be

184

transformed from Victorian to what passed as colonial, the new "in" style. But nobody considered replacing modern bathrooms with privies or turning in automobiles for horse-drawn vehicles. Quaintness had its limits.

War again

The dawn attack on Pearl Harbor, on December 7, 1941, forced America to enter the Second World War at a much earlier stage than it had entered the first, less than a quarter-century before. But that was only one difference. This time there was no idealistic illusion about making the world safe for democracy, no eagerness to die for one's country, no bitterness over being left out when friends were being drafted. The scale of operations was also much greater, not limited to western Europe and the north Atlantic but extending to Africa and the entire Pacific region. And it greatly affected the noncombatant population, virtually conscribing it to war-related industry and business and rationing food and gasoline.

Cultural activities did not grind to a halt; but if culture was much less adversely affected than in parts of the world where there were air raids and actual fighting, freedom of movement, and of choice, was severely limited. Vacation travel was discouraged, and both coasts were darkened by strictly enforced blackouts. Social life was of necessity curtailed. In a time marked by such a vast mobilization of goods, manpower, and energy, taste was of minor concern. All that really mattered was bringing the ugly war to an end and restoring peace.

On V-E Day in 1945, May 4, and even more on V-J Day, August 14, the American people shared the worldwide relief in an exuberant celebration, not unlike that of a typical New Year's Eve but of longer duration and with a deeply felt satisfaction. Peace restored meant the chance to pick up the pieces, to revive hopes and dreams deferred too long, to enjoy again the free exercise of choice that is the essence of taste. The year marked not only the defeat of the Axis powers but also the beginning of what may properly be called the modern era.

If Americans expected life to be a renewal of what it had been before Pearl Harbor, they were both right and wrong. They could be confident of resuming the old pace and the old freedom but, being Americans, the pace was one of change and the freedom was one of new choices. As for the direction the culture would take, the only safe prediction would have been that taste would continue to evolve.

Opposite: *Typical bungalow; ca. 1930. The relatively high roof and full upstairs are not found in the first bungalows.* Above: *Chrysler automobile; 1935.*

VII

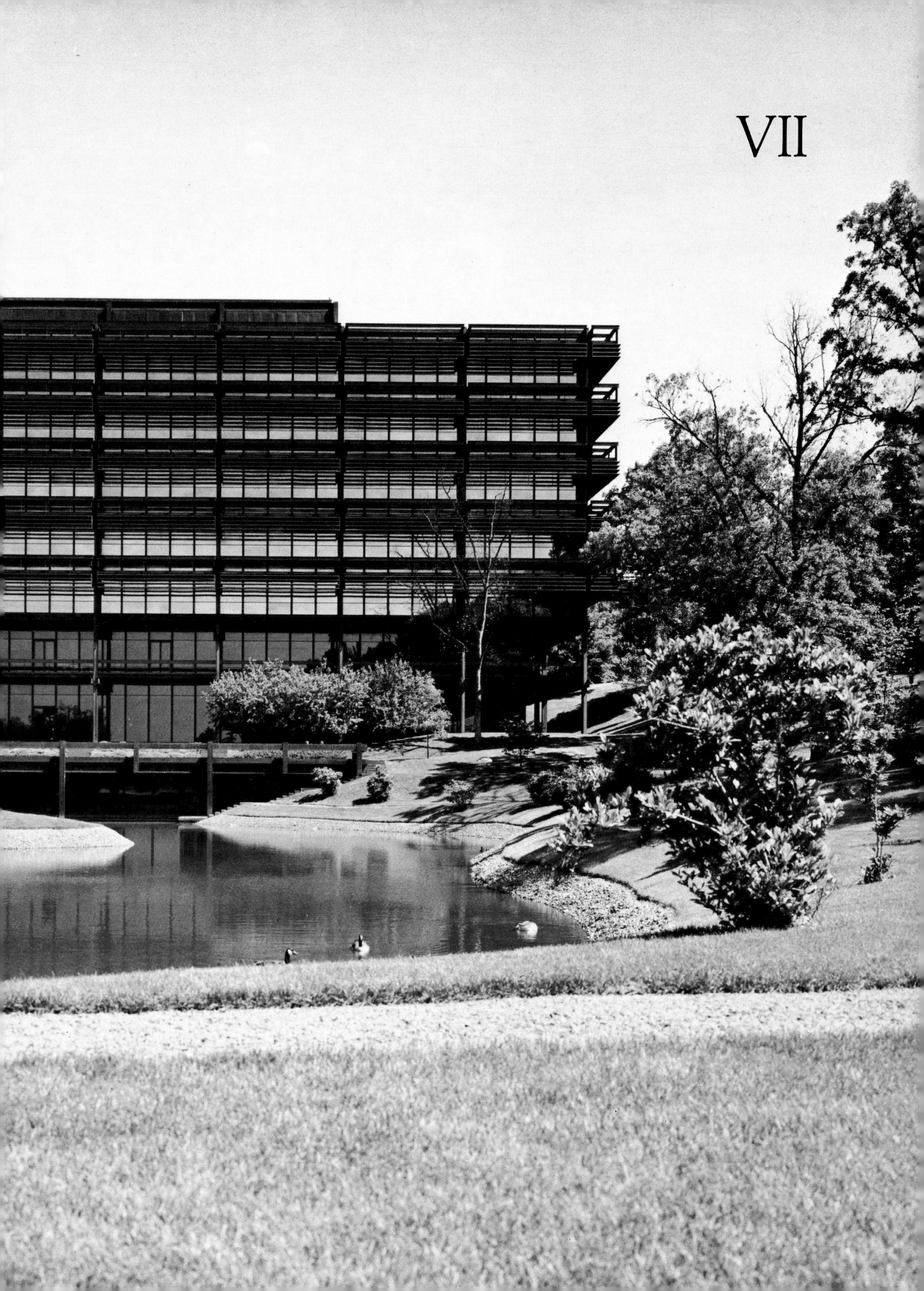

Anything Goes

(since 1945)

Preceding pages: *Administrative Center, John Deere Company, designed by Eero Saarinen; Moline, Ill.; 1964.* Above: *Saint John's Abbey, Saint John's University, designed by Marcel Breuer; Collegeville, Minn.; 1961.*

With the lifting of wartime restrictions, late in 1945, Americans were free to resume their pursuit of happiness and to enjoy the blessings of liberty. In the thirty-odd years since, that pursuit has taken diverse paths, and the taste marking the prewar years has been altered almost beyond recognition.

For those who revel in a society that tolerates and even encourages individual choice, this is the best of all possible worlds, and a great improvement over any former time in the nation's history. For the more conventional, wedded to fixed principles, the rapid acceleration of change and the more extreme forms of individual behavior it produces are evidence of cultural anarchy. Such people tremble at the thought of where such permissiveness may lead, but for the postwar generation and individuals in other age groups who share its attitudes, the current freedom can lead only to an ever brighter future. Both camps agree that taste is dead, if taste is understood to mean a single set of standards accepted as a guide to behavior and as a basis for choice.

The generation gap

The postwar generation—the generation that is now in early adulthood—grew up with no personal memory of the Great Depression, the war that ended it, or the McCarthy years that quickly followed. For these young adults, the most pivotal event within memory was the Vietnam War, which put in jeopardy, year after year, the free exercise of choice that people in an era of affluence expect to enjoy. Ideology apart, this undeclared war in Southeast Asia narrowed the focus of attention to the immediate present, to the exclusion of serious interest in yesterday or tomorrow. It also undermined respect for tradition and authority and encouraged overt rebellion against all standards.

It was sobering to learn, from the findings of the 1970 census, that the median age of the population at that time was twenty-seven. The last time the median had been so low was in the seventeenth century, when life expectancy was far short of the biblical three score years and ten. By 1970, about a tenth of the population—some 20 million people—were over sixty-five, but even with unprecedented increase in longevity, the baby boom of the 1940s and 1950s created a striking bulge on the population charts.

This rising generation, conditioned almost from birth to expect fulfillment of every impulse, could hardly be aware of what their parents and grandparents had had to endure in the recent past—especially the lean years of the 1930s and the restrictions required by the Second World War. Those parents and grandparents, for their own part, were glad that the children were spared such harsh realities. With no letup in the nation's traditional glorification of youth, or in the old belief that parents should sacrifice for the young, this first postwar generation grew to maturity with a marked sense of its own importance and a general indifference to older values.

The prewar years, to this new generation, were a time when life was less pleasant, a time deserving only to be forgotten. Emphasis on the immediate present spawned a rejection of history, and taste changed from being an enduring guide to choice and behavior to being an acceptance of whatever was "in" at the moment.

Oblivious to protests from whatever source, the postwar generation simply "did its thing," setting its own standards or none at all. In so doing, it discovered its power to redirect general taste, and it used that power not defiantly but with great casualness. Older people, in considerable numbers, were at first dismayed but gradually came to accept much of this freewheeling behavior. The result has been not the creation of a new national standard of taste but a multiplicity of overlapping tastes.

These youths, of course, could not influence standards that were set before they were born. Nor could they adopt their independent ways until their members were old enough to know their own minds— in their early teens or when they neared college age. As a result, for roughly fifteen years after 1945, culture continued its evolution without the benefit of their input. Certain events occurring in that decade and a half were important enough to need examination. One was the McCarthy nightmare.

McCarthyism

Wars, especially when fought on foreign soil, tend to stimulate a country's economy, and the United States, as it emerged from the Second World War, was at a peak of unprecedented prosperity. Fred Vinson, director of War Mobilization and Reconversion, stated the facts accurately when he observed that "the American people are in the pleasant predicament of living fifty percent better than they have ever lived before." Young couples who had fared well on wartime incomes but who had had to defer children and homes particularly welcomed the release from restrictions and made up for lost time with all the zest of youthful energy. The baby boom began, and continued for the next decade.

This period should have been one of universal happiness, but there was one ominous cloud in the otherwise bright blue sky—the Communist "menace." The Soviets had helped win the war, but once it was over, the old fear of Communism resurfaced, and it was stronger than ever. It was further encouraged by ambitious politicians who had no scruples about exploiting the fear for their own personal advantage. The grand master of this game was Joseph McCarthy, junior senator from Wisconsin.

McCarthy won national attention in February, 1950, when he charged that the State Department was infiltrated by Communists. Although he refused to present specific evidence, then or in subsequent sweeping accusations, he rode high until 1954, when his fellow senators finally censured him for arrogant abuses. By then, however, he had ruined hundreds of reputations.

Among those most seriously affected by the Great Depression were people in the arts, for whom the Works Progress Administration, maligned by well-to-do conservatives as useless "make-work," was a welcome support. With hindsight, we can appreciate

Cylindrical tower of the Peachtree Plaza Hotel, designed by John Portman and Associates; Atlanta, Ga.; 1974.

the contributions to art and taste made by those talented individuals —handsome murals on post office walls; an excellent series of state guidebooks; drama and music written and performed by young artists who subsequently became leading figures in their fields. Because many of the creative individuals were of liberal political tendencies, though, they were conspicuous targets for the virulent anti-Communist drive.

Much of the experimental work in the visual arts was incomprehensible to people without some training, just as the modern French painting at the Armory Show had been in 1913. For that very reason, it was suspected of being subversive. In the verbal arts, meanings were less abstruse, and writers who were in any way critical of contemporary America were quickly threatened with official censure. Questionable books were removed from libraries and school curriculums, and some were even burned. The same sort of harassment also extended to include some of the most respected actors and playwrights, both in Hollywood and on the Broadway stage.

Lillian Hellman, famous for such plays as *The Children's Hour* (1934)and *The Little Foxes* (1939), was asked by a congressional committee to name acquaintances suspected of belonging to allegedly subversive groups. She refused. "I cannot cut my conscience," she said, "to fit this year's fashions." Arthur Miller suffered even greater indignities. In 1954, he was denied a passport on the grounds that he was "believed to be supporting the Communist movement," and in 1956, when he declined to identify individuals he had seen at Communist front meetings he was cited for contempt of Congress.

Lesser figures than Hellman and Miller, not as secure in their repu-

tations, saw the expediency of curtailing their progressive impulses. The result was a constriction in all areas of American cultural life, an increasing blandness of production as writers feared to express what they really believed. But not even such prudence could save them from the inquisitors, who became adept at quoting out of context whatever might damn them. The list of artists and intellectuals ruined by self-seeking political opportunists, including members of the House Un-American Activities Committee exploiting the

fear of Communism, is a shameful record of a period as dark as the Salem witchcraft trials of the 1690s.

The play must go on

What may have roused the vicious attack on Arthur Miller was his 1953 play, *The Crucible*, a realistic account of the persecution of accused witches in Salem two and a half centuries earlier; many people viewed the play as a parable of the McCarthyite persecutions. As seen today, *The Crucible* still evokes audience horror, but no

Summer and Smoke—all first produced between 1945 and 1955. And few plays approached Miller's *Death of a Salesman* for sheer horror born of blasted dreams.

A few critics faulted both Miller and Williams for their version of tragedy. Aristotle had said that a hero or heroine must have two qualities to be considered tragic: he must be noble and he must have some flaw in his character through which fate can act to doom him. But since few people in the twentieth century believe in fate, tragic heroes have become antiheroes, ordinary individuals who are destroyed by familar modern traps rather than by fate. Contemporary audiences also approve of antiheroes being carried to extremes, in the form of psychotics such as Blanche Du Bois in *Streetcar* and hollow men such as Willy Loman in *Death of a Salesman*.

Television

Television, which reached the market shortly after the Second World War, is one of the most important facts of modern living. It is so much a part of modern America—of the modern world—that it is difficult to assess its effects on taste and culture. Some people argue that television mirrors our world—in which case it would be a clear window on contemporary American taste; others insist that it is a cultural trend-setter; still others feel that it is a major block to cultural growth. Whichever it is, it can neither be denied nor avoided —its images enter nearly every American home.

With the exception of public television, a recent development in which programs are financed largely by private donations, television in the United States is financed by advertisers and serves the purpose of promoting sales. Scientific testing of which programs attract the most viewers—

longer is it seen to be connected with McCarthyism. To today's viewers, it simply shows the dramatic genius of Miller, whose *Death of a Salesman*, produced a few years earlier, in 1949, had been one of the great hits of the stage; like every great play, it is timeless in its audience appeal.

Eugene O'Neill, who in 1920 had led American drama out of its prolonged adolescence, was still productive after the Second World War, furnishing *The Iceman Cometh* in 1946 and, ten years later, *Long Day's Journey into Night,* an autobiographical tragedy.

By that time taste in the theater had been firmly redirected toward serious themes that were treated in depth. But only with the emergence of Arthur Miller and Tennessee Williams, after 1945, could it be said that O'Neill had worthy successors in probing the darker passions of man and in moving audiences deeply. Few playwrights in any period, in any country, have been able to create the atmospheric quality of *The Glass Menagerie* or such other Williams successes as *A Streetcar Named Desire* and potential customers—determines which programs will be aired. The great majority of the programs thus selected are a form of entertainment that only the least sophisticated viewers mistake for reality. Wise fathers manage to settle family crises as few can in actual life, detectives invariably catch their man, and lawyers always manage to win their cases.

The effects of television can be readily seen in the areas of sports telecasting and news coverage. Pregame and postgame interviews, instant replays and analyses have taken away some of sport's romance and replaced it with a scientific clarity.

Television news has sped up the process of news reporting to the point where millions of viewers can actually watch an event take place —as happened when Jack Ruby shot Lee Harvey Oswald. Detractors of television claim that it creates news—that the sight of television cameras, for instance, instigates riots.

Variety in drama

Although television has replaced radio as a major home entertainment, it has yet to replace newspapers, sports stadiums, opera, and theater. Live theater maintains its hold on taste largely because the actors are present in their three-dimensional reality whatever the nature of the action. Taste for the older live theater and the newer taste for the kind projected by what its detractors call the idiot box can coexist amicably, however, for they fulfill quite different needs—the one for . what the Greeks called catharsis, the other for relaxed make-believe.

The old dramatic troupes, touring the nation and presenting tried-and-true plays on one-night stands, are gone. But summer stock and permanent professional repertory groups throughout the country have more than adequately replaced them. If famous plays are no longer performed at "the old opera house" in every town, modern audiences travel for some distance to see old and new plays acted by professionals or by amateurs in training for theatrical careers. Established (or "provincial") companies offer much the same fare as Broadway; sometimes they also include more experimental and original plays.

Summer stock usually offers light fare, intended to entertain people on holiday, and the leading roles are often played by well-known Broadway stars who, like the audience, are enjoying vacations in idyllic resorts. A representative summer season might approximate that of the Durham Summer Theatre at the University of New Hampshire, which offered for its fourteenth season, in 1977, Shakespeare's *Much Ado about Nothing,* Miller's *A View from the Bridge,* Shaw's *Arms and the Man,* and Tom Stoppard's *The Real Inspector Hound,* along with *South Pacific* and another musical, *Celebration,* and two pops concerts as well.

Dramatic music

Musicals, and the taste for them, have also become more sophisticated. *Oklahoma!,* first staged in 1943, had a strong grass-roots appeal that earned for it, among sophisticates, the reputation of being corny; but it pioneered the integration of music, song, and dance with a detailed plot. Of numerous outstanding successors, *South Pacific* (1949) and *My Fair Lady* (1956) not only rival *Oklahoma!* for stage immortality but contain serious ideas. The first, based on James Michener's *Tales of the South Pacific,* conveys a strong indictment of American racial prejudice, and the second, adapted from Shaw's *Pygmalion,* is a parable of the interrelation of dialect and social status.

That both *South Pacific* and *My Fair Lady* were converted to moving pictures and television spectaculars with extravagant success suggests that taste has developed for entertainment with a social message. But that is not the whole story. Unlike its progenitor, the operetta, a theatrical piece of light and sentimental character, the musical in America since the Second World War has led taste along divergent paths. Leonard Bernstein's *West Side Story* (1957) with its exceptional choreography ventured into the thorny problem of ethnic tension in Manhattan, and the advent of rock music encouraged the rock musical, greeted with enthusiasm. *Hair,* in 1967, was initially shocking with its stage nudity, which was taken in stride during a revival in 1977. Two with religious themes—*Godspell* and *Jesus Christ Superstar,* both in 1971—would have been no less shocking to conventional Christians a quarter-century earlier, but tolerance for unfamiliar forms had developed, and only a minority of viewers found them distasteful.

Few operas in the standard repertory have any element of ethical significance. They survive at the pinnacle of cultivated taste for other reasons—the glory of the world's finest voices, the high quality of the music, the splendor of the stage settings. Most of the best loved are tragedies—*Carmen, La Bohème, Il Trovatore, Tosca,* profoundly moving but without the true catharsis of high tragedy produced by such plays as *Oedipus Rex, Medea,* and *Othello.* Carlyle Floyd's *Susannah* (1955), based on a biblical incident, represents a recent effort by American opera composers to infuse ethical content. But despite its enthusiastic reception in many cities, the *Har-*

Spring Valley toll barrier; Spring Valley, N.Y.

vard *Dictionary of Music* dismisses it as a folk opera, and it is unlikely to be given ranking with the famous works of Puccini, Verdi, and Wagner. Operas sung in English, it seems clear, are handicapped. If sung in foreign languages, the sheer inanity of most librettos is lost on audiences, or dismissed as irrelevant to the total effect.

Musical taste in America exists on a broad range of levels, each with large numbers of enthusiastic adherents. Two centuries ago the choices were very limited, and few people formed a taste for any kind of music at all. Now that every home and most automobiles are equipped with some sort of sound system, or at least a radio, and "canned" music is to be heard in supermarkets, hotel lobbies, restaurants, and even hospitals, we can hardly avoid exercising the faculty of discerning excellence, even if we never attend a concert.

Vast numbers of Americans do attend concerts, though. The greatest crowds are of young people who gather at open-air rock concerts and jazz festivals, or pack the largest auditoriums, to hear particular singers or, more likely, particular groups. Today's youth has an insatiable appetite for new talent, raising one singer or rock group to the very peak of popularity only to turn quickly to another that offers a fresh interpretation.

The music that young Americans listen to—that the youth of the whole world listens to—is a peculiarly American product. Like jazz, popular music today— whether rock, disco, country and western, or any of its other myriad kinds—owes most of its form and sound to the musical heritage of black Americans. It began in the 1950s as rhythm and blues—part gospel shouting, part *a cappella* street-corner serenade, usually with the soulful wail of a saxo-

The first Holiday Inn; Memphis, Tenn.; opened August, 1952.
The modest pioneer of a major industry geared to the
tastes of mobile Americans. Memphis now has 15 Holiday Inns.

phone. The lyrics were of secondary importance—the important thing was the beat: loud, driving, and rhythmic, it was highly rated for its danceability. Such music did not remain a black institution for, long—white performers, such as Elvis Presley, made its popularity soar.

The style of contemporary music changed as its listeners changed. When the postwar generation was immersed in the civil rights struggle and antiwar activity, the music exchanged its juvenile lyrics for the more mature words of such songpoets as Bob Dylan. The songs became polemics, vehicles for political ideas of peace, love, and brotherhood.

When this idealism met head-on with the entrenched system, frustrations boiled over, and drugs and dropping out of society became popular. Again the music followed its listeners, adapting itself to strobe lights and a bigger sound.

Today the music, again reflecting the mood of its listeners, has become more entertaining and less political.

Victims of television

Radio suffered a serious setback when television became generally available early in the 1950s. But it has regained some of the ground it lost, with the development of FM and the factory-installation of radio receivers in most automobiles made in the United States. Even when driving, people can, with a flick of the switch, satisfy their demand for instant news or music ranging from the classics to the latest rock.

For a time it seemed that the moving-picture industry was doomed. It was, in terms of producing films to be shown in huge theaters. But ingenuity produced a solution—a series of small auditoriums contained under a single roof. Called "cinemas," these offer simultaneously a variety of films that appeal to different tastes. With retail trade moving away from downtown, where the old theaters were, cinemas also have the advantage of being more conveniently located, commonly in or near suburban shopping plazas that provide ample space for parking. More and better drive-in outdoor theaters have also been a success, but they cannot operate in inclement weather.

Taste for the grandiose decora-

tion of large theaters had been strong before the Second World War, but it declined as both films and their viewers became more sophisticated. The industry also grew bolder, producing films that were much franker than ever before, both verbally and in the situations they portrayed. Adult taste responded favorably. Television was at last at a disadvantage. Like the general magazines of a century earlier, television is meant for family entertainment and must obey certain taboos that do not extend to moving pictures.

Frankness that would have been universally condemned before 1900, or even 1950, has now gone about as far as it can go. The industry's use of key letters—G for general viewing, PG for parental guidance, R for restricted, X for pornography—to denote the amount of frankness, usually sexual explicitness, a film displays is no doubt an advance over the days when Will Hayes and others simply censored a film or the parts of it they considered objectionable. The new system, however, is of little help in distinguishing trash from cinematic excellence. G and PG films, incidentally, share with television the freedom to project to minors violence of the worst sort but sexual themes and nudity are forbidden, even if they are handled artistically.

Readily available hard-core pornography may be less perverting to morals, it is sometimes argued, than such underground publications as *The Pearl* in Victorian England, which encouraged a high level of hypocrisy. All advanced civilizations in the past have had outlets for so-called prurient tastes, and cinematic frankness might be taken as evidence that the United States, in this respect at least, is approaching that ultimate stage of sophistication. Nobody is forced to attend X-rated films. They may be Exhibit A in the "anything goes" syndrome, but merely by existing, they contribute to the present multiplicity of choices.

No one, even with time and money enough, could sample everything available in modern culture. But no wise person would ever try, for a particular choice, once made, might rule out the alternatives. On the other hand, too narrow a taste can limit the pleasure in living that individuals of more catholic tastes learn to savor. Anything goes today, but it is one thing to deplore the extremes of taste and another to welcome the variety and choose what seems most conducive to a rich, full life.

American literature

If corner newsstands and drugstores display magazines and lurid paperbacks meant to gratify a variety of sexual appetites, the shelves of bookstores and libraries are crowded with recent fiction that better represents American diversity than any written in the past. There is something for every taste—science fiction; "gothics," usually set in old castles and dramatically combining terror and ro-

mance; feminist novels; stories of mismatched couples; fantasy; social satire; serious experimental writing; brutally realistic narratives of slum life and gang warfare; detective stories and other mysteries; fictionalized history and biography—Gore Vidal's *Burr,* for example; and the newly popular "sweet, savage love" novels that combine gothic-style romance with a mixture of masochism and sadism.

Whether we are in the midst of a new renaissance of creative writing, only the future can decide; but we have certainly been undergoing a literary revolution, one result of the rapid advance of democratic egalitarianism.

The earliest writing in the colonies was the work of immigrants—transplanted Europeans. Once the colonies were well established, however, native-born writers emerged. Most were of English descent, and until the Second World War most American writers held in highest esteem were Anglo-Americans, despite the fact that they represented less than half the total population, and had since the 1880 census. When American literature was first added to school and college courses in literature after the Civil War, it was judged by the standards of English classics, and until well after 1900, it was given a subordinate place to them. Textbooks and anthologies used in classes before 1950 tell the story: one must hunt through them for authors from minority groups. Prior to 1976, moreover, every American winner of the Nobel Prize for Literature has been of English or northern European extraction: Sinclair Lewis (1930), Eugene O'Neill (1936), Pearl Buck (1938), T. S. Eliot (1946), William Faulkner (1950), Ernest Hemingway (1954), and John Steinbeck (1962).

The *Cambridge History of*

American Literature, completed in 1921, did not totally ignore "ethnic" writers, but the attention it paid them was minimal. Of its 1,488 pages, exactly half a page is devoted to black literary figures: "an orator, two prose writers, and one poet of merited eminence"—Frederick Douglass, Booker T. Washington, W. E. B. DuBois, Paul Laurence Dunbar. The final two chapters of this scholarly and influential history concern "Non-English Writings," almost as an afterthought, and summarize works of German, French, Yiddish, and aboriginal authorship.

The second great American work of scholarship, *Literary History of the United States,* published in 1948 in three volumes, substantially reshuffled the literary reputations accorded a mere quarter-century in the past. For the first time, Herman Melville was given thorough coverage, while the beloved old "household poets"—Longfellow, Whittier, and Lowell—ceded space to Emily Dickinson, Walt Whitman, Edwin Arlington Robinson, and the New Poetry of Robert Frost, Vachel Lindsay, Edgar Lee Masters, and Carl Sandburg, whose work was collectively dubbed "bizarre and not always sincere" in the *Cambridge History of American Literature.*

Now that another three decades have passed, it may be time for another such survey of American literature. In such a study, the section on writing since 1945 would show a remarkable broadening in both talent and reader taste.

For one thing, the hypothetical major new history would offer much more than the two earlier surveys about black writers past and present. It is now generally recognized that writers of African descent have contributed far more to American literature in the past than anyone in 1921 or even in 1948 was aware of. The 1948 history referred to Richard Wright as "one of the most powerful and promising American novelists in the forties," but merely named eleven other black writers as "an established and versatile group of contemporary Negro writers." This was only slightly more obtuse than the *Cambridge History* had been. By mid-century, neither scholars nor readers were ready to give black writers the same standing as white.

Born in Natchez, Mississippi, in 1908, and raised in Memphis, Wright first gained attention in 1938 with *Uncle Tom's Children,* a prize-winning collection of short stories. *Native Son* (1940) won even greater praise and made its luckless hero, Bigger Thomas, almost as famous as Natty Bumppo or Huckleberry Finn. Wright was the first black writer to be considered as worthy of prizes and respect as his white counterparts. From then on, doors began to open to other black talent. Wright's chief successors have been Ralph Ellison, whose *Invisible Man* won the National Book Award in 1952, and James Baldwin, too strident for some readers' taste but powerful. Baldwin's numerous books include a novel, *Go Tell It on the Mountain* (1953); a book of essays, *Nobody Knows My Name* (1961); and a volume of short stories, *To Meet the Man* (1965). The great success of Alex Haley's *Roots,* in both book form and a week-long television series, confirmed in 1977 the nationwide awareness of black writers.

An equally significant expansion of interest attended the virtual explosion of Jewish literary genius. When Saul Bellow became the eighth American—and the first non-Aryan—to win the Nobel Prize in Literature, nobody was astonished who was abreast of recent writing. Born in Canada of Russian Jewish parents and a graduate

of Northwestern University, Bellow has been a leisurely writer, producing eight novels between 1944 and 1973, the date of *Humboldt's Gift.*

Norman Mailer, who grew up in Brooklyn and graduated from Harvard, shares Bellow's gift for ironical humor but displays a bitter streak in his writing. *The Naked and the Dead,* set on a Japanese-held island during the Second World War where thirteen American infantrymen struggle to survive, makes all earlier war fiction seem rather tame. His *Armies of the Night,* granted a Pulitzer Prize, recounts and analyzes the 1967 peace march on Washington, and the same fierce opposition to America's tragic involvement in Southeast Asia prompted his *Why Are We in Vietnam?* The fact that readers by the hundreds of thousands made best-sellers of such books suggests a remarkable shift in taste, and in public attitudes toward war.

On a less political note are the writings of Malamud and Singer. Bernard Malamud, another son of Russian Jewish immigrants, gives his fiction a tone suggesting the great Russian novelists of the nineteenth century. *The Natural* (1952) applies comic irony to a baseball hero (and may suggest to John Updike fans a parallel to *Rabbit Run*). *The Assistant* (1957) traces the wretched life of a loser who works in a shabby Brooklyn grocery. *The Fixer* (Pulitzer Prize, 1966) is even closer to the Russian greats, for it follows the miserable career of a peasant in the Russian countryside. As for Isaac Bashevis Singer, born in Poland and an immigrant at age thirty-one, we acknowledge a curious fact: he writes in Yiddish, then makes revisions after he and a collaborator have made an English translation. Such is the greatly broadened taste in literature that his strange other-

worldly characters and plots make an indelible impression.

One other recent immigrant from eastern Europe who has been even more widely accepted by American readers is the elegant Vladimir Nabokov, who died in 1977. Born in Russia of patrician parents and educated at Trinity College, Cambridge, he taught Russian literature at Cornell from 1949 until 1959, when his success as a writer prompted him to resign. Like Joseph Conrad (who was born in the Ukraine of Polish parents) before him, he not only acquired a perfect command of English but developed a highly distinctive style—witty, complex, ironic, and often satirical. The great popularity of his *Lolita* in 1958 tended to overshadow such other books as *Pnin* and *Invitation to a Beheading,* and his many sophisticated short stories.

It is amply evident that American literature since the Second World War has been greatly enriched by the special talents of blacks and so-called ethnics, and by reader readiness to accept them. But representatives of older groupings have not been pushed aside—Gore Vidal, scion of a prominent Tennessee family; Joyce Carol Oates, who teaches in Canada but is considered an American author; John Updike of an old Pennsylvania Dutch family; and Robert Penn Warren, Carson McCullers, Eudora Welty, and other stalwarts of the "Southern Renaissance." Recent decades, indeed, have produced the phenomenon of a highly competitive literary fraternity open to all, and a far richer variety of writing than ever before.

Poets' corner
The one relatively weak point in current writing is in poetry. There are many fine poets today, but none with the stature of Frost or

Amsterdam Addition; New York, N.Y.; 1974; 175 units. A recent project in New York City's commitment to provide well-designed public housing for people with modest incomes.

Sandburg or Robinson. In the mid-1950s, the Beat Movement, centered in San Francisco, Los Angeles, and New York, claimed public attention. It was a bohemian rebellion against middle-class values and the blatant commercialism of the day. Jack Kerouac was by far its best prose writer, especially with his *On the Road* (1957), but the major literary expression of the Beats was in poetry. Allen Ginsberg made a considerable impact with his *Howl and Other Poems* (1956) but offended many readers with its scattered obscenities. William Burroughs also alienated conservative readers by his frank account of drug addiction in *The Naked*

Lunch (1962), a novel using odd experiments in structure. The best of the Beat poets was Lawrence Ferlinghetti, who published Ginsberg's *Howl* and whose City Lights Bookshop in the Haight-Ashbury section of San Francisco became a virtual headquarters for the gathering storm of youthful rebellion. The Beat Movement as such did not endure, but served as a prelude to what proved to be the greatest student movement in American history.

Campus unrest

Modern poetry varies greatly in style and content but has, as booksellers know, gained a new audience by becoming intimate and

personal. In this respect, it parallels, or reflects, the recent "search for identity" in a civilization viewed as increasingly mechanistic. Assignment of numbers—for zip codes, driver's licenses, Social Security, bank accounts—applies to everyone. For the generation eligible for induction during the unpopular Vietnam War, becoming a number in a draft lottery was especially objectionable.

The campus unrest of the late 1960s was a culmination of the frustration that generation felt at having its individual identity suppressed, its voice ignored. Striking out at this alienation, students organized protests—against the war in Vietnam, in which they especially stood to lose much, and also against campus administrations, the nearest defenders of the status quo. Many faculty members approved their intransigeance; some joined the protest marches and spoke out at rallies, and a few risked losing their positions by encouraging stronger action. Faculty members as a national group were closer to unanimity than were student bodies in opposing that war, but since they had less to lose, they were more inclined to avoid activist roles.

Opposition to the war had no visible effect on the nation's decisionmakers, which only added to the feelings of frustration and alienation. Students next turned to demanding a voice in campus policy, even in the content of courses and the assigning of final grades. Faculties acceded, with mixed results. On many campuses, students were admitted to faculty meetings and appointed to faculty committees. The curriculum was enriched by the creation of area programs, as in black history and women's studies. Student evaluation of teachers became part of the system of merit raises and promotions. Taking roll at each class

meeting was abolished almost everywhere, and attendance became a matter of individual choice. Whatever the gains that students enjoyed, however, academic standards declined, sometimes disastrously.

Departments of English were particularly vulnerable. The writing requirements were drastically reduced despite overwhelming evidence that few entering freshmen could write with even minimal coherence or grammatical correctness. By the late 1970s, the tide had turned; some high schools were withholding diplomas until their graduates could demonstrate at least a tenth-grade reading competence, while colleges began to restore the former stress on fundamentals. By then, however, student activism had passed its peak, partly because it had succeeded on many fronts, partly from fatigue. Most students today are amenable to this redirection.

One of the triumphs of the student activist movement was the substitution of "Introduction" courses—in the novel, the short story, the poem—for the traditional courses in English and American literature. Younger faculty members drew large enrollments to courses in which a few works by currently popular writers said to have maximum "relevance" were discussed intensively and extensively. The intention was to develop skill in meaningful reading of similar writings, but too often the works studied, chosen for their momentary popularity, were the only "classics" the students became familiar with. Instead of taste, they acquired a method, and instead of discovery of great literature, they learned the joys of individual judgment and self-expression. Such courses ideally suited this generation imbued with indifference to the past and its values, and gave fresh sanction to the insistence on immediacy.

The postwar generation was not limited to college students. Among its most rebellious members were academic dropouts who, while in high school or after a brief exposure to college, decided that formal education was training for conformity. But it was on college campuses that young Americans, born after the Second World War, collided head-on with authority, with traditional standards, with established arbiters of taste. Also, whatever form of protest they chose to adopt was well reported in the press, and activities on one campus stimulated similar activism on others.

It would be too much, probably, to credit rebellious youth with the stepped-up campaign for equality or civil rights, but the same idealism and desire for equitable treatment are fundamental to all such movements. Women of all ages and blacks had been struggling for civil equality for more than a century, but it is only recently that they have made significant headway. American Indians and other minority groups, and the great majority of physically or mentally handicapped individuals, have begun to express themselves forcibly. Special-interest groups have multiplied; the old American habit of forming clubs has expanded to put pressure on the social and political establishment. Things that would have shocked the nation's taste in earlier times have come out into the open and demanded recognition— women's liberation, abortion, homosexuality, lesbianism. Old and new causes attract strenuous supporters—conservation, now renamed ecology; antimilitarism; accountability in elected officials; lowered age limits for voting and drinking; human rights in general, both at home and abroad. What is more, the general indignation at extreme changes in behavior has softened to tolerance and, here and there, to open approval. The culture is very much in flux, fragmented as never before, and anybody trying to keep up with the times might have difficulty discerning just where good taste lies. One of the keys may be the use of emotional, straightforward honesty rather than controlled intellectual rationalizing.

Back to the land and God

Emerson had urged nonconformity in the 1830s, but if students rebelling in the 1960s had a historic patron, it was not Emerson but his young friend Henry David Thoreau, who not only defied convention in his time but wrote "Civil Disobedience," a virtual handbook for subsequent rebellion. His modern young disciples took from him what they chose, including a deep respect for Far Eastern mysticism and philosophy. Yoga and T M— Transcendental Meditation—cannot be traced to his influence, but the back-to-the-land movement can be. Dropouts from the society they considered corrupt, some of them college graduates, chose to move to rural or wilderness areas, turning their backs on the materialism and conveniences of modern civilization and subsisting on the work of their hands.

This wave of new philosophy has had its effect on religion. Staid old churches supported by large endowments have not been seriously affected, but many others, alarmed by the declining attendance, have adopted novel methods especially attractive to youth, including the introduction of rock music to Sabbath services. A new music industry has developed: "Jesus Rock" groups—as many as a thousand of them nationwide, according to one estimate—that perform in churches and lure repentant sinners to the rail with

electric guitars and such lyrics as this:

> I don't have to play to get glad.
> I get plenty glad when I pray.
> I don't have to go somewhere to
>   find God,
> 'Cause I'm with him every day.

The groups have names as interesting as any others in the rock business—The All Saved Freak Band, for example, and the Second Chapter of Acts.

Church weddings sometimes take on what conservatives view as a carnival atmosphere, with bride and groom and attendants writing their own scripts and introducing song and dance to the ceremony. Some of the young have rejected organized religion altogether by forming their own worship groups that gather at odd times on week-days for serious Bible reading and informal prayer. Others combine religion with strenuous sports activity; it is not uncommon today for prominent professional athletes to declare their faith in public and urge emulation. The traditional line between religious and secular interests has been breached at many points. Billy Graham, the nation's leading evangelist, has led prayer meetings in the White House and has played golf with presidents with full exposure to television cameras.

No brief summary could exhaust the recent and current trends in American religiosity—or, to use the language of William James, the increasing varieties of religious experience. Far-out clergymen perform marriages for couples of the same sex, while priests and nuns defect from the Catholic Church to marry. The more extreme young enthusiasts, called "Jesus Freaks," adopt odd practices and behavior as if intent on proving their freakishness. Some blacks repudiate American religions altogether by becoming Muslims and adopting Arabic names, and the Reverend Moon of Korea has had little difficulty in winning thousands of converts to his Unification Church, not recognized as Christian.

In religion today, as elsewhere in the culture, anything goes, in a range from traditional orthodoxy to the most extreme radicalism. The majority of the population belongs to no church at all, as has always been true in the United States; but church membership is growing if we count as a church every kind of deviant worship.

Heritage Hills, designed by Walz & McLeod; Somers, N.Y.; 1975.
An example of cluster housing, with 3,100 condominiums scattered
over 1,100 rural acres. The minimum age for a resident is 18.

Wearing what you believe in

The postwar generation's ideas and ideals have had a great many effects on American taste. In addition to political demonstrations, young people rebelled in their choice of clothing and manner of personal appearance. The appearance of the people in power—double-knit suits, polyester shirts, and well-combed hair—was rejected for the more simple look of blue jeans, denim workshirts, and long hair. This outfit—the same for both women and men—became a uniform of nonconformity. Coupled with the "back-to-the-land" movement, it eventually led to a general desire for unaffected simplicity and the naturalness of things homemade. Peasant shirts and skirts, Mexican serapes, and Indian shirts were added to the blue jeans and workshirts.

Today, college students have returned to their studies, and as in the past, both hairstyles and clothing distinguish male from female.

Free choice in building

Gothic, long the preferred style for new church construction, is seldom chosen today. Most new churches are given a central plan whereby the congregation can face itself. Some of these modern designs are strikingly beautiful, such as St. John's Abbey in Collegeville, Minnesota. For most other public buildings, taste generally favors rejection of all historicism and its replacement by sleek, clean-lined structures based on engineering principles and using new materials.

The term *modern* means different things in different periods, and even in the same period when applied, say, to dress and music and theology. What most of us consider a modern house, moreover, has little in common with a contemporary office building or tall apartment house. For such buildings, taste now generally favors the styles displayed at the International Show mounted at the Museum of Modern Art in 1932. It was marked by extensive use of reinforced concrete, glass in corner and ribbon windows, bands of glass brick, and elevator shafts as hubs of design. It had visually satisfying balance without artificial symmetry and was commonly angular or boxlike, with no cornices to accentuate roof lines.

Taste for this style, which totally rejected historicism, developed faster in Europe, where most of the progressive designers lived, than in the United States. Here it met stiff resistance, especially for dwellings. Frank Lloyd Wright applied some of its innovations to modest houses, but very few

Americans found them tasteful. There was more tolerance for innovation applied to large structures, and some of the big Art Deco projects, notably Rockefeller Center, were quite close to the International style.

Interest in the style began to accelerate in the late 1930s after several of the most gifted European architects were invited to teach at

architectural schools and settled permanently in America—Miës van der Rohe and Walter Gropius from Germany, Eliel Saarinen and Alvar Aalto from Finland. They left behind in Europe some of the most distinctive monuments of creative design, but soon created in America a new synthesis of the International style. Collectively, these men viewed architecture as a primary force in shaping culture and in creating new life-styles, and their successors have continued to develop their ideas.

One American innovation was the glass curtain wall for office buildings. The pioneer was the Halladie Building in San Francisco, designed by Willis Polk in 1918. Although it had Victorian ironwork for cornices and balconies, like many other structures in that era of transition from old to new, it also had a great expanse of glass that permitted maximum penetration of light. It was the forerunner of Lever House (1952) and the Seagram Building (1958) in New York and the many other later glass-faced office buildings.

An even more recent concept, of similarly designed buildings connected and surrounded by plazas, plots of greenery, and pools of water, as in the older Rockefeller Center, has had an enormous appeal, especially when the cluster thus landscaped is the end product of urban renewal.

Old forms and new

The new breed of architectural designers has been imaginative enough to distinguish between wretched old structures deserving only of demolition and monuments of historic styles worthy of preservation. They have been in the vanguard of one of the most interesting developments of recent years, the rescue of good old buildings threatened by the wrecking ball to make room for new and more productive structures.

Local and regional historical societies have had a long history of fund-raising to buy such old structures—meetinghouses, town halls, abandoned churches and mansions, gristmills, covered bridges, and other relics. In 1949, the National Trust for Historic Preservation was founded, a nonprofit private organization chartered by Congress and partly funded by federal agencies. Growing fast, especially during the bicentennial period, it now has well over a hundred thousand members and the professional staff and resources to help local groups preserve buildings and sometimes entire districts.

This ground swell of interest is a strange phenomenon, coupled as it is with the American passion for the new. It could not succeed without the skill of professional designers, for its chief reliance is on "adaptive use"—renovation,

Top right: *Aerial view of residences; St. Augustine Shores, Fla.; 1970. A Deltona Corporation community with modest one-family homes.* Above: *LaGuardia Airport, New York, N.Y.; opened 1939, named after Fiorello LaGuardia in 1947.*

McDonald's restaurant; Clarkstown, W.Va.
Today there are 4,712 McDonald's restaurants—the
first one opened in Des Plaines, Ill., in 1955.

mostly of interiors, to give the old buildings a new life of income-producing, tax-paying activity. The net result is that all across the land, communities large and small are keeping their architectural past alive at the same time that the International style is fully accepted for large new structures.

Uneven progress

In the 1940s, it was still possible to charge architects with neglecting to develop appropriate forms for the burgeoning travel industry—airports, motels, service stations. They have since made up for their neglect, particularly at airports, where the ideas of space and flight have inspired some spectacular designs. As for motels, the results have been mediocre or worse, with few exceptions. Travelers and builders alike have been more concerned with interior luxury and

comfort than with facade aesthetics. The best motel chains cling to an approximation of the Georgian style or erect lifeless "modern" blocks without any hint of the International style. Service stations, meanwhile, are not so much architecture as efficient machines, which is what motorists prefer.

Much more attention has been lavished on city hotels. The Hyatt Regency on the Embarcadero in San Francisco must be one of the most awesomely exciting buildings in the modern world. It has a vast interior atrium rising the height of an eighteen-story main block, above which is a revolving restaurant that provides a panoramic view of city and bay. The atrium is like an enclosed city, with a huge square pool, copious greenery, scattered clusters of tables, and expansive open spaces. The Hyatt Regency is a worthy successor to

the nearby Palace Hotel—the nation's most modern when it was completed in 1876—and has the same emphasis on ample dimensions, especially in lobby, corridors, and glass-roofed interior court. Most hotels built after 1876 stinted on space, a trend that the Hyatt and several other hotel chains are reversing. As for top-story restaurants, numerous cities now boast of them. New York has several, with the loftiest atop one tower of the World Trade Center in lower Manhattan. Seattle has a restaurant on a tower of its own, with no functioning building beneath it. For many diners, it would seem, elegance is enhanced by the distance above street level.

Open space has become an important consideration in cities that have become severely overbuilt and congested. In New York, where every square foot of ground space has a fantastic dollar value, open space laws are now strictly enforced. The welcome pockets of sunlight and fresh air, and ground-level or sunken gardens, fountains, trees, and walkways temper the stark, unadorned design of the buildings and enhance the general ambiance. A prime example of such innovative design is the row of lofty office buildings that Rockefeller Center has erected, one to a block, on the west side of Avenue of the Americas, all set well back from the street. Lawmakers and imaginative architects have collaborated in creating a new taste in urban architecture.

Nor is New York alone. Open space has been integrated with clusters of new buildings in numerous other cities, with or without prodding from municipal officers. In Boston, close to such historic structures as Faneuil Hall and the Quincy Market, the recently completed Government Center is a classic of urban renewal. Its large plaza, brick-paved, suggests the ancient Roman forum. Other cities, partly or largely in an effort to reverse the flight of taxpayers to the suburbs, have added new grace to their central cores with distinctive efforts—Seattle, Minneapolis, Atlanta, Cincinnati, San Diego, Kansas City, Detroit. Whether or not the taxpayers are lured back, the result has been to reduce urban blight and create new forms attractive to everyone's taste.

Multiple housing

Wholesale demolition of most housing units in the nation, and their replacement by modern housing, might, in the view of one minor sage, produce the greatest era of prosperity this country has ever known. Few people, presumably, would prefer the present crowding in most city cores, with block after block of private residences and apartment houses touching each other on both sides and windows only in front and in back. Steps have already been taken to alleviate this condition with the building of residential clusters that provide adequate light and air and open areas between units. Some of the best are for the benefit of the urban poor, dispossessed of their former tenement life by the steady demand for ground space for commercial buildings. For the middle economic classes and for the wealthy, however, the same thinking has produced the high-rise condominium, which is as likely to be found where ground space is not at a premium as it is in crowded cities. High-rise condominium apartment houses are especially numerous in the Florida sun belt, where the flat landscape makes them conspicuous for miles around.

The condominium principle has a special attraction for older couples, who can sell roomy houses that they no longer need or wish to maintain, use the proceeds to buy an apartment of a few rooms containing every latest gadget and having plenty of cross ventilation, and not have to worry about mowing the lawn or keeping aphids off the shrubbery, let alone shovel snow in the winter. Of course, there may be unexpected drawbacks to condominium living, such as having hard-of-hearing neighbors who turn up the volume of their television sets late at night to observe the antics of Johnny Carson. An even greater drawback for families with limited resources is the steady rise of the monthly maintenance fee to cover all the services the condominium promises to provide. But no sensible American expects perfection.

Another kind of condominium to become popular in recent years is the retirement village, usually set in a rural area, well supplied with shops and recreational facilities— tennis courts, golf courses, whirl-pool baths, bosky dells—and often barring residents under the age of twenty-one. The word "Heritage" in the name of several of these communities hints at a return to a former time when life for all was more leisurely. The buildings themselves somewhat recapture the colonial past, thereby providing reassurance of stability. Such communities tend to be rather expensive and therefore accessible only to families with higher-than-average incomes. Like the high-rises, they are often governed collectively, with elected representatives deciding such matters as when dogs may run loose and the schedules for bus trips to the nearest city.

Most of these retirement communities in the North consist of units with a variable number of apartments under one roof—six or eight, perhaps. Elsewhere, especially in Florida but also found in the north woods, single-house projects are increasingly available. Some of them differ little from the tract houses of the 1950s, with the monotony of a single design and narrow, identical lots. The better ones permit a choice of styles and colors, and offer more amenities such as walking and bicycling paths, clubhouses, and open land. Unwary prospective customers are often gulled by high-pressure sales tactics and elaborate brochures showing sketches of streets and buildings that are still merely in the proposal stage. Well-planned communities, whatever their particular form, have wide streets already paved and curbed, sidewalks, fully sodded lawns, and sewers and utility lines all in place before the sales pitch begins.

Shopping centers

For working Americans, past their years of revolt if they ever had them and not yet ready for retire-

ment, the common goal is to own a home large enough to house a growing family and its pets, with a two-car garage on a paved driveway and grounds for unrestricted gardening, in a neighborhood relatively free of traffic but convenient to shops. This last is perhaps the most important single factor, without which neither outlying tract developments nor retirement communities would be feasible.

The huge shopping centers, some in urban settings but more in what was recently open country, are a phenomenon of the postwar period. In part, they are the outcome of urban sprawl, which changes countrysides to vast residential areas, but they also thrive on the absence of mass transit and the American love for automobiles. In fact, many are the result of the linear development of highways rather than the planned expansion of townships. They represent a decline of the urban way of life and even of the old village pattern; in both, shops and residences were closely mingled, and people, mostly on foot, knew each other or easily formed new friendships.

The new shopping centers vary in gracefulness of design. Only a few have trees and shrubs to alleviate the bleak vastness of their parking areas. The shoddiest deteriorate rapidly until they become, like western ghost towns or unprofitable filling stations, permanent rebukes to local planning, or to the lack of it. The larger the shopping centers become, the likelier it is that sheer size defeats their original purpose—to shorten walking distances for tired shoppers and to protect them from the weather. In the late 1970s, small neighborhood stores like those in built-up cities, began to make a comeback, although local zoning ordinances, meant to protect the residential neighborhoods, often thwart this trend.

One recourse for refugees from urban crowding who discover disadvantages in "country living" is to move back into town, where there are buses, subways, and taxis to move individuals from place to place. Cities that have lost taxpayers to new outlying areas would gladly welcome them back, and much of the effort spent on urban renewal is based on this hope. But as Herbert Hoover asserted in 1932, "To own one's home is a physical expression of individualism, of enterprise, of independence, and of freedom of spirit." All these sterling qualities would be sacrificed, by inference, if families in any large numbers were to reverse their exodus to regain urban advantages.

The modern homestead

If individualism and freedom of spirit are distinctly American qualities, as Mr. Hoover supposed, we might expect more variety in domestic life-style than is evident in the great middle class. What is evident, in most neighborhoods where families own their own homes on their own lots, is a

Contemporary breakfast area with molded chairs and bistro table.

curious combination of the "anything goes" syndrome and a new compulsion to conform. There is welcome freedom from the enforced restrictions of retirement communities, and from the physical limitations of high-rise condominiums; but even in the open country, what passes as good taste betrays a singular impulse to avoid too much deviation from neighborhood or national norm.

The average builder or buyer of a contemporary house would probably not acknowledge his conformity any more than student activists would have admitted theirs when they donned the uniforms symbolic of rebellion. The style most favored today for single-family dwellings has no name but is a distant variant of the one-story vernacular farmhouse with pitched roof parallel to the street and a lower extension on one side. Unlike the designs of most public buildings, the current taste for dwellings commonly extends to include details from various foreign and historic styles. There seems to be something reassuring about having such a mixture, although not many of the people who adopt it are aware of what they are mixing. Certainly, few of them would prefer a new house in any standard older style—Greek Revival, Victorian Gothic, Italianate, Queen Anne. But there is widespread taste for evocation of what people assume to be colonial, however remote this style of house is from anything built during the days before independence.

As a 1976 exhibition at the Renwick Gallery in Washington, D.C., made almost painfully clear, what makes a house look like a house today, in the thinking of most people, is the presence of "elements of architecture [that] have symbolic meaning and give messages about the environment that make it comprehensible and

therefore usable by people in their daily lives." The title given to the exhibit was "Signs of Life: Symbols in the American City," but the sections about taste in dwellings referred as much to suburban and rural homes as to those within city limits, and such styles are more conspicuous in suburbia.

All across the country, these symbols are easily recognized. Doorways vary but commonly imitate some historic style. In wealthier neighborhoods, where most houses have two stories, the doors are likely to be topped by broken pediments. Nonfunctional shutters frame the windows, especially those on the main facade. Siding is of brick in plain or intricate patterns, or of treated fire-resistant material made to look like old shingles or clapboards. The front walk may be bordered by small plants evoking Colonial Williamsburg, and where it meets the sidewalk, there is apt to be a metal post supporting a coach lamp that matches one by the door, with bulbs shaped like candles or the wicks of primitive oil lamps.

The manicured front lawn is often adorned with other artifacts recalling olden times or distant lands: wagon wheels partly buried in the ground as if left there when the wagon got mired down; fluted Greek columns, truncated, supporting birdbaths; imitation well covers, holding flowers, and sometimes even a well sweep. Along the entire block, the same smooth lawn continues, broken only by driveways or groups of shrubs. If a fence exists, it is of split logs, suggesting young Abe Lincoln's era. Signs proclaim the family names, commonly misspelled—"Andrew's," "The Bruce's." The facade of the typical house bears further evidence of the taste for historical detail: an American eagle over the door, a Pennsylvania Dutch hex sign, Mediterranean

grill railings flanking the steps and the tiny porch. There may be window boxes of plastic molded to resemble wood.

No single house flaunts all such details. A judicious sampling seems to satisfy most families. Interiors are somewhat less standardized, perhaps because the range of choices is much broader. Most rooms display a casual freedom unknown since the late Victorian period; unlike typical Victorian interiors, however, the choices are from established periods of taste. Consistency of style within a room is preferred by sophisticates, perhaps, but not by average American homemakers, while functional modern furniture, imitative of Scandinavian design, has only limited attraction for the majority of Americans.

The formal parlor may have a well-stuffed Chippendale sofa, a coffee table resembling a Renaissance buffet or a legged tray from eighteenth-century France, an étagère in one corner containing much the same jumble of curios as a Victorian whatnot, a Federal side table holding an Art Nouveau lamp, a domestic Oriental rug or wall-to-wall shag carpeting, a television set in what resembles a Flemish chest, and heavy Georgian draperies that can be drawn to cover the sliding glass doors that have succeeded the picture window of the 1950s. On the fireplace mantel, small glass or ceramic animals may be flanked by huge hurricane lamps. Over the sofa is a large framed print of a rural scene.

Most families who build or buy such houses belong to the rising middle class, beneficiaries of the rapid increase in national affluence since the Second World War, and eager to secure their status as substantial citizens. Most, moreover, have never had any acquaintance with early American houses, and have no family heirlooms. Many

Americans do, of course, but the great majority do not—there simply are not enough antiques around, and the good pieces sell at auctions for prices average families cannot afford.

In a very real sense, this middle-age generation—a huge one—has had no exposure to taste as it existed in the past, and has been forced to create a taste of its own based on free choice of available consumer goods. Advertising, of course, helps form taste, as do the designers of objects for sale. Inventive as such people are, they tend to exploit the great demand for articles representing the past—including snap-in plastic window dividers that give the impression of nine-over-six Georgian windows or even the diamond panes of colonial casement windows.

Every house in the middle-class range is an efficient machine for living, well equipped with the latest products of technology. In a Wright-designed house, those products were complemented by structural materials no less advanced and by innovative furniture and furnishings with no debt to period styles. But such consistency has slight appeal today. Strictly modern houses are built for particular clients, by architects in the Wright tradition, and taste for this type of dwelling is limited.

Making taste today

In different periods of the past, successful men and their wives invited envy by furnishing their grand mansions in the latest European mode. But since the latter years of the nineteenth century, the very rich have lost interest in performing the role of tastemakers. They are even reluctant to have their homes featured in magazine articles as was common before and for some time after the First World War. The interiors most frequently illustrated today

in magazine articles are those of a new breed of national heroes and heroines—leading professional athletes with million-dollar contracts and stars of the entertainment world who seek constant exposure in order to retain their hold on the public's favor. Their homes are more often than not extravagantly furnished, in no particular style, and confirm, for the millions of families without the same incomes, the propriety of mixing styles at will.

Central to this huge market from which consumers can chose their own style, and perhaps the most striking feature of contemporary American living, is internationality. Following the First World War, the United States retreated back to its boundaries and remained there until war again brought it out. The Second World War—and the division of the world along cold-war battle lines that followed it—has left the United States inextricably tied with the rest of the free world. The American economy is solidly joined, in particular, to the economies of Europe, Japan, Taiwan, and most recently, the OPEC nations.

Almost anything an American buys may well have been made outside the United States. The label "made in Japan," once taken as a sign of an inferior product, now signifies something else entirely: almost all televisions sold in the United States are made in Japan. The same holds true for radios. Clothing, silverware, coffee cups, and myriad other products made in Taiwan can be found all across the United States.

Although Americans no longer follow the direction of Europe, it sometimes seems that by following their own desires, Americans end up with European-made products. When bicycling became popular in the United States, the old "English racers" were replaced by foreign-

made ten-speed sport bikes. When better sports shoes were needed for the new interest in jogging, tennis, and many other sports, the product, again, was European. In furniture, Scandinavian designing has had its share of the American market for many years. Foreign designer clothing shops line the avenues in most American cities.

The most obvious example of Americans following the foreign lead is the automobile. Because of their better gas mileage and cheaper prices, foreign cars have been successfully invading the American market for years. Partly in response to this preference on the part of consumers and partly as a reaction to strong energy regulations, American car manufacturers are beginning to follow the foreign example.

This influx of foreign-made items has made the range of choices open to American consumers almost boundless.

Museum practices

Complementing the growing interest in preserving old buildings by adaptive use and the taste for furniture vaguely imitative of historic styles is an amazing current interest in museums that exhibit not only prized paintings but lesser artifacts from the past. The old concept of a museum as a place to display acknowledged masterpieces and thereby instruct ambitious art students has long since been abandoned. A new kind of curator has emerged, professionally trained and as interested in new styles and forms as in historic treasures. Instead of crowding walls with as many pictures as possible, these curators select a few for emphasis, light them carefully, and change them frequently. The modern museum is something like a theater, offering changing programs with a high order of showmanship. Special exhibits travel from one museum to another, and individual pieces are often exchanged on a loan basis. The greatest attractions are such unusual loan exhibitions as the art of ancient China, King Tutankhamen's treasures, and early Irish art.

If museums no longer view their role as dictation of taste, they still inform and let viewers decide for themselves which styles and artists are to their individual tastes. However, the traditional notion that works of art must have specific literal meaning is still very much alive in many quarters. Since much in modern art deliberately avoids such literalness, sometimes to the point of total abstraction or pure design, taste for it has been slow to develop, and, for some Americans, obscurity is still a barrier to acceptance.

Among the newer forms of art produced in recent years are the mobiles pioneered by Alexander Calder, so perfectly balanced that they change position when touched or moved by air currents; the massive metal sculptures of Calder and other artists; and the constructions, now renamed "assemblages," by such innovators as Louise Nevelson. Their primary home is the Hirshhorn Museum and Sculpture Garden in Washington, D.C., just east of the Smithsonian Castle. But they can also be found in libraries and skyscraper office buildings, on college campuses (notably the University of California at Los Angeles), in parks, and alongside interstate highways—as in rural Nebraska, where they have caused considerable controversy.

When the Hirshhorn opened in the fall of 1974, its contents took second place in public awareness to the building itself. One eminent architectural critic, Ada Louise Huxtable, found the round concrete structure raised above ground level on four immense stanchions totally lacking in "the essential factors of esthetic strength and provocative vitality," and called the style "neopenitentiary modern." Washingtonians had other names for it: a bunker lacking only gun emplacements; a gas tank without its Exxon sign. Its defenders insisted that the building was itself a work of functional sculpture and an innovative, elegant addition to the Mall. But taste often reacts unfavorably to anything too unusual, as it did in 1959 when the Guggenheim Museum, also of poured concrete in a design by Frank Lloyd Wright, was opened on New York's Fifth Avenue. Nor should we forget the denunciation of the Smithsonian Castle in the 1850s as a desecration of the Mall. Today the Guggenheim is viewed as one of Wright's masterpieces, and most Washingtonians are fond of the Castle. Familiarity seems to soften contempt as often as it breeds it.

On any good day, the Hirshhorn is crowded, and at noon visitors lunch in the sculpture garden amid pieces they may not understand but accept for what they are. Museum-goers have developed a casual attitude toward whatever modern art produces, in what might be called a passive form of taste. They know that not even the strongest expression of distaste can drive what they dislike out of sight, but they are by and large willing to look at it, and to be persuaded that it has some value.

Yet some art can still excite controversy. Female nudity no longer offends, but male nudity does, in painting if less so in sculpture. More conspicuous is Pop Art, first displayed in the early 1960s by such painters as Andy Warhol. The chief objection to it is that it virtually eliminates the gap between traditional art and the advertising art that relates directly to daily living. In this respect, it resembles the singing commercials that help sell products over television and radio.

Defenders of Pop Art call it a manifestation of the modern taste for realism, and insist that it has a welcome relevance to actuality that "serious art" simply does not have. A historic precedent would be the multiform chromos of the last century, meant to please but frankly ephemeral. Andy Warhol would be the first to applaud if his photographically realistic painting of Campbell Soup cans were forgotten, replaced by a continuing series of fresh works. Pop Art lays no claim to permanent value. Its appeal is to the sense of immediacy that today's young people have established as one of the national norms. But despite the disclaimers of Pop artists, some of their works may stand the test of time and earn the reputation of significance.

New foods

Scientists love to remind us that technology has made greater advances in the last fifty years than in all previous human history. The impact of those advances on culture is too obvious to need explication here. Choices available are far more numerous than at any period in the past, and tastes are necessarily multiplied. But if we all accept what we wish from the vast diversity, not everything can be credited to technological advance—the things we eat, for example.

In 1949, Clarence Birdseye perfected a quick-freezing process that made it possible for housewives to serve seasonal food any time during the year. They could do so, however, only with the introduction of freezer sections in refrigerators, or separate freezers. Earlier, canned foods had been the only way to provide a varied diet, whether home-canned or factory-produced. But neither the availability of prepared foods nor the in-

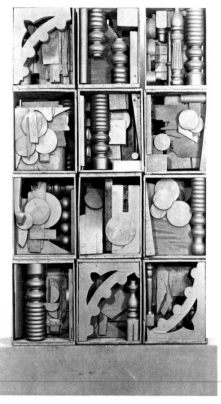

Top: Black Wall, *by Russian-born*
Louise Nevelson; 1964.
Above: Racoon # 1, *by*
German-born Karl Zerbe; 1968.

fluence of the advertisers that tout them explains the gradual shift from hearty meals three times a day to the present more or less standard pattern of breakfast, lunch, and dinner, or breakfast, dinner, and supper. That change came only with the tardy awareness that people in most occupations live more healthful lives without heavy meals. Not everybody is happy about the role advertising plays in determining eating habits, or with the bright packaging, artificial coloring, and chemical preservatives used to sell meats and vegetables. Concerned Americans have expressed their dissatisfaction with standardized foods that have little nutritional value. The interest in foods that are more natural—that are treated with fewer chemicals—has been bolstered by a barrage of scientific discoveries about cancer-causing agents found in many commonly used chemicals. Most Americans accept the packaging and processing that add to the cost of food but simplify preparation.

Most of us, in addition, have welcomed the new variety of foods once called "ethnic" but now well established as American—Chinese menus, for example, and all the different pastas of Italian origin, not to mention Norwegian herring, olive oil from Mediterranean countries, and cheeses from Greece and Finland, France and Italy. "Ethnic" restaurants abound not only in New York, where most immigrants first put down roots, but in cities with almost none of these recent newcomers. The admission of Hawaii as a state in 1959 stimulated interest in Polynesian dishes, and the influx of Puerto Ricans and Mexicans has popularized Latin American foods. Wine-lovers, meanwhile, have learned that not all excellent wines come from France. German, Italian, Spanish, Greek, and Yugoslav wines now

compete with the French, and native varieties, from California and the Finger Lake region of New York, have their loyal enthusiasts.

Sports and leisure activities

A comparable explosion has occurred in sports. Horse racing, baseball, golf, tennis, and basketball have become even more popular with professional organization. Ice hockey, soccer, football, and skiing have expanded even faster, and to skiing on snow has been added water skiing. Although some people decry the tendency of Americans to observe rather than participate in sports, a parallel interest, part of the general concern for health, has developed in physical fitness—jogging, cross-country running and skiing, swimming, skating, scuba diving, mountain climbing, camping, sailing, bowling, and numerous "racket" sports. Such activities multiply the need for special clothing and equipment, including the ubiquitous sleeping bags. The variety of these essentials and the volume of their sales attest to the affluence sports-minded young Americans take for granted.

Not every sport is universally admired, and with their multiplication, friction is inevitable. Small-boat sailors abominate high-power speed boats, pedestrians are not overly fond of joggers and bicyclists, people in rural areas are annoyed by the nerve-shattering noise of snowmobiles on still winter nights. But most Americans today have leisure enough to participate in at least one sport and to play one or more of the popular games.

Among card games, bridge is still the most popular, although poker is the favorite of many men who find it a good substitute for costlier kinds of gambling. Monopoly, favored in the 1930s and 1940s, has yielded to Scrabble, a sophisticated cousin of the nineteenth-century game of anagrams. Still champion of skilled board games is chess, which has remained in fashion since the time of the Medes and the Persians; but backgammon is posing a challenge to its primacy.

Vacationing away from home has steadily grown in favor, until today almost all Americans consider it one of their inherent rights. More and better highways and the development of efficient, comfortable trailers and campers have made vacations on wheels a popular annual sport. With competitive air fares, foreign travel—once restricted to the upper echelons of society—has now become feasible for a much larger segment of the population. Until a few years ago, Europe was the chief mecca of American tourists, but now the desire to see new places takes many to other continents, at a cost within the means of students, working people, and retirees.

Hundreds of thousands of middle-income northern families now spend part of each winter in far-southern regions of the United States or in the Caribbean. Hawaii, as far from the West Coast as that coast is from the Atlantic, draws other tens of thousands of mainland visitors all year round. Nor is it uncommon for ordinary citizens to take off for three-week trips to Machu Picchu high in the Andean mountains of Peru, to China and Southeast Asia, up the Nile to Luxor and other monuments of ancient Egypt, or to wild animal preserves in Kenya. Taste for travel has never been so easily indulged, and the choice of potential destinations is almost completely unlimited.

Freedom and courage

The national anthem speaks of the United States as "the land of the free and the home of the brave."

Freedom and courage—twin qualities that were well distributed in generations before our own. In this age of unprecedented affluence, it is sometimes easy to forget the long, hard struggle that was necessary to get us where we are.

We Americans today tend to take for granted the abundance of consumer goods, and the incomes that enable us to choose freely from among the almost limitless range of options—in life-style, the arts, entertainment, travel, food, clothing, religion, and everything else in this land and age of plenty. What need there is for individual courage is hardly comparable to the kinds needed in the past—to cross the Atlantic in small ships and create footholds in a wilderness, to defy a great European power and win independence, to extend the frontier three thousand miles westward, to create a complex system of institutions and government. All that is history now. Success has pushed it aside, and courage takes the modern form of aggressive demands for group and individual rights and for a greater share of the national wealth.

The key word to present actuality is not courage but freedom, which we implement by choosing from among a plethora of objects. One of the most important aspects of that freedom is that the American people no longer depend on foreign dictation in forming their taste. Another is a greatly reduced responsiveness to authoritarian pronouncements.

And we have graduated from our adolescent contempt for indigenous forms, such as Shaker chairs and folk art, to a genuine appreciation of their intrinsic beauty. We have come to recognize native music, especially that of Afro-American origin, with its original tempos and melodies, rather than rejecting it as something infe-

rior. The Armory Show of 1913 shocked the nation out of its ignorance of modern painting, and redirected artistic taste toward tolerance of innovation and experiment. Eugene O'Neill pioneered modern drama and changed theatergoers' ideas about what drama should be. Literary standards have undergone a comparable change with the New Poets, the giants of fiction between the two world wars, and the recent emergence of creative talent in a broad ethnic spectrum.

Amid all these changes, and with the unrestricted freedom of groups and individuals to make their own choices, it may be that present multiplicity and independence of taste will lead to chaos. In an age when anything goes and no single standard is generally accepted, taste as it has been recognized in all past ages is threatened with extinction. Whatever we may privately think about taste in the past, it at least provided a certain stability, which is something that fragmented and shifting taste cannot do. One reasonable hope is that what is valuable amid the present diversity will endure and serve as the firm base for a new national taste.

But does America need redirection, or restoration of what it has forgotten? Is there any time in our past that any number of us would consider a golden age of taste, one we wish we could return to? What ground is there for believing the nation is on the wrong course?

Future students of culture may decide that the present multiplicity of standards, and the freedom of choice that we share today, is the ideal the American people have been striving to attain these three and a half centuries. No one now living can be certain. All we can be sure of is what these chapters have tried to record—that taste in America has undergone a continuous and fascinating evolution.

INDEX

Adam, Robert, 77
Adam Thoroughgood House (Va.), 26, 41
Adams, Abigail, 78
Adler, Dankman, *130*, 132
Adobe, 22
Advertising, 182–83
Age of Reason (Paine), 73
Alarm to Unconverted Sinners (Alleine), 63
Aldrich, Thomas Bailey, 154
Alfred Avery House (Ohio), 97
Alger, Horatio, Jr., 152–53
Allen, Ethan, 73
Alna Meeting House (Maine), 73, *74*
Alsop, George, 12
America's Cup, 99
Anderson, Sherwood, 162
Anglicans, 25, 26, 30, 40–41, 68
Annapolis (Md.), 25
Armory Exhibition (1913), 150–51
Art Deco, *163*, *168*, 170–71, 174–75
Art Nouveau, 148
Art of Sound Building (Halfpenny), 44
Ashcan School, 148–49, *151*, 160
Audubon, John James, 89
Austin, Henry, 113
Avery-Hunter House (Ohio), *98*

Babbitt (Lewis), 164
Bacon's Castle (Va.), 26, 41
Baldwin, James, 196
Balloon construction, 132
Bank buildings, 95, 97–99
Barlow, Joel, 74, 76
Barnum, P. T., *100*, 122
Bartram, John, 87–89
Bascom, Ruth Henshaw, 84
Baylis, Richard, 44
Beards, 115–16
Beaux-Arts style, 127, 135–41
Belasco, David, 157
Bellamy, Edward, 153
Bellow, Saul, 196
Bellows, George, 149, *157*
Benjamin, Asher, 97
Bennett, William, 87
Berkeley (Va.), 44
Beth Elohim Synagogue (S.C.), 98
Bierstadt, Albert, 108, *138-39*
Billings, William, 62
Biltmore (N.C.), *134*, 135
Blackburn, Joseph, *33*, 61
Blacksmiths, 12–17
Blair House (Wash., D.C.), *77*
Bloomer, Amelia, 117
Bogardus, James, 114
Bok, Edward, 143
Book of Architecture (Gibbs), 44, 52
Books and literature, 31, 63–64, 73–76, 100–103, 106–109, 114, 147, 152–55, 161, 195–96
Boston rocker, 117
Brackenridge, Henry, 74, 76
Bradstreet, Anne, 24–25, 31
Bradstreet, Simon, 24–25
Brancusi, Constantin, 176
Brannan, Sam, 109

Breakers (R.I.), *134*, 135, 173
Bremo (Va.), 80
Brewster chairs, 28, *54–55*
Brewster, John, Jr., *88*
Brick, 17, 23, 44–45
Broadsides, 65
Bryant, William Cullen, 89, 106–107
Bulfinch, Charles, 77, *77*, 78–80
Bungalows, 143–45, *184*
Burnett, Frances Hodgson, 152
Burnham, Daniel, *133*
Burroughs, John, 131
Butterick, Ebenezer, 117
Byles, Mather, 61
Byrd, William, 64

Cabinet Maker & Upholsterer's Guide (Hepplewhite), 80
Cabriole, 53
Canova, Antonio, 85
Capt. Keyram Walsh House (N.H.), *75*, *79*
Capt. Lord Mansion (Maine), 79
Carrére, John, *130*, 131
Carter's Grove (Va.), *41*, 44
Casa Grande (Calif.), 173
Cassatt, Mary, 148, *151*
Cast-iron facades, 114, 132
Cathedrals, 110–11
Catlin, George, 108
Cemeteries, 106
Centennial Exhibition (1876), 126–28, *138–39*
Central Park (N.Y.C.), *96*, 105
Charlotte Temple (Rowson), 75
Chewing tobacco, 115
Chicago Stock Exchange, 141
Chimneys, 41, 47, 50
Chippendale furniture, *54–55*, 80, *81*
Chretian Point Plantation (La.), 96
Christ Church (Maine), 104
Chromolithography, *72*, *120*, *138*, 146–47
Chrysler Building (N.Y.C.), 171
Churches, *16*, *18*, 22, 26, *42*, 51–52, 68–73, *74*, 97–99, 104, 109–11, *128*, 171
Churchill, Winston, 152
Cider, 58
Clipper ships, *96*, 99
Clothing and fashion, 21, 30, 32, 45, 58–59, 90–91, *103*, 116–17, *126*, *137*, 152, *173*, 200
Cole, Thomas, 107
Colonial colors, 45
Columbiad (Barlow), 74
Columbian Exposition (Ill.), *124–25*, 135–41
Commons, 25
Common Sense (Paine), 65
Complete Book of Architecture (Ware), 44
Condominiums, 203
Congregationalism, 45
Conwell, Russell, 153
Cooking and utensils, 12
Cooper, James Fenimore, 100–101
Copley, John Singleton, *50–51*, 61, 85

Coquette (Foster), 75
Corcoran Gallery (Wash., D.C.), 112
Corn, 12, 57
Cottage Residences (Davis & Downing), 104
Country Georgian, 49–51
Country Sheraton, *35*
Crane, Stephen, 154–55
Crawford, Thomas, 121
Crewel work, 29–30
Cummings, E. E., 161
Currier & Ives, *92–93*, 96
Currier, Nathaniel, 107–108
Customs House (N.Y.), 104

Dance and ballet, 166–67
David Gamble House (Calif.), 145, *153*
Davis, Alexander Jackson, *99*, 104–105, 114
Davis, Rebecca Harding, 103
Day of Doom (Wigglesworth), 31, 63
de Mille, Agnes, 167
De Wolfe, Elsie, 174
Deists, 73
Delineator, *137*, 152, *173*
Denison Homestead (Conn.), 96
Dickens, Charles, 114
Dickinson, John, 63
Don Raimundo Arrivas House (Fla.), *16*
Doorways, 45, 49–50, 77–78, 95
Dormer windows, 41
Dos Passos, John, 161, 164
Doughty, Thomas, 107
Downing, Andrew Jackson, 104–105
Drama and theater, 65, 76, 123, 156–57, 163, 190–91, 192–94
Dreiser, Theodore, 155, 164
Durand, Asher, 107
Durgin House (Maine), *105*, *116*
Durrier, George, 107, 108
Dutch influences, 17–21
Dvorak, Anton, 156
Dwight, Timothy, 74
Dyckman House (N.Y.), 19

Eads, James Buchanan, 101
Eakins, Thomas, 148, *151*
Eastlake, Charles, 142–43
Eastlake style, 117, *148*
Education, 64–65, 118, 197–98
Edwards, Jonathan, 61, 63
Egyptian style, 112, 174
Elevators, 133
Eliot, T. S., 162
Ellison, Ralph, 196
Embroidery, 29–30
Emerson, Ralph Waldo, 101–102, 115, 121, 131
Empire style, *35*, 79
English influences, 23–27, 48–49, 53–55
Ephrata Cloister (Pa.), 47–48
Etchers, 30–31
Executive Office Building (Wash., D.C.), 112
Exhuming the Mastadon (Peale), 86

Farms, 17–19
Federal age and styles, *35*, 52-53, *66–67*, 68–91, *77*, *81*
Feke, Robert, *60*, 61
First Baptist Meeting House (R.I.), *42*, 52
Fithian, Philip, 64
Fitzgerald, F. Scott, 163–64
Flagg, Ernest, *133*
Flatiron Building (N.Y.C.), *133*
Folk art, 83–85, 118, 174–75
Food, drink and diet, 11–12, 21, 57–58, 115, 207–208
Foster, Stephen, 122
Fraktur, *70*, 85
Francis Wyman House (Mass.), *18*
Frankel, Paul, 171
Franklin, Benjamin, 63, 73
Franklin Crescent (Mass.), 79
Freedom of the Will (Edwards), 63
French, Daniel Chester, *97*, *126*
French Directoire style, 81–83
French influences, 22–23
Freneau, Philip, 74–75, 76, 87–89, 90
Frost, Robert, 162–63
Fry, William Henry, 122
Furniture, 19–21, 26–28, *54–55*, 80–83, 117–18, 119, 142, 171, 184–85

Gadsden House (S.C.), 80
Gambling, 63
Gambrel roof, 17, 45
Gardner-Pingree House (Mass.), *78*, 80, *81*
Gateleg table, 28
Generation gap, 189
Genteel Tradition, 153–54
Gentleman & Cabinet-Maker's Director (Chippendale), *54–55*
Gentleman's Magazine, 65
Gentlemen's Classic, 45–46
Georgian age and styles, *37*, *38–39*, 40–65, *41*, *43*
German influences, 21
Germantown (Pa.), 47
Gibbs, James, 44, 49, 50
Gibson, Charles Dana, 146–47, *149*
Gingerbread style, 128–31
Glassware, 59–61
Gold Rush Gothic, 109
Goodman, Benny, 165
Goodwin mansion (N.H.), 79, *106*
Gothic, 73, 103–105, 109–15, 171
Gottschalk. Louis Moreau, 122
Governor's Palace (Va.), 44
Grace Episcopal Church (N.Y.C.), 110
Grandma Moses, 169
Granville (Ohio), *96–97*
Gravestone carving, *27*, 30, *60*, 61–62, 85
Greek Revival, 89, 95–99
Greene, Charles and Henry, 145, *153*
Greenfield Hill (Dwight), 74
Greenough, Horatio, *116*, 120–21
Gropius, Walter, *177*
Grosz, George, 169
Grove Plantation (Fla.), 96
Guy, Francis, 87

Hadley chest, *20, 28*
Haggard, H. Rider, 152
Hamilton House (Maine), 52–53
Hancock, John, *33,* 59
Hangings, 32, 63
Hardware, 14–17
Harrison, Peter, 52
Hart House (Mass.), 41–42
Harte, Bret, 108–109
Hassam, Childe, 148
Hastings, Thomas, *130,* 131
Hawthorne, Nathaniel, 102, 121, 131
Held, Anna, *126,* 157
Hellman, Lillian, 190
Hemingway, Ernest, 161
Henry, Joseph, 101
Hepplewhite, George, 80–83
Hepplewhite style, *79*
Herner, James A., 156
Hesselius, Gustav, 61
Hicks, Edward, 84
High Jacobean structures, 26
High Victorian style, 112, 117–19, 123, 128–31
Hints on Household Taste (Eastlake), 142
Hitchcock, Lambert, 117
Hitchcock chair, 104
Holy Trinity Church (Del.), 26
Homer, Winslow, 147
Hope, Anthony, 152
Hopkinson, Francis, 62, *64*
Horse racing, 32, 63, 99
Horticulture Hall (Pa.), 127
Hotels, *130, 131, 173, 190–91, 194,* 202
Houdon, Jean Antoine, 85, 120
Howe, Samuel Gridley, 95
Howells, William Dean, 154, 161
Hudson River School, 107, 108
Huguenots, 22
Hunt, Richard, *133,* 133–35, *134*
Hunting, 32, 63

Immigration, 99, 150
Industrial designing, 176–78
Interior decorating, 174–75
Ironwork, *11,* 14–17, *56*
Irving, Washington, 76, 89
Italianate style, *102,* 112–14
Ives, Charles, 156
Ives, James Merritt, 108

Jackson, Andrew, 99–100
Jackson, William Henry, 108
Jacksonian Revolution, 100–101
Jamestown (Va.), 11–12
Jane Dillon House (Conn.), *13*
Japanning, *46,* 55
Jarvis, Samuel, 73
Jazz, 165
Jefferson, Thomas, *34,* 80, 89–90
Jewett, Sarah Orne, 108
John Brown House (R.I.), 47
John Paul Jones House (Maine), 45
John Whipple House (Mass.), *13,* 24
Jones, Inigo, 32, 52
Joplin, Scott, 165

Kensett, John, 107
King's Chapel (Mass.), 52
Kitsch, 175
Knitting, 118
Krehbiel, Edward, 155–56
Kühn, Justus, *29,* 30

Lane, FitzHugh, 107
Language, 76
Latrobe, Benjamin, 85, 95, 104, 112,
L'Enfant, Pierre, 89
Levi Hayes House (Ohio), 96
Levine, Jack, *166,* 169
Lewis, Sinclair, 162, 163–64

Lind, Jenny, *116,* 122
Lindsay, Vachel, 161–62
Lithography, *92–93, 96, 97, 99,* 107–108, *116, 121,* 146, *149, 157*
Log houses, *14,* 21–22
Louis XV style, 117
Louis XVI style, 117
Lowell, Amy, 162
Lucius Mower House (Ohio), 97
Lyndhurst (N.Y.), *98,* 104
Lyon, Mary, 101

McBean, Thomas, 52
McCarthyism, 189–90
MacDowell, Edward, 156
McIntire, Samuel, 52, 77, 78–79, *79, 80*
McKim, Charles Fullen, 136, 141, *144*
Madison, Dolley, 90
Madison, James, 90
Magazines, 65, 151–52, 164–65
Mailer, Norman, 196
Major, Charles, 152
Malamud, Bernard, 196
Mansard roof, 112, *143*
Mark Twain House (Conn.), *94, 113,* 118–19, *148*
Martineau, Harriet, 114, 116
Mason, Lowell, 122
Masonic Temple (Pa.), *100,* 111
Massachusetts General Hospital, 80
Masters, Edgar Lee, 161–62
Mather, Cotton, 29, 31–32
Mayor Girod House (La.), *16*
Mead, William Rutherford, 136, 141
Medway Plantation (S.C.), *14,* 23
Melville, Herman, 102
Memorial Hall (Pa.), 127, *138–39*
Mencken, Henry Louis, 165
M'Fingal (Trumbull), 65, 73–74
Middleburg House (S.C.), 23, 41
Millay, Edna St. Vincent, 162
Miller, Arthur, 190–91
Mission Church (N.M.), 22
Mission furniture, 145
Mitchell, Maria, 101
Modern architecture, 171, *186–87, 188, 190–91, 193, 194, 197, 199, 200–201, 200–206, 201.*
Modern art, 150–51
Modern Chivalry (Brackenridge), 76
Modern dance, 166–67
Monroe, Harriet, 161
Monterey Colonial, 22
Montez, Lola, 109, *121,* 133
Moore, Marianne, 162
Moran, Thomas, 108
Morgan, Benjamin, 97, *98*
Mormon Gothic, 109
Morse, Samuel F. B., 86
Morse-Libby House (Maine), *102,* 113–14
Motion pictures, 181–83, 194–95
Mucha, Alphonse, 148–49
Muckraking, 155
Multiple housing, 203
Mumford, Lewis, 17, 41, 136, 141
Museums and art galleries, 127, 146, 206–207
Mush, 57
Music, 30, 47, 62, 121–23, 155–56, 165, 167–69, 192–94

Nabokov, Vladimir, 196
Nathan Parker House (N.H.), 78
Nathaniel Hawthorne House (Mass.), 45
National Trust for Historic Preservation, 201–202
Neagle, John, 87
Near Eastern style, 112
Needlework, *8–9,* 28–30, *51, 64, 81, 84, 110*

Nevelson, Louise, *208*
New Amsterdam, 17–21
New England Primer, 31
New-England Psalm Singer (Billings), 62
New Orleans, 22
New Poetry, 161–63
Newport (R.I.), 52
New Rochelle (N.Y.), 23
New Sweden, 21–22
Newspapers, 65
Norris, Frank, 154–55
Novels, 75–76

Oaklands (Maine), 109
Ocean liners, 176
Octogon (Wash., D.C.), *77,* 80
Old Ship Meeting House (Mass.), 26
Olmsted, Frederick Law, 105–106, 135
O'Neill, Eugene, 163, 191
Open space laws, 203
Orchestras, 122, *164,* 167
Oriental influences, 54–55, *106*
Oval Office (White House), 78

Paine, Tom, 65, 73
Painting and art, 30–31, *33, 49, 50–51, 56, 60,* 61, *64, 69,* 76–77, 85–89, *87, 88,* 107–108, *138–39,* 140, 145–48, 150–51, *151, 158–59, 160, 164, 166,* 169–70, *208*
Palace of Governors (N.M.), 22
Palladio, Andrea, 48–49, 95, *144*
Palm Beach (Fla.), 173
Panama-Pacific Exposition (1915), 151, *154*
Paper ephemera, 147
Parks, 105–106
Patent Office (Wash., D.C.), 104
Patternmakers, 117
Peabody-Silsbee House (Mass.), 80
Peale, Charles Willson, 85–86
Peirce Mansion (N.H.), *77,* 78
Peirce-Nichols House (Mass.), 52, 80
Pelham, Peter, *29,* 30
Pennsbury (Pa.), 41
Pennsylvania Dutch, 47–48
Pepperrell House (Maine), 41, 42–43
Period houses, 183–84
Pewter ware, 59–61
Philadelphia, 25, 47, 97–99
Philipsburg Manor (N.Y.), *10,* 21
Philipse, Frederick, 21
Photography, 108, 149–50
Phyfe, Duncan, *81,* 82–83
Planned communities, 145, 178
Plantation Greek, 96
Plastics, 175–76
Poe, Edgar Allan, 102, 123
Pollock, Jackson, *140,* 169
Ponce de Leon Hotel (Fla.), 131
Pope-Leighey House (Va.), *170*
Porter, Eleanor, 152
Portraiture, 84
Portsmouth (N.H.), 78–79
Pottery, 59–61
Pound, Ezra, 161–62
Powers, Hiram, 121
Practical House Carpenter (Benjamin), 97
Practice of Piety (Bayly), 63
Press cupboards, *20,* 28
Prince of Parthia (Godfrey), 65
Prior, William Matthew, *69,* 84
Progressive architecture, 132
Pueblo, 22
Puritans, 24–25, 30, 31, 40–41, 45, 68

Quakers, 25, 26, 30, 73
Queen Anne styles, *46,* 54–55, 80, *81,* 128

Quilts, 118
Quincy, Josiah, 48, 59, 62
Quincy Market (Mass.), 98

Radio, 167, 179–82, 194
Radio City Music Hall (N.Y.C.), *164*
Railways, 99, *149,* 176–77
Realism, 87–89
Records and recordings, 167
Redwood Library (R.I.), 52
Renaissance style, 117
Renwick, James, 110–12
Retirement villages, 203
Revere, Paul, *24,* 51, 60
Richardson, Henry Hobson, *130,* 132
Rimmer, William, 121
Ringling Estate (Fla.), 173
Robie House (Ill.), *177, 181*
Robinson, E. A., 162
Rogers, John, 119
Rolfe-Warren House (Smith's Fort Plantation, Va.), 26, *34,* 41
Roman Revival, 89–90
Romanesque Revival, *130,* 132
Romanticism, 87, 95, 100
Rosecliff (R.I.), 141, *144*
Rum, 57–58

Ste. Genevieve (Mo.), 23
St. James Church (S.C.), *19*
St. John's Cathedral (N.Y.C.), 110–11
St. Luke's Church (Ohio), 97
St. Luke's Church (Va.), 26
St. Mary's Chapel (Md.), 104
Saint-Mémin, Charles de, 89
St. Michael's Church (S.C.), 52
St. Patrick's Cathedral (N.Y.C.), 110
St. Paul's Chapel (N.Y.C.), 52
Samplers, 84
San José de Gracia Church (N.Mex.), *16*
San Xavier del Bac (Ariz.), *16,* 22
Sandburg, Carl, 162–63
Sargent, John Singer, 147–48
Satire, 31, 73, 76, 163–64
Saugus Iron Works (Mass.), 15
Sawbuck table, 28
Sawmills, 24
School and college buildings, *2–3,* 37, *38–39,* 43, 80, 97–99, 188
Schwarzmann, Herman, 127
Scotch-Irish influences, 21
Sculpture, 30, 61–62, 76, 85, *97, 116,* 119–21, *124–25,* 136, *163,* 170, *208*
Sea Cliff (N.Y.), 131
Seafood, 11–12
Second Empire style, 112
Sedgeley (Pa.), 104
Seven Oaks (La.), 96
Shahn, Ben, 169
Shakers, *82, 83*
Shaw, Richard Norman, 128
Sheldon, Charles M., 152
Shellstone, 22
Sheraton, Thomas, 80–83
Sheraton style, *81*
Shingle style, *2–3,* 128, *128, 129*
Ship figureheads, *60,* 61, 80
Shirley (Va.), 44
Shopping centers, 203–204
Sibelius, Jean, 168
Silverware, *24,* 30, *51,* 59–60
Simons, Benjamin, 23
Sinclair, Upton, 155
Singer Building (N.Y.C.), *133*
Sketch Book (Irving), 76
Skyscrapers, 133
Slat-back chairs, 28
Smibert, John, *56,* 61
Smith, F. Hopkinson, 152
Smith, John, 11
Smithsonian Institute (Wash., D.C.), 111

Social status, 32
Spanish influences, *16, 22, 181*
Spelling Book (Webster), 76
Spindle chairs, 28
Sports and recreation, 32, 63, 179, 208–
    209
Stagecoaches, *96, 99*
Stead, William Thomas, 152
Steeples, 52, 99
Steffens, Lincoln, 155
Stenciling, 84–85, *88, 104*
Stepped gables, 17
Stevens, John Calvin, 128, *128*
Stewart, A. T., 145
Stickley, Gustav, 143–45
Stiegel, Henry William, *56,* 61
Stieglitz, Alfred, 150–51
Stiles, Ezra, 73
Stowe, Harriet Beecher, 102–103
Strawbery Banke (N.H.), *43, 46, 66–
    67, 75, 78–79, 106*
Streamlining, 176–78
Stuart, Gilbert, 85–86
Stuart furniture, 53–55
Suburbs, 178–79
Sullivan, Louis, *130,* 132, 136, 141, *144*
Swedenborgian Church (Maine), 98
Swedish influences, *14,* 21–22
Symmetry, 45, 49–50, 73

Tarbell, Ida M., 155
Taylor, Edward, 31
Tea, 58
Television, 191–92, 194
Thomas Larkin House (Calif.), *16*
Thoreau, Henry, 103, 132
Tiffany, Louis Comfort, *113,* 148–49
Tombs, (N.Y.C.), 112
Tools, 12–17
Toscanini, Arturo, 167
Touro Synagogue (R.I.), *42,* 52
Town & Davis, 112, 114, 128
Transportation, 99, 176–78
Travels (Bartram), 89
Treadwell, John, 87
Tribune Building (N.Y.C.), *133*
Trinity Church (Conn.), 73, 104
Trinity Church (Mass.), 132
Trinity Church (N.Y.C.), 109–10
Trollope, Frances, 114
Trumbull, John, 65, 73–74, 76
Trumbull, John, 86–87
Turkey work, 30
Turkish styles, 117

Un santo, 85
University Hall (Mass.), 80
Upjohn, Richard, 109–10

Van Arrsens, Jan, 23

Van Cortlandt, Stephanus, 21w
Van Cortlandt Manor House (N.Y.),
    14, 21
Van Rensselaer, Kiliaen, 21
Vanderlyn, John, 86, *88*
Vaux, Calvert, *100,* 105–106
Vernacular, 49–51
Virginia, 25–26, *34,* 43–44

Wainscot chair, *19,* 28
Wallace, Lew, 152
Wallpaper, 80, *81*
Washington, D.C., 89–90
Watts, Isaac, 62
Weathervanes, 30
Webster, Noah, 76
Wedding Cake House (Maine), *99,* 104–
    105
West, Benjamin, *64,* 85
Western Reserve style, 96–97
Westover (Va.), 44
Wheatley, Phillis, 65
Whistler, James McNeill, 147–48
White, Stanford, 132, 136, 141
Whitman Walt, 101, 102, 106
Whittier, John Greenleaf, 107
Widow walk, 45
Wieland (Brown), 76
Wiggin, Kate Douglas, 152
Wigglesworth, Michael, 31, 63

Wilder, Thornton, 162
William Harrison House (Ind.), 80
William and Mary College (Va.), 37,
    41, 43
William and Mary furniture, *43, 46,* 53–
    55
Williams, Tennessee, 191
Williamsburg (Va.), 37, 43–44
Wilson, Henry, 143–45
Windows, 12, 45, 48–49, 50, 77–78, *181*
Windsor chairs, *46,* 55–57, *81, 83*
Wine, 57, 208
Winslow-Crocker House (Mass.), *54–
    55*
Wistar, Caspar, 61
Wister, Owen, 152
Wood, William, 11–12
Woodcarving, *1, 71, 85*
Woodlawn (Va.), 80
Woodshed (N.Y.), 131
World's Fair (1939), 178
Wren, Sir Christopher, 32–37, 41, 43
Wren Building (Va.), 37, *38–39*
Wright, Frank Lloyd, *170,* 171–72, *177,
    181, 183*
Wright, Richard, 196

Yachting, 99

Zerbe, Karl, *208*

ACKNOWLEDGMENTS

The author expresses his sincere thanks to the many individuals, too many to be listed here, without whose help this book could never have been written.

The following photographs were taken by Allan Mogel. The cooperation of curators and other individuals who made materials available is gratefully acknowledged.

The following abbreviations are used:
BSM: Brick Store Museum, Kennebunk, Maine
PF: Peirce Farm, Waterboro Old Corner, Maine
SB: Strawbery Banke, Inc., Portsmouth, N.H.
SHR: Sleepy Hollow Restorations, Tarrytown, N.Y.
YIM: York Institute Museum, Saco, Maine

2–3: Photographed at location 10: SHR 13: (far left) PF 15: SHR 20: (top left *and* above) SHR 43: (left) SHR; (right) SB 46: (above) YIM; (below) SB 48: PF 51: (left) SHR 54: SHR 66–67: SB 73: PF 75: (top *and* above) SB 77: (top left) Photographed at location 79: YIM 81: (left) YIM; (above) SHR 87: PF 88: (above) BSM; (right) YIM 96: (center) BSM 98: (bottom) Photographed at location 103: (right) BSM; (all others) PF 105: Willowbrook at Newfield, Newfield, Maine (a Victorian village museum) 106: SB 110: BSM 111: PF 116: (above right) Willowbrook at Newfield 126: (above *and* above far right) PF 128: PF 129: (below) Photographed at location 137: PF 138: PF 143: (left) PF 168: Photographed at location 169: Photographed at location 173: PF 180–81: Photographed at location 208: (bottom) PF

The following abbreviations are used:
HABS: Historic American Buildings Survey, National Park Service
HMSG: Hirshhorn Museum and Sculpture Garden, Smithsonian Institution
IAD: Index of American Design, National Gallery of Art, Washington, D.C.
MFAB: Museum of Fine Arts, Boston
NGA: National Gallery of Art, Washington, D.C.
PP: Prints and Photographs Division, Library of Congress, Washington, D.C.
SPNEA: Society for the Preservation of New England Antiquities, Boston

Chapter 1
1: IAD 4–5 Scripps Institution of Oceanography, University of California, San Diego, Calif., photo by Larry Ford 8–9: MFAB, M. and M. Karolik Fund 13: (top *and* above left) HABS; (above); PP; (left) IAD 14: (top) Courtesy, Sleepy Hollow Restorations; (center *and* bottom) HABS 16: (above right) Bancroft Library, University of California, Berkeley, Calif.; (all others) HABS 18: HABS 19: (left) HABS; (above) MFAB, Samuel Putnam Avery Fund 20: (top right) MFAB, Charles Hitchcock Tyler Fund; (left) Bennington Museum, Bennington, Vt.; 24: MFAB 27: PP, Allan Ludwig Collection 28: Maryland Historical Society, Baltimore, Md., 29: (above) PP; (left) MFAB, M. and M. Karolik Collection 33: Bowdoin College Museum of Art, Brunswick, Maine 34: Virginia State Travel Service 35: *Catalog of American Antiques,* Rutledge Books, photos by John Garetti 36: Peabody Museum of Salem, Salem, Mass., photo by Mark Sexton

Chapter 2
38–39: The College of William and Mary, Williamsburg, Va. 40: HABS 41: (top) Colonial Williamsburg; (bottom) HABS 42: (top) HABS, photo by Jack Boucher; (bottom) Rhode Island Department of Economic Development 46: (right) SPNEA, photo by Richard Cheek at Winslow-Crocker House, Yarmouthport, Mass. 49: NGA, gift of Edgar William and Bernice Chrysler Garbisch 51: (far left) NGA, Andrew W. Mellon Fund; (top) MFAB, John Wheelock Elliot Fund; (above left); The Library Company of Philadelphia; (above) MFAB, gift of

James Longley 54–55: SPNEA, photo by Richard Cheek 56: (above) MFAB, gift of Hollis French; (above right) MFAB, M. and M. Karolik Collection; (right) Essex Institute, Salem, Mass. 60: (above right) Brooklyn Museum, Dick S. Ramsay Fund; (right) PP, Allan Ludwig Collection; (far right) IAD 64: (right) Historical Society of Pennsylvania, Philadelphia, Pa.; (below) NGA, gift of Edgar William and Bernice Chrysler Garbisch; (bottom left) from *The History of the Ancient and Honorable Tuesday Club,* preserved by the John Work Garrett Library, Johns Hopkins University; (bottom right) American Antiquarian Society

Chapter 3
69: Shelbourne Museum, Inc., Shelbourne, Vt. 70: IAD 71: IAD 72: photos by Transparencies, Inc. 74: HABS 75: (above left) HABS 77: (top right) PP; (center) HABS; (above) PP 78: Essex Institute 81: (top) Essex Institute, Salem, Mass. 82: (top) PP; (all others) HABS 88: (top) Courtesy of the Pennsylvania Academy of the Fine Arts

Chapter 4
92–93: PP 94: Mark Twain Memorial, Hartford, Conn. 96: (top *and* bottom) PP 97: PP 98: (top) Park National Bank, Granville, Ohio; (center) HABS, photo by Jack Boucher 100: (above *and* above right) HABS; (right) HABS 101: HABS 102: HABS 104: (left) HABS; (right) Peirce Farm, photo by Arthur Straughn 113: Mark Twain Memorial, Hartford, Conn. 116: (top left *and* bottom) PP 120: PP

Chapter 5
124–25: PP, Frances Benjamin Johnston Collection 126: (above right) PP 129: (left) California State Library 130: (above) National Trust for Historic Preservation, photo by John Blumenson; (above right) HABS; (right) State Photographic Archives, Strozier Library, Florida State University; (below right) HABS 133: PP 134: (top) PP; (above) The Preservation Society of Newport County, Newport, R.I. 139: (above) Brooklyn Museum; (right) photo by William P. Randel 140: HMSG, photo by John Tennant 142: (left) PP; (right) HABS 143: (far left) HABS 144: (top) Rhode Island Department of Economic Development; (above) PP; (right) HABS 146: (top) PP; (above far right) HABS 148: (top) Minnesota Historical Society, photo by Truman W. Ingersoll; (bottom) Mark Twain Memorial, Hartford, Conn. 149: PP 151: (top left) NGA, gift of Chester Dale; (top right) Philadelphia Museum of Art, gift of Mrs. Thomas Eakins and Miss Mary A. Williams; (bottom) NGA, Chester Dale Collection 153: Courtesy, Greene and Greene Library, The Gamble House, University of Southern California, Los Angeles, Calif., photo by Marvin Rand 154: (top) PP, Frances, Benjamin Johnston Collection; (above) HABS 157: PP

Chapter 6
158–59: HMSG 160: HMSG 163: (top) Radio City Music Hall, New York, N.Y.; (all others) Collection of Lillian Nassau 164: Radio City Music Hall, New York, N.Y. 166: HMSG 170: HABS 172: HABS 177: (top) HABS; (center) PP, Frances Benjamin Johnston Collection; (bottom) SPNEA, photo by Robert Damora 181: HABS 184: Photo by Arthur Straughn 185: Chrysler Corporation

Chapter 7
186–87: Deere & Company, Moline, Ill. 188: Courtesy, Saint John's University, Collegeville, Minn. 190–91: Peachtree Plaza, Western International Hotels 193: New York State Thruway Authority 194: Holiday Inns, Inc. 197: New York City Housing Authority 199: Heritage Development Group, photo by Martin Tornallyay 200–1: LaGuardia Airport, the Port Authority of New York & New Jersey 201: Deltona Corporation, Miami, Florida 202: Courtesy, McDonald's Corporation 204: Syroco, Syracuse, N.Y. 208: (top) HMSG